To : Cathy;

Hope this helps!

Lorrie

Blue, Baseball, Virginia

The Journey of an Alzheimer's Patient and Caregiver!
A Journey of Humor, Help, and Hope!

Lorrie Davis McDonald

WESTBOW®
PRESS
A DIVISION OF THOMAS NELSON
& ZONDERVAN

WestBow Press books may be ordered through booksellers or by contacting:

WestBow Press
A Division of Thomas Nelson & Zondervan
1663 Liberty Drive
Bloomington, IN 47403
www.westbowpress.com
1 (866) 928-1240

All Scripture references in this book are taken from the King James Version of the Bible.

ISBN: 978-1-4908-5990-3 (sc)
ISBN: 978-1-4908-5991-0 (hc)
ISBN: 978-1-4908-5992-7 (e)

Library of Congress Control Number: 2014920426

Printed in the United States of America.

WestBow Press rev. date: 01/07/2015

Contents

This book is dedicated to Jenna Green Christian, my partner in crime. Thank you for helping me "steal" Granny back from this horrible, terrible disease.
"Lucy, you're the greatest!"—Cha Cha

Foreword

Caregiving can happen to you—unexpectedly, for which you are not prepared. This book will help you get through the challenging experiences of being a full-time caregiver for a loved one, friend, or neighbor. It happened to me—my husband was diagnosed with myasthenia gravis three years ago; it has been a shattering experience. All the support you can find will help, including materials like this book.

Lorrie has provided an incredibly detailed log of my sister's decline, all the way up to her unexpected sudden death, the shock and grief of which she efficiently and passionately handled. Listening carefully to Lois, my sister, Lorrie thought critically about what she heard and observed. Over time, she came to question and ultimately challenge many of the popular conventions about treatment of older adults with declining mental and physical ability.

Her book will challenge you to think critically, and you will learn how to escape from the tension and demands of an overloaded schedule and focus on the needs of a loved one. Lorrie expanded the horizons for Lois. This began by undoing many popular, well-intended but counterproductive reactions to a sick person. She heroically documented, with photographs and narratives, the journey they went on together.

This is the only book I remember completely reading at one time. Every event led me to want to know what happened next. I believe that this documentation of her experiences will definitely help any caregiver.

—Ruth Garrett, PhD, MPH, MEd

Dr. Garrett is a retired associate professor from the University of Georgia. She retired a second time from the Meharry Medical College and is presently a gerontology education consultant for both medical colleges in Nashville, Tennessee—Vanderbilt University and Meharry Medical College. She is a guest lecturer of gerontology and environmental health at the Tennessee Valley Health Care System, Trevecca, Belmont, Tennessee State University, and civic and church groups. She is the author of the book *Embracing Aging*, has written over 450 newspaper and journal articles, and is active on several boards of directors. She is a keynote speaker for major local, national, and international aging organizations.

Acknowledgments

This book was nine years in the making. How do I possibly thank everyone who helped or encouraged me in that span of time? I will try.

First, I would like to say thank you to Jesus Christ for not only being the author and finisher of my faith but also the author of this book. I feel that every word came straight from His guidance. I often sat down to a blank screen, not knowing what to write. Eight hours later, I would read what I had just written and knew it was all Him. I am eternally grateful.

Second, thank you to my family. Thank you to David and Marilyn for trusting me to do what I felt was best for your mother. David, I feel like we faced unbelievable odds to get through this book, but we did it. I love you and the wonderful life we have built together. I can't wait to grow old with you. Better than ever!

Collin, Connor, and Delanie, thank you for putting up with me for the last few months. Life has been crazy, and you have handled it like the troupers you are. I can't wait to see what God has in store for each of your lives. Collin, God will use your flying to take you far in life (literally and figuratively). Connor, He has given you an unbelievable love of true American history. You are a born leader. I am excited where that will lead you. Delanie, you are the best friend I have. Your words of encouragement and song list over the past few years have kept me going. Keep singing for Jesus! Thank you for keeping our home running smoothly when I'm running wild. I love you all three!

Cory, Meg, Ellie Beth, and Annsley, I am *so* thankful to be your Cha Cha. The four of you make my life complete. I am so excited that grandbaby number three is on his/her way. Tripp, I love you already! Thank you for all your encouragement and prayers.

Thank you to Aunt Ruth and Aunt Mary for reading and rereading this book. I am blessed to have you in my life and to be a part of your family.

Thank you to Nana and Poppie who fed my family when I was stuck at a computer. Thank you to all who ever lent a hand with Granny and Papa. Thank you to Pastor Ron Ralph and Cornerstone Baptist Church for being the closest thing to a New Testament church I have ever found. Thanks to our very dear friends Mike and Lucinda Phillips, Mark and Gina Dillon, Dan and Jill Garner, and all the others who have been a part of our journey. Your labor was not in vain. Thank you!

"The memory of the just is blessed …"—Proverbs 10:7

Introduction

If you are reading this book, chances are you know someone who has Alzheimer's disease. Chances are even greater that you are the caregiver of someone with Alzheimer's. That's how this book came to be. My mother-in-law was diagnosed with AD (Alzheimer's disease) several years ago. I began reading up on AD. I began pouring over information on the Web and in books galore to get insight into what we were going to be facing. It was not pretty. None of these sources of information could give me what I so desperately needed—a day-to-day guide on what to expect as the disease progressed. There was a *ton* of information out there—more than I wanted to know. I found statistics, charts, and medical jargon, but that wasn't what I wanted. *I wanted hope.* I wanted to know that life could go on, even after the "A word" had been used. So over the past several years, I talked with doctors, neurologists, and reflexologists. I developed a game plan for helping my mother-in-law to get better for as long as possible, and guess what? She got better! Cured? Not by a long shot. But she improved to the point that her neurologist said she was better than she had been in eighteen months, so much so that he even thought that perhaps he had misdiagnosed her. He had not. But the things we did with her significantly improved her condition.

So this is our story—the journey I have gone on with Granny (that's what everybody calls my mother-in-law). The more I have spoken with others who were thrust into the position of caregiver to someone with AD, the more I realized that the whole world is facing a very real medical epidemic. I don't know of a single family who has not been touched somehow by this terrible disease. I have learned it is okay to laugh at the disease, but we have had our share of cries too.

If someone gave you this book, it is because that person wants you to know what I have found out. This is not a book with more medical terms.

It is intended to be a book of humor and of help. To those of you who are a part of this story, some of you are mentioned by name, and sometimes I have left you anonymous in order to protect the guilty. I have tried to be as honest as I can without being intentionally hurtful, knowing that all families are going to face the challenges we have faced.

This is a book about the journey that the patient, the caregiver, and the family all go on. You will laugh, you will cry, and you will see … there is *hope*.

Preface

Help!

Some of you may be desperate. This book is written not only to entertain you but to enlighten you. If you need help with an AD patient, then let me suggest skipping straight to chapters 7 and 8. Those are more of how-to chapters, and the rest of the book is more biography style. You and your patient may greatly benefit from going to those chapters first. I have been incredibly blessed in that one of Granny's sisters, Dr. Ruth Jean Garrett, speaks all over the world on gerontology. Amazingly, when I first started my war on this disease, I didn't have all these resources or the clinical findings that have since backed up what I implemented with her. I did lots of trial and error and went on gut instinct. Some of it works today but not so much yesterday. You, the reader, will get the benefit of all those experiments.

Disclaimer

When you read this book, you may come away thinking that I hate nursing homes. That is *not* true. As a matter of fact, I would like to take this opportunity to personally thank everyone at the Smith County Nursing Home for their excellent care of Lois during her brief stay there. Jody Gammons and her physical therapy workers did a wonderful job of trying to help Granny, and I thank them for that.

I do believe that many people have been placed in nursing homes out of convenience, not necessity. Our family has been involved with nursing home ministries for years, and I have been saddened by some of the people who have been placed there. Sometimes, there is a legitimate need for a patient to be there; in fact, I know of several incidences where that was the case. Too many times, though, I think families have been lead to believe that they cannot care for their loved one at home. That is especially true in the case of AD patients. Take hope! You *can* keep them at home and help them live a productive life. I know because we have accomplished just that.

I also know there are some wonderful assisted-living facilities out there that are the next best thing to being at home. This book is written to show what can be done. It was not meant to beat you up over a decision you may have had to make. In the long run, each story will be unique. If you are involved in the nursing home industry, do not be offended by my opinion. It is indeed just that.

Chapter 1

Meet Granny

Icie Lois McCall McDonald was born August 25, 1927. She was the oldest daughter in a family of nine children. She was born and raised on a farm in Middle Tennessee. It was the end of the Roaring Twenties, and her childhood memories were of growing up during the Great Depression. I once asked her about the Depression, and she laughed. She explained that when you lived on a farm, you took care of yourself and yours. The economy didn't have a lot of bearing on your day-to-day living. As long as the chickens were still laying, and the cow was still producing milk, and the garden still grew crops, life on the farm didn't crash with the stock market. She did learn, however, some very frugal habits and obtained something that has helped her overcome life's hardships—a sense of humor. With five brothers and three sisters, you learn to laugh at the pitfalls of life and work together to make the world a better place for those you love.

Lois is my mother-in-law. I have never called her anything but Granny. She was already in her sixties when I married her only son, David, and she had four wonderful grandsons who had already lovingly dubbed her "Granny." We live in a small town. When a baby is born, we all make the family a meal. When someone dies, we carry a pie to the funeral home. So when you are well known in the community, if your family calls you Granny, then everyone calls you Granny.

It didn't take me long after marrying into the family to find out that Granny was a character. I want you to know her—the *real her*. Not the person who repeatedly asks the same questions. Not the person who sits and stares out into space at times. Not the person you will read about in the following chapters. The real Granny is such a colorful figure that she deserves to be remembered and celebrated. Plus, it might help you, if you are helping a loved one with AD, to remember that once upon time; your loved one was lively also. This disease is a horrible thief. One of the cruelest things it does is steal our loved ones away from us, one small memory at a time, until, if we are not on guard, we look on with pity at a person we once admired. When you are caregiving day after long day, you begin to forget how smart and active that person once was. Remind yourself and others involved of the wonderful qualities about your loved one. You may have young children who do not remember your loved one any other way. Don't let this monstrous disease steal your precious memories. Hold on to them for dear life! You will all be better for it in the long run.

One of the first things I learned when I began helping Granny was that you get what you expect out of people. I am a teacher by trade. The same is true with an eighth-grader or an eighty-year-old. If you expect very little, you get very little. By trial and error, I began to remind Granny of what she *could still do*, and then I expected her to do it. Voila! I learned one of the greatest secrets to success in life. It always seems to help Granny remember who she really is too.

"For as he thinketh in his heart, so is he." (Proverbs 23:7)

Enjoy reading about some of the things that make up this wonderful, wild woman I have grown to know and love. I feel it is an honor to be the one to care for her. The longer I care for her and try to give her some worth to living, the more I find that I am the one who is enriched, far above what I am doing for her.

D. T. and Amy McCall with their nine children,
spouses, and grandchildren, circa 1959.
Lois (Granny) is on the far left.

Anyone who knows the McCall family knows what a group of pranksters they are. Granny's father, D. T. McCall, is worthy of a book all to himself. The nine children learned to work and (gasp!) to enjoy it, from working alongside him. He did that by making work fun. The McCalls thrive on practical jokes. That is one way I gauge Granny's progress now. If she is cracking jokes, we're good. If she's lost her sense of humor, I know it's going to be a bad day. *"A merry heart doeth good like a medicine." (Proverbs 17:22)* A study done in 2011 at the University of Maryland by Michael Miller, MD, says, "The merrier you are the more benefits to your health."

The mind is a fascinating thing. There seems to be a blur between reality and a memory, especially once dementia sets in. Your patient may be sitting there freezing because she is recalling a winter snowstorm from fifty years ago. So it is with joy. Some days, when Granny's feeling down, I do what the famous song says: "When I'm feeling sad, I simply remember my favorite things, and then I don't feel so bad." I have long since fought fire with fire. Just know that when you find out something your loved one enjoyed so much as a child, draw on that now.

Practical jokes were a way of life for the McCall children. When I can get Granny to recall some of those pranks, she relives that joyous time again. Body, soul, mind, and spirit all go back to that happy moment and we get to reap the health benefits today from the "happy hormones" that get released when she recalls these stories.

One of her favorite stories that she tells us is about one of her brothers, Albert. When you have a large family, desserts—or food of any kind, for that matter—are hard to come by. Albert had a habit of going through the kitchen and grabbing the largest dessert. So one day, Granny and her sister Mary Nell were in the kitchen, dishing out the banana pudding (Albert's favorite). Granny had an idea. Sitting on the table was a bowl of leftover biscuits from breakfast. Granny discussed with Mary Nell and their mother how that they should teach Albert a lesson. She placed the biscuit in the bowl and then spooned a little of the banana pudding over the top. It looked perfect. It appeared to be a very large helping of creamy heaven. Just as Granny had predicted, Albert swiped it from the counter with a sneaking grin and a sly shake of the head. As the family finished up their supper, everyone dug into the decadent dessert. As Albert bit into his, there came a stunning surprise! What he thought was going to be creamy pudding was a dry biscuit. The entire family roared in laughter as Albert learned a lesson in greed and gluttony.

L to R: Mary Nell, Ruth, Albert, Mildred, Ray, Frank, John, Dave, Lois

Granny loves to tell that story. She has such a wonderful sense of humor that up until the last couple of years when her health hinder it, Granny would make Albert a large banana pudding and take it to him on his birthday at the family-owned furniture store. Then they would stand around and tell anyone who would listen, "Did I ever tell you the time ..." Sixty-five years later, that practical joke still gets a laugh.

Humor is one of the things that has made the McCall family so close-knit. Their mother and father helped their children realize that you can laugh or you can cry. Why not find the humor in any situation? If you look closely enough, it's there.

They have all grown up to lead very different lives, but that doesn't mean they cannot appreciate their differences and still laugh at funny stories of their childhood, as well as at each other and—perhaps more important—at themselves.

L to R: Dave, Lois (Granny), Frank, Mildred, John, Mary Nell, Ray, Ruth Jean, Albert (banana pudding thief)

Granny was a local schoolteacher for over twenty-seven years. After she retired from school teaching, she made it her personal mission to feed the teachers at the end of the school year. I hate to think of the pounds Granny is responsible for putting on the educational system of Smith

County. She made cinnamon rolls from scratch and took them around to the teachers by the dozens.

There is also no telling how many trips she made to the funeral home with a plate of those delicious rolls. She took them by whenever someone in the community passed away. Granny ministered with food. When she didn't know what to say or what to do, she said and did it with a plate of ham and homemade biscuits. She learned a long time ago what my generation just doesn't appreciate: when a family is hurting, they just need to know they have a community that is there for them. They might not be hungry after the funeral, but somehow, just seeing all that food in the kitchen at Sanderson's Funeral Home brings about a sense of comfort. One of the grandest gestures of love is the boxes of food that Jackie Carver loads into the grieving families' cars after the funeral. It shows that a whole community is grieving with them. One pecan pie at a time.

—◦◊◦—

Granny also fed the neighbors. I can't count the number of people over the years who have said, "You know, Mrs. Lois was the first person I met when we moved to Carthage. She came walking up the driveway with a plate of ham and homemade biscuits. She invited us to church too. She just made us feel so welcomed. She was so genuinely glad we were here. I'll never forget that as long as I live!" Knowing this about her helped me form part of my game plan that you will read about in later chapters. Think about the person you are caring for. What things did he or she love to do when in perfect health? If you try hard enough, there are very few things that you can't adapt to bring some normalcy into a life that has become anything but normal.

The longer I live and the more people I meet, the more I am convinced that most people need to feel needed. People need to feel as if they are part of the solution, not part of the problem. Granny loves to show people love. Some of the hardest people to care for later in life are those who were themselves the caregivers. It just goes against their grain to be on the receiving end. So once again, I had to outsmart this disease!

I began to make Granny feel like *she* was helping *me*, instead of the other way around. As the disease has progressed, I have often kept her from being alone at her house for long periods of time by simply telling her that I desperately need her to help me keep an eye on the kids. Bingo! She's happy to come help me, whereas if I had told her that I was worried about her being home alone, she would have resisted. You just have to outwit the disease. We are beating it. Several times a day, I can get Granny to do things that she shouldn't be able to do, if you believe everything you read about the capabilities of Alzheimer's disease patients. I don't take limitations very well. Neither should you. When you feel like you are going to lose your loved one, remember ... there is hope. Granny is proof!

———⟡⟡⟡———

When Granny was a school teacher, she taught practically everyone in Smith County at one time or another. Those she didn't have in class, she had in the library when she was the school librarian. As Granny's mind began to slip a few years ago, she sometimes would forget things that had happened but remember things that had not!

My good friend Gina Dillon pulled me aside at church one Sunday night and told me, "You know how Granny always tells me I was one of her best students."

"Yeah, which I'm sure is a lie!" I joked.

"Well, here's the deal. I always smile and say 'Yes, ma'am' to her out of respect, but to be honest, Mrs. Lois was never my teacher."

"What? Are you sure?" I questioned her, knowing that Granny had been telling Gina this for years. She had told Gina this since long before she was diagnosed with any type of memory problem.

"That's just it. I *know* I never had her, but Mrs. Lois is so adamant about it that I actually called Momma this afternoon and asked her to be sure," Gina said.

"And?"

"Momma said it didn't sound like Mrs. Lois was having problems with her mind but that maybe I should see a doctor if a little ol' woman could convince me I was in a classroom I never was in," replied Gina with her usual smirk.

———⟡⟡⟡———

Granny loves music. She single-handedly brought a music program to Carthage Elementary when she first started teaching. Several of her fellow retired teacher friends have told me that Lois thought all children should be exposed to music. So she purchased cheap flutes and distributed them to the students, and then she taught them songs for a program they would hold for the parents. Did I mention that Granny had to first learn how to play the flute herself? Not a problem! No challenge was too hard for her. The program grew and grew, and finally, years later, they hired a music teacher on staff. But all those budding musicians out there have Granny to thank for being able to play "Three Blind Mice" on a plastic flute. And who knows what that has done for people's résumés over the years?

She loves music and church. She also loves children. This led to another of her legacies. If she could bring music to the children in the public school system, then she could bring it to the children in the Sunday schools. And so she did. One of the things she is most famous for is the All Kid Kazoo Band for the King of Kings. Oh, that may not have been the name on the marquee, but that's what it was. Can you imagine the sound of dozens of kids, ranging in age from two to twelve, humming through "Joy to the World"? I'm sure it was off-key, off-time, and probably aw-ful. But not to Granny.

———◈◈◈———

She also began doing an annual Church Children's Choir program. I have been an assistant —or should I say a partner in crime- to some of these. By the time I married into the family, Granny had put on dozens of these award-winning programs. She had all the confidence in the world in these children. I soon learned that there were some staples to all these performances. First, family got lead roles. In Granny's early years, it started off with her casting younger brothers and sisters as Mary and Joseph. Then, as she grew older, she cast her own children, and then, what red-blooded grandmother wouldn't thrust her talented grandchildren into the spotlight? Never mind that my dear stepson cannot even play the radio in tune, much less sing a musical measure in key. Those are minor issues that just needed a little tweaking. So Cory soon became the narrator. "Let's just face it," Granny would say with a wink. "He's both articulate and cute as a button!"

Another staple were sheep. When all the good parts had been given to those grandkids who could speak and to the few kids with some actual talent, then everyone else could be a sheep. Lots of lambs in Bethlehem—at least in the 1980s and early '90s. No child was too shy to be in the play. Just hot glue a dozen or so cotton balls to a white sweatshirt, and there you have it—a star is born!

Many a Saturday morning, I'm sure the pastor would slip off to his church office and fall down upon his knees. He would no doubt beseech God to please bring order to the chaos he had just witnessed in the sanctuary during the dress rehearsal. Kids running about. Mrs. Lois, seemingly in charge, but not really aware of the impending doom around her. And why were there more sheep in the choir loft than most wool farms owned? But somehow, some magical way, the next night's performance was always a grand success. Cameras clicked. Video cameras hummed. Sheep bleated. Granny beamed. Surely beauty was in the ear of the beholder.

Granny working at Cornerstone with the two- and three-year-olds

Granny not only loves music, but she also loves playing the piano. Back in her day, all young ladies received some type of formal piano instruction. Granny got to where she could play fairly well. One of the most unselfish and comical things I have ever seen her do is go up to the local nursing home to visit the "old folks." She doesn't necessarily visit anyone in particular, but after living in a small town for several years, I realize that you will always know someone wherever you go.

Once a month, with a plate of homemade cinnamon rolls in hand, she heads off to be a blessing to the old people. She goes into the community room, sits down at the piano, and opens up the hymnal. She starts off with some of the classics, such as "The Old Rugged Cross" or "Amazing Grace." Something they could all sing along to. Then, without fail, after six or seven church songs, she breaks into "The Boogie Woogie Song." ("You know, just to liven the joint up a bit," she always says with a wink.)

Granny and Papa were so excited when David
signed with the University of Georgia!

Granny loves ball. Not that she herself was an outstanding athlete, but she did cheer and play basketball while in high school. She also took up golf after we bought the golf course, and she became a fairly decent golfer. But that is not why she loves ball. She loves ball because her son and grandchildren love ball. Her son, David, my husband, was an outstanding ballplayer. Papa, his dad, was his coach in most sports, and Papa and his brother, Uncle Douglas, had both gone on to play college ball as the kickers at Tennessee Tech University.

David says he remembers, as a child, needing someone to throw a baseball with or to catch the football for him, and more times than not, it was Granny who got out back in the yard with him. I still have the scrapbooks she filled with all of his newspaper write-ups. When he was in high school, he made the All Mid-State team in football, and Granny was so proud of that, she framed not one copy of the clipping but three.

She could hardly contain herself when David was offered a football scholarship to the University of Georgia. She and Papa would work all week and then hop in the car right after work on Fridays and drive down to Athens, Georgia, to be there for the next day's game. This was back before the interstate system made it a quick six-hour drive from Carthage, Tennessee. There was a time, as a freshman, when David didn't even play. That didn't stop Granny from insisting they make the trek. "Cordell, he needs to know we support him and that we are there for him. And you never know when that sweet Ray Goff or Matt Robinson might break a leg or something, and they'll let David in!" Granny—always the optimist!

David, #15, playing for the University of Georgia

Granny supports her grandkids' athletic endeavors too. She has always gotten all of the grandsons' ball schedules, and her days and nights are planned around when she needed to be at the ball field. Our town obviously needs more optometrists because according to Granny, there are an awful lot of umpires and referees who desperately needed glasses. Her grandson was *not* out!

My stepson, Cory, has the same athletic gene that comes with being a McDonald. Two very distinct memories come to mind about Granny's watching him play baseball. The first one I should probably be ashamed to laugh at, and if Granny had gotten seriously injured, I wouldn't find it so funny. We were sitting at the ballpark on the left-hand side when we heard someone yell from the field behind us, "Heads up!" Well, we all ducked and covered our heads with our arms—all of us except Granny. As I turned to look at her, she was shielding her eyes from the sun and staring straight toward the incoming foul ball. It popped her right on top of the head! Everyone around us rushed to see if she was okay. She was. When I leaned over and said, "Granny, they yelled 'heads up.' Why didn't you cover your head?" She replied in total seriousness, "Well, why in this world didn't they yell 'heads down'?"

When I say Cory has the ball gene, what I really mean is that all the men in this family take ball just a tad too seriously. Always have. Always will. Cory was twelve when his daddy and I started spitting out his siblings. One of the first things I had to teach our three younger ones was that when Cory was playing ball, they should leave him alone. He was not going to do a lot of chitchatting with us. He had "his mind on the game." So imagine my surprise when, during a baseball game, Cory ran toward the fence, yelling, "Lorrie! Lorrie! Come here! Lorrie! Hurry! Come here!" What in the world? Was he sick? Was there an emergency? How unsettling.

"Lorrie! Do something about Granny! *Now!*" And he was off and running, back on to the field.

Do something about Granny? What in the world was he talking about? I turned to see what he had seen. Granny had gotten up from the stands, walked out to her car, and was returning with a bright yellow Dollar General Store bag tied around her head—pointed end up, no less. What I wouldn't have given for cell phones with cameras to have been invented back then. Talk about a picture being worth a thousand words.

I walked toward her, doing all I could do to stifle my laughter. "Um, Granny, whatcha doin' with that bag on your head?"

"Oh, honey, I forgot my toboggan at home." (For those of you who are not sports inclined, it was baseball season, the middle of July. One hundred degrees in the shade. But in Granny's defense, it was a night game, when the scorching sun did finally set. It might even have dipped down to a chilling eighty-five degrees.) "And that night air just kills my head. And I am *not* going to miss this game for anything."

"Well, Granny, you're not going to be able to wear that bag on your head," I calmly explained to her.

"Well, I'd like to know why not." She did not even try to hide her irritation.

"Because I think it might be a slight distraction for Cory."

Shoulders slumped. A woeful sigh escaped her. "Oh. Well, honey, I don't want to do that. But ..."

"Granny, I tell you what. You can use Connor's baby blanket and wrap that around your head instead."

"Won't he be needing it?" she asked as she looked down at her adorable grandson, who actually had sweat dripping off of him.

"No, ma'am."

"Don't you think that might be a distraction, too?" she queried.

"Comparatively speaking, I think not," I assured her.

"Well, if you insist."

"Oh-h-h, I insist!"

———

Granny was brave. She single-handedly saved Cory's beloved dog when Cory was just a little boy. When the first Dooley was being attacked by a Doberman pinscher, Granny jumped in and yanked him free from the attacking dog. It didn't matter to Granny that *she* could have been attacked. That probably never entered her mind. All she knew was that her sweet grandson needed a super hero—immediately. Since there was a shortage of those around that day, she became Cory's Wonder Woman. (Note: All our dogs have been named after Coach Vince Dooley, David's football coach at the University of Georgia. This one was a ten-pound wire-haired dachshund, as opposed to our current one-hundred-pound golden retriever.)

David said Cory was only about five years old then, and he told his daddy that Granny had saved Dooley's life. "Wow, Daddy! You should have seen Granny! She wasn't afraid of that mean ol' dog! She's the bravest person I know!" A lot of time has passed since that day, but if you were to ask Cory, I think he would still feel that she's the bravest person he knows.

—◦◦◦—

Granny with me on one of our many riding adventures

Granny loves horses. I have met very few women who have a passion for them as much as my mother-in-law. Her father, D. T. McCall, instilled that in her from an early age. He was part of the movement that swept across our region with the rise of the famous Tennessee walking horses. Oh, how Pa loved his horses! Granny grew up a "daddy's girl," so it was only natural that she acquired his keen sense of working with them. One of the reasons I fell into such good graces with her after I met her son was because I ride horses. Any doubts she may have had about me flew out the barn window when she learned she would now have a riding partner.

Over the years, we have had dozens of the finest Tennessee walking horses on the farm. Granny took care of them all by herself. I guess it never dawned on any of us that she might need some help with them. She made it abundantly clear that she had it completely under control. I can remember the few times I did actually help her do some fence mending. Boy, was that a sight!

Granny's farm truck was a white four-door Chevy Lumina. Not exactly built for off-road excursion. Not a problem for Granny. She has always been the queen of improvisation. Growing up through the Depression or not, this was a woman who could fix a five-hundred-dollar problem with a fifty-cent paper clip. I can't tell you the number of times we mended a broken-down spot in the fence with whatever was on hand in the trunk of that Lumina. We have used many a string of twine off a hay bale. And I'll bet you had no idea that a pair of Hanes pantyhose can keep a 1,500-pound horse in a pasture. With or without a run in them, now *that's* a support hose!

Granny and her grandsons

I'm glad I knew the real Granny for several years before I started sensing something wasn't quite right. She was such an unbelievable person then. When I stop and look at her today, I make myself remember that she's still in there. I know she is.

Be careful that you don't degrade your patient. Most of these people have lived remarkable lives to which we can't even hold a candle. One of the things that makes me madder than anything else is to hear someone say, "Oh, it doesn't matter. She doesn't know the difference. She can't remember anyway."

I heard something very interesting once: if you can't respect the person in authority, then respect the position. In other words, you may have serious issues with people who hold positions of power, but if they hold a position of authority, your job is to respect that position.

"Render therefore to all their dues: tribute to whom tribute is due; custom to whom custom; fear to whom fear; honour to whom honour" (Romans 13:7).

If the patient for whom you are caring happens to be a parent, then honor your father and mother. If you don't honor them because it is a commandment, then perhaps you'd better do it because *your* kids are watching to see how *you* handle their grandparents. You are teaching them how you want to someday be treated. Something to consider.

"Honour thy father and thy mother: that thy days may be long upon the land which the Lord thy God giveth thee" (Exodus 20:12).

There is nothing more important to Granny than God and family. She loved growing up in a big family, and even though she and Papa only had David and Marilyn, her quiver is full of grandchildren–she looks for any excuse to get together. Holidays, birthdays, or just a day in general are all good reasons in Granny's mind for us all to get together.

Granny has seven grandchildren: Cory McDonald, John Steven Wilmore, Michael Wilmore, Jay Wilmore, Collin McDonald, Connor McDonald, and Delanie McDonald. Cory married Megan, and they had Granny's first great-granddaughter, Ellie Beth. John married Abbey, and they had Jordan, Granny's first great-grandson. I hate that Ellie and Jordan will never get to know the Granny that their daddies knew. Even the last three or four grandchildren have only a few "Granny" memories. Those are memories of the stunts that Granny pulled with them that we still sit around and laugh about at those many family gatherings.

Our family Thanksgiving 2008

The great-grandkids, Ellie Elizabeth McDonald
and Jordan Cole Wilmore, 2009

It's not that she is so incoherent that they don't enjoy spending time with her. It's just that the old Granny was as fun as a barrel full of monkeys. My children still like to spend time with her, but Cory, John, and Mike *really* got to enjoy her antics.

Like the time Granny took Cory golfing and his club slipped out of his hands and went sailing out into the pond. *"Oh, no!"* exclaimed Cory in his ever-present overly dramatic tone. Did Granny panic? Absolutely not! She did what Granny was famous for: she improvised Granny style! She sat down, took off her socks and shoes, rolled up her pant legs, grabbed a putter, and waded out to it. She wasn't afraid of any old snapping turtles. After all, she was the bravest person he'd ever known.

When it snowed, the older boys would call Granny and ask her to come get them. She would make her rounds and end up slip-sliding up my driveway to fetch Cory.

I feel that I should stop the story here to help you appreciate this in its truest sense. There should be a whole chapter devoted in this book to Granny's driving skills (or lack thereof). As a caring parent, it was a little nerve-racking to watch my stepchild climb into the front seat of a woman's car who I didn't trust driving on a mild, sunny June day, much less with three inches of snow over a bed of black ice. Granny didn't listen to the driving warnings on the news; she was a woman on a mission. Just as nothing stops the postal service from getting through, nothing could stop Granny from picking up her grandkids for a snow day!

Granny with Cory, John, and Mike, building
snow forts and having snowball fights

She would pile the boys into her living room with their sleeping bags. Then she would commence the cookie-baking process. (Can you imagine how many chocolate chip cookies these abominable snowboys could eat?) Granny would join in the backyard snowball fights and then drive the boys up the steep road behind her house and let them sled down to the bottom. The bottom, I might add, was a state highway. I think one of the boy's thrills was to see who could swoop down the hill the fastest and closest to the highway. I joined them a few times, and I was always worn out at day's end. Not Granny. "Who's up for some checkers?" she'd say as she poked her head in the living room, with a cookie in her hand.

Granny with Collin and Connor.   Granny with Mike.

Granny loved to fish. She still does. She spent countless hours taking her grandchildren fishing. She loved nothing better than for all of us to meet at her house and head down to the pond. She was from the old school. She taught the boys how to dig up worms from around the barn and then use those worms and chicken livers to catch some of the biggest catfish you've ever seen.

Later, I will share how continuing to cultivate this love in her has turned some of our worst days into some of our greatest days. It's just a matter of having the right attitude as a caregiver and the right bait for the patient.

—⁌⁌⁌—

As a family of an Alzheimer patient, we must go through a slow grieving process. When my grandfather died suddenly of a heart attack a few years ago, I wept uncontrollably for several days. We lost him, and we would never get to see him again, this side of heaven. A few nights ago, I wept uncontrollably again. This time it was for my sense of loss over Granny—the real her. It is not a sudden loss but a slow slipping away that you can see happening right in front of your very eyes, and it makes you feel helpless. Sometimes I compare it to a helium balloon. You can actually see the life just slowly leaking out. You realize that AD is not a disease made up by pharmaceutical companies (one of the theories I read about in my initial research). It is a very real and slow-moving leech that sucks the life out of its victims. You almost get a sense of panic when you see it happening to someone you love. Yet even deep into the disease, I still see glimmers of hope.

Some days, it will be healthy for you to just grieve. Sit and cry as though you just left your loved one's funeral. (Do this out of the sight of the patient, of course.) Grieve over the loss of the person he or she once was—and then get a grip. You will need to have a warrior's mentality. It's you against the disease. Be vigilant, and your effort will pay off. Many days, you will get a glimpse of the old "Granny" again. Live for those days. Relish those days. Videotape those days.

I am glad that we videotape everyday events. I feel sorry for those families who only keep a video journal of the major holidays. I know some moms who videotape their children only on Easter and Christmas and special events. Not me! Sometimes I grab the video camera and just walk through the house to the kids' rooms, and walk in, and have a thirty-second chat with them. You will be amazed how much your kids change and just how precious those moments are. I videotape Granny as often as possible. I capture her reading to the kids, playing with Play-Doh, baking cookies, and fishing. She has always been such an incredible grandmother, and I know a day will come when she will be gone. Somehow, as adults, we tend to push out some of our most cherished memories to make room for the nonsense data we all need to function in our jobs. I don't want my kids to forget what a blessed childhood they have had. I also wanted them to remember those people who helped mold them into who they will become.

Don't fret if you've missed those opportunities. On days when it's a good day, just videotape him or her while asking questions about his or her childhood and young adulthood. These are the things which the loved one normally retains consciousness until the very end. When I first started writing this book, there was no such device as a smartphone. But today's smartphones make it even easier to catch spontaneous moments to save and share. If your loved one is at the beginning stages of AD, take advantage of the opportunity you have and video the everyday small moments. Someday you will look back and realize that the little stuff was the big stuff. When I sense that the kids only know the Granny who tends to be repetitive and burdensome, I pull out old home movies, and we remember her for who she was.

This has many benefits. One of the best ones is that it gives them a springboard for a conversation with her the next time they go see her. "Granny, remember the time when ..." And being Granny, she always declares, "Of course I remember that, honey! Why, Granny won't *ever forget* that." Oh, if only that were true.

This disease is a lot like trekking down the side of a steep mountain. We travel along at a very slight downgrade for a few weeks, and then, almost as if hitting a mudslide, we move at warp speed downward. Then, just as suddenly as that avalanche started, we level back out and are steady for several more weeks. The doctors don't have clear-cut answers to why this occurs. It just does. You must come to grips with the knowledge that there will not be many positive advances with this disease. We actually improve Granny's health significantly at times, but the reality is that we linger in the conversations we have with her today because we never know if those conversations may be a memory of the forgotten past.

Remember not to lose focus on the person for whom you are caring. The weak, pitiful person that you deal with, day in and day out, is only a shadow of the real person. You will reap benefits for your diligence. I think the Lord gives us little handfuls of purpose so that we will not be weary in well doing. And in the end, when those moments of seeing the real "them" become less and less, you will know you have done what you could. Someday, when your loved one is gone, you will look back and have a grand sense of accomplishment at the dignity you gave to another human being. In Granny's case, because she has had such a servant's heart all her life, I can't imagine anything less than giving my all to help her final years be filled with laughter, adventure, love, and respect. After all, she spent a lifetime caring for others, as I tell her on a weekly basis. This is her payback for all those people she spent her life helping. What goes around indeed does come around.

"And let us not be weary in well doing: for in due season we shall reap, if we faint not. As we have therefore opportunity, let us do good unto all men, especially unto them who are of the household of faith" (Galatians 6:9–10).

Chapter 2

First One Thing and Then T'other (Realizing There Is a Problem)

Because Granny grew up in the Depression, she learned how to handle money—and learned it well. When I married David, he and his parents owned a golf course at the local country club. David's main focus was the basic upkeep and appearance of the course. I can't tell you how many rounds of golf he played with a weed-eater in the back of his golf cart. I took over the swimming pool at the country club and became head lifeguard. We have often joked that McDonald children are born with gills because of the number of hours they were at that pool.

Granny and Papa ran the pro shop. They had both retired from teaching and set out on a second career. They had worked out quite a system for running the country club. Granny went in on Tuesdays, Thursdays, and Saturdays. Papa worked Mondays, Wednesdays, and Fridays. He also would go in on Sunday mornings while Granny went to church, and then she would relieve him when church let out. A high school student usually helped out, but Granny and Papa kept the place thriving.

Even though Granny was good with money, I noticed that a few scoundrels took advantage of her memory lapses. One day, while I was helping out in the pro shop I watched Granny take money from a golfer and then give him his change. She left the twenty-dollar bill on the open register drawer, and then turned to get him the Diet Coke he'd requested. When she came back, she saw the money on the register and counted out his change again. He actually took it from her and began putting it in his pocket—until I rounded the corner and reminded her (and him) that she had already given him his change. He looked like a cat caught with the canary, and he reluctantly handed over the loot. I surmised that as smoothly as that had occurred, it had probably had happened before. Who knows how many times? That was my first siren that went off that told me Granny was a little too forgetful. This is a woman who knew the value of a dollar. She thought the eleventh commandment was "Thou shalt not waste money." Even through some of her forgetfulness, though, the golf course was a great endeavor for both her and Papa. It helped keep both of them as vivacious as they were for so long.

The golf course was the first place I noticed the pattern in the notes she would leave herself. If someone came in and reminded her of something, she would jot it down on a piece of paper by the register. She might scurry back to her desk and as it crossed her mind, she'd grab another piece of paper and jot it down again. Then, as if in a comedy sketch, she would be in the kitchen area, and I would hear her remind herself of it yet again, saying that she had better write that down, just to be sure she didn't forget it.

You may be thinking, "Oh, no, I write stuff down all the time!" Don't make that appointment with the neurologist just yet. The older I get, the more I realize that a good memo book and a sharp pencil make good companions too. But Granny took note-taking to the extreme. What concerned me was not her need for a reminder note but that she seemed to not remember that she already had written the note … six other times.

At the golf course for a family meal

The golf course became a second home for Granny and Papa for the fifteen years we owned the country club. It was easy to figure out whose day it was to work by opening the pro-shop door. If it was Papa's day, he'd be in his ugly green chair in front of the TV, watching football, baseball, basketball, or golf. He would gladly hop up and wait on you. Most golfers knew Coach (as they called him) well enough to wait until the commercials to get waited on. One day in 1995, a regular at the golf course called us to say that Coach didn't look well. He was in his chair, but he wasn't acting quite right. He was, in fact, having a heart attack. We got him to the doctor, he had a quadruple bypass, and a few weeks later, he was back at the golf course, holding down the fort. And his ugly green chair.

When Granny was on duty, the golfers would come in the door, see the door behind the counter open, and yell, "Mrs. Lois, you back there?" She'd call out, "Be right there, honey!" Out she'd come, scurrying from the banquet room's kitchen, apron on, flour from here to there, and a smile spread across her face. She always had a plate of something on the counter that she'd whipped up in the back. Most of the time, she kept those goodies out in case the kids stopped in, which they did on a regular basis.

All our kids had the run of the place—they learned to swing a golf club before they learned to potty. The local patrons were great sports about the kids being there. David and I made sure the kids all knew proper golf etiquette, and if Granny saw that they were getting in the way, she would put them to "work," helping her.

Granny loved to cook for her family. She wasn't about to let something like running a business stand in her way. On the days when she worked, she would bring the stuff to cook a huge meal for all of us, and we would congregate in the pro shop when everyone got off work. Because she was a multitasking woman, she always had a lot going on. She made me tired sometimes, just watching all she had going on, and this was when I was in my twenties. When she was in her late sixties and early seventies, she was conquering the world around her.

Because she was always in a whirlwind, she came across as a little … how to put this delicately … scatterbrained. She would be fixing Jay a sandwich and refilling Cory's glass, all the while taking greens fees and renting carts. So when I began to notice little things about her forgetfulness, I was met with a lot of skepticism. "Ah, honey, that's just Granny. She's got too much on her mind." Things like that. Plus, Granny was very sly. I begin to realize she was doing things to cover up the problem she knew she had with her memory. She always wrote everything down. One of her favorite sayings was, "The dullest pencil is better than the sharpest mind."

I begin to notice she wrote the same thing down, over and over again. I would find little scraps of paper on which she'd written "milk, bread, pick up Cory on Friday at 3:00, potatoes." She might make six notes for the very same thing. One by the register. One on her desk. One on the front seat of her car. One on the kitchen table. I found it strange that each note always was written in the same order: "milk, bread, pick up Cory on Friday at 3:00, potatoes." Years later, after the diagnosis, I realized that was the pattern her brain went through with her statements and questions.

Anytime she gets in what I call her "broken record" phase, she asks me exactly the same question, over and over. Or perhaps she'll tell me something funny, pausing always at exactly same moment to laugh, and then continue on with the tale. She might do this a dozen times or so. I feel that those earlier notes I found were a big indication that she realized something was going on long before we did.

One of the hardest parts of identifying a problem with a family member involves family dynamics. In a family, there is no real hierarchy system. At work, you have an employee who answers to a supervisor, who typically reports to a manager, who gives an account to the boss. Families are different. When you have a family with so many different personalities, sometimes people tend to tiptoe around people's feelings, to the detriment of the greater good. You have people who are more outgoing, take charge, and are accused of being bossy. Then you have those who are more emotional and seem to take every statement as a personal attack on them somehow. Then you have those who are AWOL until big decisions need to be made, and then they show up to the family meeting with their opinion. You have those who mean well but quite frankly are either uninformed or simply clueless. No matter what your situation is, you will have to pray for guidance because these are tricky tasks to face. Even if you are an only child, chances are there are other relatives who will hold your caregiving under a microscope and will critique your efforts. Be prepared to hear the criticism.

Be open to suggestions, but just because someone "thinks" doing it his or her way might be the best, that doesn't mean it works in the real world. I have had to come to terms with the fact that *I am* the one taking care of Granny. Me. Even when I got to the point of hiring daytime help, I had to make everyone understand that there needed to be one person in charge. Since I have been taking care of her for the last four years by default, it makes sense that I am the one who knows what works with her and what doesn't.

One more thing: it's important to understand that what works for one patient doesn't necessarily work with another. More important, what works with the patient today doesn't necessarily mean it will work tomorrow. That is why it is so important for there to be *a chief caregiver.* You, as chief caregiver, get to know the signs. Don't let people shame you into believing you are power-hungry because you want to be in charge. If your heart is in the right place and your motive is pure, then you can make a huge difference in someone's life. (Just be prepared for the criticism.)

Don't expect to be taken seriously either when you confront family members that you suspect a problem with a loved one. I would mention Granny's problem to my husband at least once a week, but nobody wants to believe that someone they love has the beginnings of Alzheimer's disease. I realized it is actually worse than hearing that someone has cancer. When you hear the word "cancer," the first question you ask is, "Is it treatable?" Living in the modern medical world today, most of the time there is some type of treatment. Many times, cancer is even curable. Not so with Alzheimer's disease. "Alzheimer's" is a life-altering word. The sense of helplessness you feel is so thick, it smothers you at times. If you have felt that way, do not feel guilty. Do not feel hopeless. You have many wonderful days ahead to make memories.

I will stress this, though: if you believe someone you love has the signs of AD, do something. Don't just hope that everyone else sees what you see. You may need to have a private family meeting to discuss your concerns. Keep a journal. That's what I did. I kept notes of several incidents, spread out over several months, of things that we needed to address. A lot of the people in our family were in denial. They talked behind my back, saying that they couldn't believe that I would be so mean as to say I thought Granny was getting Alzheimer's. Not sweet little Granny. I thought I would scream if one more person said, "That's just Granny! She's got too much on her mind. She just needs to slow down some. That's all. Alzheimer's? You're crazy!"

Denial does not reverse the diagnosis. It actually slows down any help that the loved one can get. The earlier he or she starts on medication (such as Aricept, which treats symptoms such as confusion, memory loss, and mental changes), the better. The disease can be slowed down. Some of the things we tried worked great. Some, not so much. But every day, we learned a little more about what works and what doesn't. The one thing I did not do was give up. Neither should you.

=◦◦◦=

The patient's personality can also be part of the problem when diagnosing him or her. A golfing buddy of David's told him something that just reiterated what a scatterbrain my mother-in-law can be at times. Again, this is not because of a lack of intelligence. On the contrary, Granny's problem was that she was so smart and involved in so many different facets of life that she lived a lifestyle conducive to forgetting things.

We have a friend named Terry Collins. Terry once told David that his job in the fifth grade was to go find Mrs. Lois's car keys just about every afternoon, thirty minutes or so before the bell rang. She would look for them and realize she had no idea where she had left them. He said he found them by the copy machine. In the front office. In the library. He even found them still in the classroom door. She always had so much going on when she first got to school that she would multitask (before anyone knew to call it that), and she would just flutter off, leaving her keys behind her. Terry says that to this day, it's still one of his fondest memories of school, those little afternoon scavenger hunts!

My father-in-law's personality also played into his not being diagnosed with some type of dementia earlier. You see, he is a perfectionist. If he can't do it well, then he feels there's no need to even try. He began to realize he was saying little things that just didn't quite make sense, so he became more introverted. Since he had always been more reserved than Granny, at first it went undetected.

—⁓⁓⁓—

I have noticed, from talking to others who have gone through this situation, that many friends and family members may have noticed signs of a problem but were just afraid to mention it. Looking back, lots of signs are easier to see now. Recently, at one of Granny's neurological appointments, I was scanning a magazine in the waiting room. Something in an article caught my eye. It said that one of the early indicators of AD is the inability to differentiate between the colors in a traffic light—forgetting that red means stop and green means go. I had a sudden flashback to fifteen years ago. It was the first and last time I ever rode with my mother-in-law when she was the driver.

My oldest son, Collin, was born on December 28, 1993. Granny was frugal, and I learned the fine art of bargain shopping from one of the world's finest. In the middle of February, the stores have huge end-of-season sales to get ready for their spring merchandise. Granny asked me if I wanted to ride with her to Rivergate—at the time, it was the closest mall to our town, and it was about forty-five minutes away. Absolutely! So off we went. Since Collin was just a few weeks old, I rode in the backseat to keep an eye on him. We live in a very rural community, so we drove for close to thirty minutes before we came to our first traffic light. The light was green, but Granny stopped at it. I said, "Granny, the light's green. You need to keep going before you get rear-ended."

"Oh, silly me! I wasn't paying a bit of attention!" came her quick response.

We had not gone two more blocks when she ran a red light! She just blew right through it like nobody's business. Cars were screeching their brakes from everywhere. My heart was racing, but all she could say was, "Well, I never! People drive like maniacs nowadays."

This happened four times on the way to the mall. She stopped at two green lights and ran two red lights. I just was in shock. But I dismissed it because I was in the back seat, and we were engrossed in conversation. When we were through shopping, I asked Granny if she would like to sit in the back and keep an eye on her newest grandson and let me drive home. I never rode with her again. Never.

—◦◦◦—

Sometimes, realizing there is a problem is subtle. Like carrots and celery. Let me explain.

I hate celery. David hates carrots. We've expressed this to Granny on numerous occasions. Granny is a healthful-eating fanatic. Her sweet tea could put a healthy person into a diabetic coma, but we'll not go there. Other than her simple syrup that she calls tea, she is big on fixing food that has very little fat—and sometimes very little flavor. But no matter what she fixed, we knew we would get a salad anytime we came to eat with her. Without fail, she put extra celery on mine and extra carrots on David's. Because, after all, that's the way we like them.

So dietary likes and dislikes are very subtle indicators there might be a problem. My father-in-law, however, was more of a "Houston, we have a problem!" indicator.

In 2000, we took our three little ones to Walt Disney World in Orlando, Florida. It was Father's Day weekend, and we were having a wonderful time. Then the phone rang.

The side of the conversation that I could hear went like this: "Hello. Daddy? Is that you, Papa? What? Marilyn? What? Mexicans? What? Daddy, are you okay? Is Momma there? Put Granny on the phone. ... Hello. Granny? What in the world is going on there?"

What I learned when David hung up, after assuring his daddy that the police probably did not have his house surrounded and that he would have a long talk with Marilyn, his sister, when he got home, was that Papa had told David that his sister, Marilyn, was having an affair with a Mexican and that her husband, Steve, had gotten a gun after him, and that the police had Papa's house surrounded. Now ... before you think we should be booked on the next Montel show, David's sister, Marilyn, is the equivalent of Caroline Ingalls in *Little House on the Prairie*. And Steve is like Andy Griffith. And at the time, there probably weren't ten people of Latin American decent living in Smith County.

We just sat there staring at each other. What in the world had just happened? Did we need to call an ambulance to check on him? Did we need to call the police to make sure the SWAT team really wasn't holed up outside their house? The one thing we did know was that something had just snapped inside Papa's brain. It was not gradual. It was supersonic speed. Granny might be a master at hiding her illness. This? Not so much.

When we got home, we made an appointment with a neurologist, who put Papa on antipsychotic medicine, and he seemed to stabilize. Which really only took the focus off Granny even more. After all, she wasn't seeing gun fights and wild trysts taking place, so she was good at hiding her problems.

Granny's sense of humor also hid her forgetfulness. I began to notice the ambiguous way she answered questions. This was very mild in the beginning, but as the disease progressed, Granny became an MVP at this game. Here's how it went. The kids and I would drop in to see her on her days off. The kids would run up to her and hug her and jibber-jabber about their day. I would ask, "So, Granny, what did ya do today?"

Granny's famous reply: "First one thing and then t'other." Then in true Granny style, she would turn the conversation to what the kids and I had gotten into that day. With three little ones, that topic kept us busy talking for hours. Because I thought that was such a cute phrase, I guess it stuck out in my mind, and so I began noticing that she used it as her catchall answer to any question for which she couldn't remember the answer.

"Where did you go before work today?"

"First one place and then t'other."

"Granny, I missed the sermon this morning because I kept the nursery. What did Brother Ron preach on?"

"First one thing and then t'other."

Hm-m-m.

When I would ask her what she had for lunch, her reply would be something along the lines of, "Way too much. Are you hungry? Here, let me bake us some cookies."

See the pattern? She was carrying on a normal conversation but never really answered anything. Because it was her nature to nurture, she normally didn't focus on herself in a conversation. She glossed over the facts, and no one ever noticed. Well, almost no one.

Chapter 3

The Scarlet Letter
(Being Diagnosed with Alzheimer's)

Someone *did* notice her memory lapses—me. I don't know why some of her quirks stood out in my mind, but they did. My bachelor's degree is in early childhood education and psychology. I guess some of my psychology classes have made me more keenly aware of certain behaviors. As I began to notice little indications, I discussed them with my husband and his only sister, Marilyn. Let me just forewarn you: if you are talking about somebody's momma, you likely will be met with opposition. I was met with a lot of denial and some hurt feelings, but that didn't change the obvious. Granny's memory, personality aside, was just slipping. I tried to be as tactful as I could but also persistent enough to raise a red flag in their minds. At least they were aware that I thought there might be a problem … which there was.

⎯⎯෨෨෨⎯⎯

In high school, I remember having to read the book *The Scarlet Letter* by Nathaniel Hawthorne. Hester had been caught in adultery, and her punishment was to wear a huge scarlet "A" across her chest for everyone to see. This was to show others the shame that her sin had brought upon her. Unfortunately, in today's society, many people tend to look at Alzheimer patients as though they should have a scarlet A emblazoned across their chests. As if they have brought shame upon themselves. This is just not so. There are as many different opinions about the causes of AD as there are websites discussing it. One thing is certain: AD is no respecter of persons.

Some of the most charming, intelligent, witty people I have ever known mysteriously come down with AD. I believe it strikes fear in the hearts of both the patient and the family; it's seen as a death sentence in today's society. Other diagnoses can be frightening, but Alzheimer's? There is so much not known about it or its causes. The unknown always has been a source of alarm. This doesn't have to be the case. There is *hope.*

Beatrice ("BB") and Frank Hire

I encourage you to take action. Most of the caregivers I have spoken with said that their patient knew something was going on long before he or she admitted it to family. Some of the people who develop AD approached their loved ones, who chose not to believe it. My brother-in-law is Steve Wilmore. His biological father passed away when Steve was just a boy. His mom is Beatrice, whom the whole community lovingly calls "BB," because that is what her grandchildren called her. She married Mr. Frank Hire when Steve was still young.

Mr. Frank had a business partner named Mr. Delmer Jent. At one time, the two of them together owned thirteen dry goods stores. After many years, Mr. Jent fell ill and was taken to a nursing home. BB said that on the way home from visiting him one evening, Mr. Frank turned to her and said, "You know, I've got what Delmer's got."

"What do you mean, Frank?" asked a confused BB.

"You know, where you can't remember things. And it gets worse and worse. I've got that. I know I do," he admitted.

"Frank! Don't say that! Why, you're just tired and working too much. You don't have that," BB assured him … and possibly herself.

But he did.

Steve said that Mr. Frank got so bad that at night, he would get up to go to the bathroom, see himself in the hallway mirror, and then rant and rave at BB that she had another man in the house. He was so adamant about it that he got her up out of bed one night to show her the man standing right there in their hallway—in his pajamas, no less!

Of course, it was his own reflection, but BB couldn't convince him of that. BB was a petite woman, and Steve and one of his stepbrothers, Gordon, began to fear for BB's safety. Mr. Frank gradually was getting worse and worse, and his fits of anger became more frightening. If he ever were to push BB down, she would be seriously injured.

Gordon arranged for Mr. Frank to be evaluated and then placed into a nursing home.

I believe Granny knew something was just not quite right. When I began my research for this book, I requested a copy of her medical records. As I sat poring over them, I saw that for at least five years before I became her medical caregiver, she consistently had gone to see the doctor with many of the same complaints.

Thankfully, doctors keep very thorough notes. They noted when she visited them alone, with her daughter, Marilyn, and with me. Most of her complaints had to do with what we thought were the side effects of an adrenal gland deficiency. She had been on cortisol for over twenty years, and it started causing deterioration of the bones, which led to osteoporosis. At the time, the doctor who put her on the medication was not aware of this and therefore never advised her to take a calcium supplement.

One of the other side effects of taking cortisol was insomnia. Record after record showed that she admitted to some mild confusion. She also stated she did well to get three or four good hours of sleep a night. This started a pattern in the notes.

"Mrs. McDonald came in today, stating she is suffering from insomnia. I note some mild confusion. I prescribed Ambien to help her sleep. Mrs. McDonald explained she didn't like to take sleeping pills, because they made her sleepy. I suggested she try them."

Six months to one year later: "Mrs. McDonald came in today, stating she is suffering from insomnia. I note some mild confusion. I asked if she had taken any of the Ambien I had prescribed her. She stated she had only taken very few of them. When I questioned why she had not taken them more regularly, she stated that they made her sleepy. I suggested she try them on an as-needed basis."

Six months to one year later: "Mrs. McDonald came in today stating she is suffering from insomnia ..."

—◦◦◦—

Two very distinct things happened that thrust me into becoming Granny's primary medical caregiver. The first one happened at my husband's dentist office.

Melanie Smith, one of David's long-time assistants, came in one morning and said, "Dr. Mac, I followed your momma home from Nashville yesterday."

"Oh, did you?" he said, as he thought that seemed kind of odd. "She mentioned that she had a doctor's appointment. I need to call her and see how that went. You mean you followed her all the way home from Nashville?"

"I sure did. Like to have gotten killed doing it too," she stated matter-of-factly.

"What do you mean?"

"Well, you know how they have widened Highway 70 through Mount Juliet?" she asked.

"Yeah, they've made a new turning lane all the way through there. Why?" he asked.

36

"Well, Granny would swerve over into the turning lane every time it was empty and drove home in it most of the way," she explained.

"You mean there was never anybody coming in the opposite direction? Why, that's a miracle."

"Oh, no, there were *plenty* people coming, but she just kept on a trucking, so they all swerved out of her way. That's why I stayed behind her all the way home. Praying, I might add. I just knew that any minute she was going to cause a head-on collision. But she never did. She finally made it to McCall Street. She was safe and sound; I, on the other hand, was a nervous wreck."

"Oh, my goodness! Thanks, Mel. I'm gonna call her right now and ask her about it."

When David called Granny at the golf course, she answered with, "Well, hey, sugar. What a nice surprise!"

"Granny, how did your visit go at the doctor's office yesterday?" David asked. "I know it's down in Nashville. Did you have any trouble getting down there or back?"

"Why, not a bit! Easiest, fastest trip I've ever made. Did you know they have a whole new lane all the way through Mount Juliet? Hardly any traffic at all in it. So how's your day going?"

And *that* is how I got my job, "Driving Miss Daisy."

—◦◦◦—

From that doctor's visit forward, David would find out when his momma's next trek to Nashville was and then have me make up some excuse why I needed to go too. Of course, with that horrible case of car sickness I tend to get when she's driving, I would be happy to *drive her*. Lots of times, we would call my sister-in-law—Granny's daughter, Marilyn—and we would all three go.

To be honest, those are some of my greatest memories ever. The three of us would drop my three little ones off with my mom, and off we would go. We would always play "Who's on first?" with Granny about how much sleep she actually got and how there was an easy cure to that. She always promised to take a sleeping pill if she needed it. Well, at least a half. If she needed it, mind you. Afterward, we would head to either O'Charley's for a grilled chicken salad or to Cracker Barrel. At Cracker Barrel, Granny would spend fifteen minutes perusing the menu, say that she was not really all that hungry, and then order fried chicken livers, fried okra, fried apples, cornbread, and sweet tea. And even though she said she *never* would be able to eat all that, she always did. And if we were at O'Charley's, she always reminded me to ask the waiter to put extra celery on my salad ... since I loved it so much.

After her prescriptions had been filled along with our bellies, it was time to go empty out some of our bank accounts. Granny loved nothing more than to go shopping. I found out early on that it was best to go to the same store every time. There were definitely some signs of confusion then, and I began putting certain tactics into play right from the start.

In those early years, we always went to Rivergate Mall. I would drop her and Marilyn off at the curb, and they'd wait right inside the door for me. I then would park the car and come back to make our game plan. I always made sure we went in the same door. Every time. No deviations. Never.

That store changed names several times over the years. It started out as Castner-Knotts, then Proffit's, then Hecht's, and now it's Macy's. But no matter what the name above the door said, we always went through the same one each time. I was so thankful when the Tennessee Titans came to town. How much easier could my job get? The entry way that we used was home to Tennessee Titan's gear. The whole foyer was nothing but navy and sky blue. (Our family even owned personal seat licenses for season tickets.) No way either one of them could possibly forget where to meet. What an ingenious game plan.

So, watches were synchronized, grandchildren's current sizes were given out, and then the huddle broke up. I would head out into the mall to go from store to store. Marilyn would be somewhere in the first store but not far off, for sure. Granny would be headed straight for the clearance rack in the children's department. In all those years of shopping with her, I remember only a very few times when she bought something that was located anywhere other than the kids department. Most of the time when she did buy something from the women's department, it was because she realized she couldn't pass it up for two reasons: one, it was such a great bargain; and two, one of her sisters just had to have it. But it was never because *she* needed it.

After a couple of hours—after I had made several passes out to the car to drop off packages in the trunk—I knew where to find my teammates; I knew exactly where to go. I would first walk over to women's accessories, where I would find Marilyn, who would say, "I have no idea where Mother is. I have been waiting here for her for at least thirty minutes." To which, I would respond, "That's okay. I think I know where she will be." Then we would walk across to the second store entrance, which was the men's tie department.

"Well, there you two are! I've been waiting right here at our meeting spot for both of you for several minutes," Then Granny would beam.

"Sorry 'bout that, Granny," I'd apologize. "You all set?"

"Sure am. I'm just so proud of the bargains I found today. Where are we headed anyway?" she'd ask as we headed across the store from the two doorways where they had been standing.

"Over this way, where the Titan's stuff is, so I can go get the car," I'd say, trying not to sound exasperated.

"Well, honey, you should have told us to meet you here, I've just been standing over there, where we first came in."

Of course you have. How silly of me.

As the disease has progressed, and the doctor's visits have increased, I have had to work at making them fun. Many times, Granny would adamantly refuse to go to the doctor. Then, I'd find that even if I left her a note, she still wouldn't be dressed when I came for her, and we would have to rush to get there on time.

Then, as if by divine intervention, my husband suggested that I just tell her *I* had to go to the doctor, and I would like her to ride with me, that she would be going to help me. After all, the truth was, I did have to go— because I had to go with her—but that's not what we led her to believe. Once she thought the appointment was for me, problem solved. She was dressed and ready to go. The only problem we ran into then was that she sure hadn't realized her son had married someone so sickly. I had always seemed so healthy. Why in this world did I have to go to the doctor so often?

The other reason I became her primary medical caregiver happened in 2002. Granny had really gotten forgetful. I had stated my case fairly adequately with David, and he had agreed she needed to be seen by someone. At that time, only Marilyn had gone to doctor's appointments with her every now and then. David called Marilyn and explained to her that he had made an appointment with Dr. Thomas Dinella at Summit and wanted to know if she could go with Granny. This would be a new doctor because Granny's regular doctor was older than her and had retired. Dr. Dinella was David's and Marilyn's husband, Steve's, doctor and very sharp. David also stated that the primary reason for the visit was to see if there was any way to test for Alzheimer's. We were really concerned about her memory. It was getting much worse.

That night when David got home from the office, he called his mother and asked her how the doctor's visit went. She said fine. She thought he was a nice young man, but he insisted she did not have a sinus infection, when, in fact, the top of her head just killed her, and she knew very well she did so have a sinus infection.

David chitchatted with Granny for a while and then he hung up and called his sister. "Marilyn, what did you think of Dr. Dinella?"

"He was nice."

"What did he say about Granny?"

"She doesn't have a sinus infection," she replied.

"I know *that*. What did he say about her memory problems? What can be done to test for Alzheimer's? What did he say about that?"

Marilyn hesitated and then said, "I don't know. … I didn't ask him about that. But he did say she doesn't have a sinus infection."

When David hung up, he told me in no uncertain terms to call Dr. Dinella's office in the morning and take Granny back down there. So that's exactly what I did.

At that visit, just nine days after her initial one, the doctor did some thorough cognitive testing. He gave her a piece of paper and had her draw clock faces on it. He asked several questions. She showed significant signs of dementia, so he prescribed Aricept. That trip began my journey. One of the things Dr. Dinella recommended was some continuity in Granny's medical records. She needed one person who went to all her doctor visits with her.

I cannot stress to you, as a caregiver, the importance of this one factor. You would not believe the number of times I was with Granny at one doctor's visit, and he'd ask Granny something about which she had no clue from another doctor's visit. One of the most important things you can do as a family is to pick one person to be the medical power of attorney. Once we did that, from that point on we began to get the game plan.

If you have a doctor who tells you that he would prefer *not* to have someone else along for your loved one's doctor visits, *find a different doctor*! I recently heard of a doctor who told an eighty-three-year-old woman that he did not want her niece coming to the doctor visits with her because she asked too many questions. How ignorant! Obviously, the eighty-three-year-old woman now has a new primary care physician. An extra set of ears is *always* a good idea at a doctor visit, no matter what the patient's age.

My sister-in-law is an unbelievable decorator. She has decorated more weddings than I care to count. She is unbelievably talented in many areas. One thing she is not, however, is mean. She's just not. If people hurt her feelings, she has a tendency to get quiet and cry. That is not the kind of person you need as a medical go-to person. You need someone whose personality is a little more stubborn and who doesn't mind taking charge when need be. That tends to be my nature. I have never been one to stand by and give a lot of consideration to what needs to be done. I usually jump in and take action when I see a problem. As I often told my children when they were growing up, "If you are not part of the *solution*, you are part of the *problem*!" When I become old and senile, I pray to God that there is a "Lorrie McDonald" in my corner. I do not mean that arrogantly; I just know that you have to be a little brazen to deal with the medical machine that exists. Everyone thinks they know what is best for the patient, when, in fact, they know very little about the patient.

I recently was reading a magazine article and came across an ad for Aricept. What was the catchy phrase for their advertisement? "You know your loved one better than anyone. Who better than you to talk to the doctor about Aricept?" *Ha!* I thought. *I was right all along!* I not only know my mother-in-law better than any doctor ever will, but I also love her more than even she ever imagined.

———◦◦◦———

It didn't take Dr. Thomas Dinella, a primary care physician, long to realize that Granny needed to see a neurologist. He referred us to Dr. Noel Lim. I thank God every day that he did. Dr. Lim is amazing. For one thing, he has to be the most patient man I have ever met. He has never been anything but gracious with Granny. There have been times when I thought I would pull my hair out while he was administering his questions to her. But he just sat there and patiently smiled his reassuring smile at her. This is how a typical visit to Dr. Lim's office usually played out:

"Hello, Mrs. McDonald. You're looking lovely today." Dr. Lim always greeted us with his signature smile.

"Well, hello there, yourself. How are you today?" Granny replied. There were very few times that she didn't return his cheerfulness, and on the few occasions when she didn't, he knew we had to deal with a new problem.

"I'm well, thank you, Mrs. McDonald. I'm going to tell you three things. I want you to repeat back to me, okay? Do you think you can do that?"

"I can certainly try." Granny was always the optimist.

"Blue, baseball, Virginia."

"Blue? Baseball? Virginia? What on earth do they have to do with one another?" She chuckled.

"Absolutely nothing. That's why I use them. It's a test we use to gauge your short-term memory skills. So let's try it. Blue, baseball, Virginia. Repeat that three times for me, please."

"Blue. Baseball. Virginia. Blue. Baseball. Virginia. Blue. Baseball. Virginia?" She repeated it but was not so sure about that last one.

"That's exactly right. Now, Mrs. McDonald, can you tell me what today's date is?" (Most of the time, toward the beginning, she got this one. After the first year, though, this one became nearly impossible for her to do. I came up with a plan to remind her every day of the day of the week and the date. More on that trick in chapter 8.)

"Good, can you tell me who our current president is?"

"Ronald Reagan." Confident. Without hesitation. Wrong, but confident.

"Okay, I see. Can you count backwards from 100 by sevens until I tell you to stop?"

(Here is a very important fact—she nailed this every time! I was counting on my fingers, trying to do simple math in my head, and she was flying—93, 86, 79, 72, 65, and so forth on. And by the way, I had to check those numbers just now to make sure I got them right. She would sail through them without hesitation. Later on, when I began reading back through the doctor's notes, it always confused the doctors that she could do the math section so well. Math skills are apparently one of the first things to go and to show signs of AD. Not with Granny. Chalk it up to her being a teacher, bookkeeper, or frugal, but she smoked this part of the test right up to the very last time they gave it to her.)

"Excellent, Mrs. McDonald. Wow! Very few people your age can do that so well."

"Thank you!" Granny beamed with obvious pride.

"Now, Mrs. McDonald, what were the three things I told you to remember?"

"When?"

"Just a few minutes ago. I gave you a list of three things to remember. What were they?"

"Oh, honey, I wasn't paying attention. I'm sorry." (Or "Oh, honey, I don't think I heard you," or "Oh, honey, I don't think my hearing aid is working very well today.") We were back to the methods she used to cover her tracks.

But the doctor was smarter than the average bear. "Yes, ma'am, you heard me because I had you repeat them three times to be sure you heard me."

"Oh."

Dr. Lim just sat there. Smiling. Waiting. Very patient. Still smiling.

"Come on, Granny! You can do this!" I would blurt out. "Dr. Lim, is it okay if I give her hints?" Did I mention that I am *not* the picture of patience?

"Sure." He'd patiently look from me to his patient.

"Granny, the first one is your favorite color," I coaxed.

"Blue?" she said, with uncertainty trailing in her voice.

"Yes!" I said, just a bit too enthusiastically. "The next one is a sport. The boys all play this." *That should jar something loose in there*, I thought.

"Football!"

"Okay, Dr. Lim, that's really not fair, because our family is *really* into football, and not so much into baseball. So I see why she would say football. Can she get partial credit for that one?"

Still Dr. Lim sat there smiling. The picture of patience.

"Okay, Granny, this last one is easy. It's not only the name of a state, but you also have a sister-in-law named this." I beamed with how clever I was to help her cheat this way.

"Helen?"

"*Helen!* Helen! Granny, since when do we have a state named 'Helen'? Are you kidding me, Granny? Virginia! Albert's wife is Virginia! You know that! Helen? Good grief!"

At this point Dr. Lim's smile has nearly turned into a chuckle. But still he conveys nothing but patience. I wish I could have said the same thing about me.

"Okay, Mrs. McDonald. We'll get some blood work and see you back in six months, okay?"

"Suits me just fine. But you had better ask my chauffeur here. They don't like me to drive in Nashville by myself anymore. I don't know why. I do just fine."

"I'm *sure* you think you do. But Lorrie needs to come with you anyway, so I can make sure you're behaving. See you back in six months."

Then Granny's big blue eyes looked up at me and said, "Okay, Lucy, where are we eating? I'm starved!"

(Granny calls everybody Lucy and has for as long as I've known her. She never has forgotten my name—though come to think of it, if she calls everybody Lucy, we wouldn't really know if she has forgotten our names.)

The saddest day of my life was one day when Marilyn and I took Granny in to see Dr. Lim. He had been Granny's neurologist for almost two and a half years and had been wonderful. Early on, when I asked him about trying different alternative things with her, he was all for it. He simply wanted me to keep a journal of what we did with her and not do anything that could be potentially harmful. I always discussed what I was thinking of trying, and then he would let me know at her next visit if there seemed to be any improvement.

Dr. Dinella had tried adding another medicine to her Aricept years before because it had worked so well with other AD patients. Not with Granny. I noticed a significant amount of confusion in her. I left her on the medication for several weeks, and she got much worse. I backed her off of it, and she improved. I told Dr. Lim, and he said maybe we should try it one more time. We did—with the same results. Drastic confusion. He and Dr. Dinella were both adamant that they had no patients that the drug made worse. If I had not been so aggressive in wanting to help Granny get better, I might have caved in, thinking, *Well, they're the doctors. They obviously know more than I do.* That just wasn't so when it came to this patient. I saw her every single day of her life. I knew it made her worse. I insisted to the doctors that it made her worse and finally, when we tried it for a third time with the same results, they conceded that she was in that slim margin of patients for whom it had reverse effects.

You know your patient. If you are the caregiver, and a doctor has changed the medicine, keep a daily journal. If, after several weeks, you are certain the medication is making your patient worse, be persistent in letting the doctor know. Not every medicine affects every patient the same way.

Now back to the saddest day of my life. Marilyn and I had taken Granny in to see Dr. Lim. I had known for several months that we were way past simple dementia. I spent hours every day with Granny. I knew it was just a matter of time before we got the news that I had known for quite some time.

We were sitting in an exam room. There was a huge chart behind my and Granny's heads. It said "The Stages of Dementia." It went from a very light shade of gray on the right-hand side, which listed mild memory loss; to a very dark gray on the left-hand side, which was full-blown Alzheimer's and the point of not recognizing loved ones. There were several shades in between. As Dr. Lim came in that day, he began his usual friendly banter, but I could see right away that he was overly concerned. He asked very few questions that day. He closed her chart and smiled his very patient smile at her.

"Aren't you going to ask her to do blue, baseball, Virginia?" I asked, my voice coming out in a tremble.

"No. I don't think so. Not today. I don't need to."

"Are you saying …?"

"Yes." He continued to smile at Granny.

My eyes welled up with tears. Then I remembered the chart behind my head. I knew he was using discretion out of respect for Granny. So I gave Marilyn what I thought was a knowing look and then turned back to Dr. Lim. "So what color do you think we are?" I asked, and I pointed up to the milder end. He shook his head no. So I pointed to a more advanced stage on the chart and said, "About here?"

He continued his characteristic smile. He gave a gentle nod of his head to confirm what I was asking. The next thing I saw was a distinct emotion I had never seen him have before. Sadness.

I tried my best not to cry my eyes out in front of Granny. I told Marilyn I would ask him a few questions out in the hall, and then we'd go. Out in the hallway, out of Granny's earshot, he basically told me to keep doing what we were doing and to know that she would begin to need more help than just Papa was able to give her. They were both nearly eighty years old, and we should think about finding them a good home. I explained in no uncertain terms that they *already* were living in a good home, and I had every intention of making sure that was the only "home" they ever would have to know. He understood but told me to be prepared for things to get much worse. Then he said that he appreciated all I had done for her over the years.

With that, I walked back into the room, and Granny said, "Where to now, Lucy? I'm starved!"

Chapter 4

Give Me a Crispy Chicken Salad
and Your Car Keys, Please

Change stinks!

Brother Steve Brogden is a very dear friend who just happens to be one of the world's greatest missionaries. He raised his three girls in the jungles of Papua, New Guinea, along with wife, Cindy, and became close to our hearts in the 1990s. He served part of a furlough as our church's assistant pastor, and during this time, he preached one of the most enlightening sermons I've ever heard. He said that life could be divided up into four seasons. Spring would be from birth until age twenty-five. Everything is new, growing, budding, really just awakening. Summer would be ages twenty-six to fifty. This is the prime of your life. Full of life. You are in full bloom. Hot as blazes. The days are long and productive. Very active time. The fall would be ages fifty-one to seventy-five. This is a lot of people's favorite time of year. Things have cooled down some, and you have more time to enjoy life. You tend to appreciate the colors all around you. There is still crispness to life. Then there is winter. This would be from age seventy-six to one hundred, if you were so blessed. It, too, has beauty and wonder to it. But too many people complain about all the hardships of winter. Few people can see all there is to enjoy about it. You tend to see lots of white stuff. You are always freezing. Everything begins to grow still. Lots of things die during this time.

I have never forgotten that message. Enjoy every changing season of your life! There truly is something beautiful about each one.

"To everything there is a season" (Ecclesiastes 3:1).

With that said, I still say, "Change stinks!"

———

Most of us don't like for things to change. We are creatures of habit. Change can be scary, especially as we get older. Not everyone has our best interest in mind, and we are old enough and wise enough to realize that. Change is inevitable, though. Many times, it is for our own good. Just as God knew when He was creating the seasons that if He left the days in fall as long as the days in the summer, we'd work until dark and never slow down enough to enjoy our families or His creation. So He made the days shorter in the fall by causing the rotation of the earth to be farther from the Sun and initiated a time for us to slow down and enjoy life more.

It irritates my husband to death when we have daylight saving time. If it were up to him, we would do away with ol' Ben Franklin's idea and leave the clocks alone. Either way, I tell him, the days are shorter—slow down!

That's what we had to tell Granny. Especially when it came to her driving.

Slow down!

———

There really is no telling how many mishaps Granny has had over the years in her cars. What would be even scarier to know are the number of fender-benders in which she would have been involved, had the fair citizens of Smith County not been quicker at the wheel than she was. We go to church with Matt and Alesha Dillon. For years, Matt would meet us at the door, wagging his head. "Brother David, poor ol' Granny done run us off into Jerome Donoho's yard again. You are going to have to say something to her. She's gonna kill a feller with slower reflexes." Well, I reckon so.

Our church is up a little country road. It's plenty wide enough for two cars to pass one another—if, of course, both drivers are actually paying attention to the road and staying in their designated lane. Granny, however, always seemed to be fooling with something in her backseat. Always! I cannot tell you the number of times I passed her, and she was leaning back, trying to straighten or grab something in the backseat.

All four of the older grandsons have been involved in minor vehicular mishaps with Granny. Once, Granny did enough damage to her car that she had to have it replaced. We all gathered down at the golf course for supper that night, awaiting Papa's return from purchasing Granny a new car. Papa had gotten it from Sonny Apple at the local Chevy dealership. Marilyn's middle son, Michael, was about ten years old then. I can remember he was bouncing around, so excited to see what Granny's "new" car would look like.

"Wow, Granny, a new car! What kind do you think Papa will get you? When do you think he will get here with it? What color did you ask him to get you?" Michael has always been a chatterbox.

"Well, honey, Granny doesn't care what kind of car I get," she replied. "I did tell Papa I would like a blue one, though. That's my favorite color."

"Blue! I love blue too. Blue would be pretty, Granny. It would match your eyes. I like blue." More bouncing around.

Finally, Papa opened the door, came in, and went straight to his ugly green chair and reached for his bag of chewing tobacco. He was flooded with grandchildren hovering around, asking all kinds of questions.

Michael, seeming to have the most vested in this decision for some reason, couldn't stand it any longer. "Papa, what color car did you get Granny?"

"White. Just like her old one," came his very serious, very aggravated-by-all-the-noise reply.

"*White?*" rang a whole chorus of voices, almost in unison.

Granny flew out from behind the counter, wiping her hands on a dish towel. "White? Cordell, I told you I wished you'd find me a blue one. My last two cars have both been white. I really would have liked to have had something different." She tried not to sound too disappointed.

"Different? Humph! I wouldn't dare do that to the people of Smith County! They're all used to dodging you in a white one. I wouldn't dare put you in something different. Lord, you'd probably kill somebody because they wouldn't know it was you coming at 'em!" And with that completely serious statement, he sat down in his ugly green chair as we all filed out the pro-shop door to see Granny's new white car.

One bright, sunny summer afternoon, David and our two younger boys were headed to the golf course when they passed Granny, leaving. David noticed a car had come to a stop several yards in front of where Granny was headed, and true to form, she was turned around, fooling with something in her backseat. He quickly told the boys to pray because Granny was about to be in a bad wreck.

He whipped his truck around and headed back, just after she rear-ended the car that was in the process of making a left-hand turn. David jumped out to see if his momma was okay and then, not knowing how badly the injuries were going to be in the other car, he told Granny not to get out of her car.

Fortunately, there were only minor injuries, but it could have been very serious.

We knew it was time.

One bright, sunny summer afternoon, David and our two younger boys

For a couple of years after I started taking Granny to see Dr. Dinella, he mentioned that there would come a time when she would need to stop driving. So she bartered with him. She wouldn't drive to Nashville anymore by herself. She always had me to take her. Then we got her to realize that she didn't need to drive after dark. That just made sense. At least it did to us. She thought it sounded like complete foolishness.

But by the time I started taking her to Dr. Lim, the neurologist, the bad wreck had taken place nearly a year earlier, and we had tried our best to talk Granny into driving as little as possible. More and more people were coming into the dentist office on a weekly basis, telling David about near misses with his mother. It was getting to the point where we knew it was just a matter of time before she either killed herself or someone else. Our problem was getting her to understand the seriousness of it. She was forgetful but still coherent.

When dealing with AD patients, there is a really hard period between when they first get diagnosed and when they get so bad that even they know they are bad off. Like I said, people don't like change. Granny had been driving for over sixty years—longer than I've been alive. So, brave man that my husband is, he would often say, "So when are *you* going to tell momma she can't drive anymore?" He'd always give me his sideways grin, the one he uses when he should be mowing the grass but really wants to go play golf.

Thankfully, we had modern technology on our side. One morning before we were on our way to see Dr. Lim, David faxed him a letter, asking him to please request that his mother have her driver's license test retaken. This way, when I got down there, she would not see me pull Dr. Lim or one of his nurses aside to say anything to them. While Dr. Lim did his memory testing, he asked Granny if she was still driving and then explained that before he could allow her to continue to drive, she would need to go to the DMV and be retested. She sat very still. She was very quiet and just nodded. Then he continued with her exam.

We left there, and I took her across the street to O'Charley's to get a bite to eat.

As the waiter came to take our order, I told him we both wanted crispy chicken salads with water to drink. After he walked off, I gently said, "Granny, did you understand what Dr. Lim said about your driving?"

She looked out the window and just nodded.

"We'll need to go get you retested so you can keep your driver's license, okay?"

She was still looking out the window when I saw it. Slowly at first and then more steadily—there was no mistaking what I saw. There were tears streaming down her quiet face.

"Granny, what's wrong? Why are you crying?"

"You and I both know I can't ever pass that test. Just like that, I'm through driving. Sixty-something years, and just like that, y'all are taking it away from me, and you don't even care," she said in hushed tones. More tears flowed than words. No anger, just more tears.

"Granny"—now I was squalling too—"we do care. Don't you see? That's why we are so afraid for you to keep driving. Don't you remember that wreck you had down from the golf course? You could have killed those people and yourself."

"What wreck?"

"See, Granny? You don't even remember."

The waiter brought our food, asked if we were okay, and then hurried off. We both were crying too hard to eat.

"Granny, I tell you what—I will personally help you study for the test, and if you can pass it, then there is no reason why you can't drive."

"Forget it. You and I both know I will never be able to pass that test. It's over. I'll just sit at home, where I won't be a burden to anyone."

"Granny, think about it. I take you almost everywhere now. It's not going to be that much different, really. I already stop and get you for church now. You're retired from the golf course, so you don't go to work anymore. Anytime you want to go anywhere, all you have to do is to call me. We're building over there on the farm right beside you, remember? It won't be any bother at all. I'm just right up the hill from you, okay?"

"If you say so, Lucy," she said, trying to appease me.

The look on her sad little face broke my heart. In two. But this was a moment of tough love. She really *was* going to hurt herself or someone else if she continued to drive. It just wasn't safe anymore. To be honest, it hadn't been safe for a while.

"I say so. It's going to be okay. I promise. Now, why don't you eat your salad so we can do some shopping?" I urged.

"Okay. You sure are good to ol' Granny. I hope I don't become a burden to you kids," she said woefully but was beginning to perk up.

"Granny, you've never been a burden. I enjoy every minute I get to spend with you," I said, meaning every word of it.

"Thank you, Lucy. You're the greatest. Now, if you'll slide your plate over here, I'll give you my celery. I know how much you love it."

D. T. McCall (Pa Dave) with Dolly

Truth be told, we were blessed when it came to Granny's giving up her driving privileges without a fight. Had her memory not failed her, she might have remembered the stunt her daddy pulled when they took his license away from him. (Apparently, poor driving can be hereditary.)

When D. T. McCall got up in his late seventies, his nine children decided enough was enough. He had caused more accidents in his two-mile jaunt to work than any of them cared to count. By this time in his life, he had built up what would become a multimillion dollar family-owned furniture business. It was just a matter of time before he bumped into someone of less than excellent character, and once that person realized who he was, the injured party would sue.

He not only would potentially hurt himself or someone else physically, but he stood to do damage to a business into which his whole family had poured their hearts and souls. So what did those big strong brothers of Granny's do? They called her and told her to deal with Pa.

She told me the story of talking to her daddy several times, years ago, and I stored that information away in a memory file. She had done everything in her power to let him keep his dignity, but she realized she loved him enough to know his safety was her first concern. After all, he was a grown, successful man. Surely he would succumb to his family's wishes and go peacefully into the sunset, right?

Not on your life! What he did do was the thing of legends. We live in a small rural community. Pa lived on the family farm, just across the river from his family furniture business. On that farm, he used two forms of transportation that his children had not considered modes of travel to and from work. He didn't become successful by being stupid. No, sir!

One day, Granny got a call at the school where she worked.

"Is this Lois McDonald?" came the voice from the other end.

"Yes, it is. How may I help you?" replied Granny.

"Well, ma'am, I'm calling from the store. Your daddy just came to work."

"And?" Granny obviously a little annoyed by the phone call that interrupted her class time. "What's so strange about that? Who brought him?"

"Dolly."

"Dolly? His *horse*, Dolly? I'm on my way!"

Pa had not been one to sit at home in a rocking chair. When Granny explained to him that it was the 1970s, and people didn't ride horses to town anymore, he agreed that he would not come to town on Dolly. Then Granny made him promise not to ride *any* of the horses to town. Which he reluctantly did.

Two weeks later, after riding his old tractor across the farm, he decided it couldn't possibly hurt to ride it across the bridge and pop into the store. After all, he had never promised anyone he wouldn't drive it—yet!

———⟨✦✦⟩———

One of the funniest things happened as the change occurred in Granny as the disease progressed. I made her a promise that I would take her everywhere, and I have worked hard at never letting her feel like she was a burden. As time passed, I would call her and say something like, "Granny, I'm running to Walmart. Do you want to ride with me?"

She would always reply the same way, which is something you are going to find happens a lot with AD patients. She would say, "You can stay home when you can't go anywhere else. I'd love to go with you."

At the beginning, that was her statement all the time. As AD has gotten worse, I sometimes have to *make* her go places. She will fight me tooth and toenail to stay home. She'll say she doesn't want to go or that she doesn't like to go places. So once I quoted her line about staying home to her, and she told me, "That is the stupidest thing I've ever heard. What idiot ever said that?"

Oh, well. You win some. You lose some.

———◦◦◦———

If you are caring for an AD patient or even just an elderly one, the time will come when you will have to deal with his or her driving privileges. I caution you to use the utmost grace. There is something very liberating in knowing that you can jump in your car and head off into the wild blue yonder. Unfortunately, when many of our patients get behind the wheel of a vehicle, the *wild* blue yonder often becomes too *wild*.

Work with your loved one's doctors. This is another reason to have a primary caregiver. You have to know what's going on daily and keep the physicians informed. Be discreet. One of the things that have always made me furious was when family members would talk to the doctor about their patient right in front of her! (Hello? She's sitting right here.) Their attitude was that she would not remember this in fifteen minutes anyway. Well, respect is due, regardless of whether the person remembers it fifteen seconds later. Your loved one does understand what you're saying. Just be gracious. You'll sleep better—I promise.

Chapter 5

A Family Affair

When the movie *The Blind Side* came out, several of my girlfriends saw it before I did. Every weekend, someone new would come up and say something to the effect of, "Lorrie McDonald, you have been captured on the big screen! You have got to go see the movie *The Blind Side*. You and Leigh Anne Tuohy must have been separated at birth!"

I asked more than one of my friends what they meant by that. One of them explained. "This woman is you. She's opinionated. She's to the point. She is passionate about the things that matter to her, her family, and those she chooses to love. She has more going on than three women. And bless his heart, her husband, Sean, is just like David. He stands back, hoping not to get in the fray when she's having an intense moment of fellowship and just loves her for who she is. He is wise enough to know that everybody needs a Leigh Anne Tuohy on their side."

Everything I heard about Leigh Anne Tuohy made me think that she and I had a lot in common. I like a woman who will go to bat for someone— anyone—who has not been as fortunate in life, and I especially admire a woman who is tenacious about taking care of her family.

After the fourth or fifth comparison to the woman, I dragged David—I mean, I gently suggested that we go see the movie. I have never been more flattered! I have to admit, several of your idiosyncrasies reminded me of me. Everyone in our row looked at me when she exclaimed that she wouldn't be wearing the gaudy orange if Michael Oher chose to play football for the University of Tennessee.

David played for the University of Georgia. We live in middle Tennessee. One hour forty-five minutes from the University of Tennessee, to be exact. We are surrounded in a sea of orange.

David with Georgia's coach, Mark Richt, and
David's former coach, Vince Dooley

When David and I married, I was somewhat of a UT fan. But that was all about to change. UT was not my alma mater, but neither was it the school of most of the 100,000 screaming fans who fill Neyland Stadium every Saturday in the fall. It's the adopted school of the factory workers, miners, truck drivers, and even true alumni, like our good friend, Randy Wakefield.

When David and I found out we were having a baby girl, we flew to Florida for the weekend to celebrate. (Hey, after a house full of boys, this was cause for celebration!) Upon returning from our trip, and UT beating UGA that weekend, we pulled up on Sunday night to five acres of trees rolled in pink toilet paper and the words "Go Vols" written across our front yard. Randy had gotten his youth class from church to come over almost all day Saturday after the game to roll our yard. We heard he even ordered pizza for them and ate it on our deck. That's how seriously Southeastern Conference football is taken here in the South!

———∽∽∽———

When my stepson Cory was a senior in high school, he came home one night after ball practice and said he had something fairly serious to tell me and Dad. Lots of things crossed my mind as I sat there and watched him pace back and forth on our very Georgia red-and-black carpet, wondering what in the world could be so serious.

He paced. I prayed.

What on earth could be causing this much anxiety in our happy-go-lucky boy? Finally, he spit it out.

"Dad, I don't know how to tell you this," he gravely began.

"Son, it's okay. We love you, and we will get through this. Whatever 'this' is. Just tell us."

He finally got the courage to blurt out, "Dad, I got a full ride!"

"What? Okay, I'm confused. You got a full scholarship to college, and that's a problem? How?" David queried, not even trying to hide his confusion. (Or relief, I might add.) "How is that bad?"

"*Dad!* It's to *Tennessee!*"

Oh, the anguish.

"You mean that's what all this is about? You are going to have to go to Tennessee instead of Georgia?" The color had just about returned to my poor husbands face now.

"But Dad, we *hate* Tennessee!"

"Train up a child in the way he should go: and when he is old, he will not depart from it" (Proverbs 22:6).

"Bub, it's okay. We can still hate them. But they can sure pay your way through school. Don't expect me to ever wear that nasty orange … but I'll take their check any day."

Other than school loyalty, why do I tell you about those comparisons to Leigh Anne Tuohy? Well, just like Michael Oher had a bulldog in his corner, that's what I became for Granny. Having a tenacious attitude comes in handy for the one you are caring for and love. Just as in *The Blind Side*, I knew we were going to need our own Mrs. Sue and a family full of loving helpers to accomplish what we needed to do for Granny.

Our situation is somewhat unique because Granny and Papa are both alive and living together in their own home. What a blessing! Although Papa was diagnosed with a very generic label of "dementia," he actually is quite capable of doing much more than a lot of people give him credit for. I realized early on that he likes to feel as if he is taking care of Granny.

One night after I got home, it dawned on me that I had forgotten to take Granny's hearing aids out. I called and asked Papa if he would go back to her room and do it for me. I told him that the case we keep them in was in the top dresser drawer. He seemed irritated but said he would do it.

The next night, when I got there for my bedtime routine, Papa told me that he had already taken Lois's hearing aids out and put them up for me. I realized he was contributing. I bragged and bragged on him about what a huge help that was to me. From that night forward, that has been his job. If I get there and he has not already done so, he hops up and goes and fetches Granny's hearing aids from her. This way, he feels like we are helping her together. It seems to give him some purpose.

Here's another cute trick: when I am working with Granny, I will say things like, "Granny, thank you *so* much for helping me take care of Papa. You do an amazing job. Why, I don't think he could make it without your help."

She always smiles at me with those gorgeous baby-blues and retorts, "Well, honey, he's a handful, but that's my job. I just appreciate your help with him."

Then, when I am leaving, I always tell Papa, "Papa, thank you *so* much for helping me take care of Granny. You do an amazing job. Why, I don't think she could make it without your help."

Then he looks up at me with those gorgeous baby-blues and retorts, "Nope. She couldn't."

And there you have it in a nutshell.

If you have children at home, you need to make your caregiving game plan a family affair. Too many kids never see their parents actively taking care of their grandparents. The children need to see your efforts in caring for those who can no longer care for themselves adequately. Remember, these are the same children who will someday be taking care of you. If they see all that you do for your mom or dad or some other loved one, then when your time comes around, you will have trained them that family takes care of family.

One of the reasons it was so easy for me to choose to take care of Granny was because I realized that she had worn herself out, taking care of everybody else. She had cared for her mother when she got Parkinson's disease. She cared for her dad when he was more than two handfuls to care for. Then she did the same for her in-laws when their time came.

She was part of what is now called the "sandwich generation." That is the age at which you care for your parents because they are aging, and you help care for your grandchildren because ... well ... they're your grandchildren. Who needs a reason to care for them?

There are several ways I got my children involved. As I mentioned before, when I needed to keep a close eye on Granny, I would often feign needing her help with my three little ones. She was more than happy to sit and watch them play, read a book to them, or tell them a story. I also never allowed them to be critical of her forgetfulness.

"Mom, Granny has told us that story a hundred times!" they might start to whine.

"Good! That means you will be able to tell it to me when I get old and forgetful. Be glad you have her around to tell you stories. Lots of children don't have that luxury."

Grandchildren are a wonderful distraction! There are days when I stop in to take care of her medicine, to make sure she and Papa have eaten a good meal, or just to say hello. I almost always make sure the kids get out of the car and go inside for just a short visit. Words on a thousand pages of a thousand books cannot emphasize enough what a great therapy spending time with children is. Especially when they just happen to be your grandchildren.

"Children's children are the crown of old men; and the glory of children are their fathers" (Proverbs 17:6).

I drilled the kids as we pulled up into the driveway. "Collin, you be sure to ask Papa if the forecast is for rain this week. Connor, you ask him who's winning the golf tournament. Delanie, just give him a big hug and then climb up in his lap. If the TV is on, wait one commercial until the next one, and then you can get down. Be sure you all hug both of them and tell them you love them. Got it? Good deal!"

You get out of people what you expect of them. I trained my children from the time they were small to carry on actual conversations with adults. They have never (cue the gasps from the audience) been allowed to walk around with any type of electronic device. No handheld games. No cell phone for distraction. I expect them to be able to perform an increasingly disappearing art ... called conversation.

Parents are increasingly raising morons in their homes. They allow society as a whole to dictate what the child should be able to accomplish and at which age certain tasks are appropriate. Raise the bar. Set your standards higher. Teach your children that there is a wealth of knowledge inside that elderly person. So few people know true history. Here is an opportunity to ask questions from eye witnesses. Today's young people don't have a clue what the older generation's lives were like. Remind them that there were no microwaves, no DVD players, and no cell phones back in their grandparents' day. It was a much different America than they grew up in and one from which your child could learn greatly.

I often go over a list of questions my kids can ask Granny and Papa. It helps give them a springboard on which to bridge the age gap and start up a conversation. With Granny, the simplest question will set her on a storytelling binge. Papa is a much harder cookie to crumble. He is more of a short-answer man, while Granny tends to be an essay. The type of answers they receive don't matter to me, as long as there is some type of banter. This way everyone involved benefits.

Here are some of the things I have them ask:

1. What year did you graduate (attend) high school?
2. Did you play sports in school? Which ones? Were you any good? Did you ever win any awards? Did you play in college? Did you play professionally? (You'd be surprised what old folks tend to keep secret.)

3. Who was your best friend growing up? What did you do for fun?
4. Did you ever have a pet? What was it? What was its name?
5. In which city were you born? Were you born in a hospital or at home?
6. What was the funniest memory you have of your childhood?
7. What was your favorite Christmas gift?
8. Did you serve in the military?
9. What was your first job? What was your favorite job?
10. If you could change one thing from your youth, what would it be?

I cannot tell you how many times the kids have jumped in the car and shared something with me that I never knew. Elderly people do not tend to talk about themselves unless prompted. So by all means, prompt them.

—⊰øøø⊱—

Have your children help out with chores around their grandparents' place. I know that not all patients are going to be grandparents—perhaps they are not even directly related to you—but that is no reason not to seize a wonderful opportunity to teach your children to put others first.

They can take out the trash. Pick-up sticks and tidy up the yard. Wash dishes. Straighten up in general. If your patient wants to "help" the children with the chores, then all the better—you are getting a two for one. Now you have two different generations feeling like they are contributing.

One beautiful sunny day, I took the kids down to Granny and Papa's house with buckets and sponges. I grabbed two yard chairs and stuck the chairs under the shade tree. Then I had Papa and Granny come out in the beautiful weather to watch. The kids and I set about cleaning the white fence surrounding their house, and they did little more than watch. Every now and then, my father-in-law would get up and wipe a little section. Even that little bit was tiring to him. But that night, when I was getting them settled in for bed, they both were glowing and excited about getting so much done that day. They had done something productive and felt alive. They were a part of the progress.

One of the worst things you can do to the elderly is take away their contribution to society. Many well-meaning people have "niced" the elderly to death.

"The sleep of a labouring man is sweet" (Ecclesiastes 5:12).

AD is a very irritating disease. It teaches you patience. My children have had to learn to use their manners. When Granny asks for the sixth time how they did in their ballgame, they smile and answer her. I cannot stress enough the trouble they have gotten in for huffing and smarting off with, "Granny, I just told you—we won." Not happening! This is a grand chance to teach respect for their elders.

If you teach your children nothing else about this disease, I emphasize that you teach them to have compassion. Too many people think life is about them, when, in fact, it is not.

—⟨∘∕∘∕∘⟩—

Another way to make this a family affair is by getting any other immediate family involved. I must forewarn you, though—do not expect everyone to share in your vision. This is when you need a dose of Leigh Anne Tuohy.

I talked with David early on about my plan for keeping Granny at home for as long as possible. He was a little skeptical, as his nature tends to be. He knew I was terribly busy taking care of our children, homeschooling, working part-time for his dentist office, and most importantly, taking care of him full time. He thought it was a noble idea but not very realistic. I assured him that it could and would be done. I have grown to love and admire my mother-in-law and knew that she would not want to be a burden to anyone.

I do not want you to be disillusioned by the effort it will take on your part to keep your loved one at home. It takes military-type precision planning and a well-trained team. It is going to take effort from everyone, and we do not always get that. In fact, there were many times in the beginning when I was faced with open opposition.

Each situation will be different, with any number of scenarios to deal with. In our family, Granny and Papa had only two children, Marilyn and David. Marilyn is two years older than David and sixteen years older than me. We all live in the same small town, just a few miles apart. All families have different dynamics, and these will have to be considered when coming up with a game plan. Again, you may not be able to get everyone to agree to what is best for the patient, and you may have to make some tough decisions.

Very few people know what goes into keeping Granny's and Papa's daily lives flowing "normally." All our family members have their own busy lives to contend with and therefore just tend to pop in when it is convenient for them. Little thought goes into what it takes for Granny and Papa to have three meals a day, clean laundry, fresh groceries, or even a bath. Because they have been self-sufficient all their lives, most of the nephews have no idea how many hours a day I put in, making sure their basic needs are met. I don't make a big scene about it, so in large part, it goes unnoticed.

If you are in this for fame and glory, you need to pass your baton and join the Peace Corps because much of what you are going to do will not be recognized or even appreciated. Not to mention that what you are doing will be criticized by those who are doing nothing. Just a reminder—it *will* happen. I talk to caregivers all the time, and this is their number-one complaint.

Encourage family members to do what they can or will. If each one of the seven grandchildren in our family call the house just one day a week and talk for ten minutes, then it only takes ten minutes out of their week, but the dividends are huge for my in-laws—the more contact they have with the "outside" world, the more grounded they can stay.

I use a simple trick. When I am in my car by myself, I have "trained" myself to use traffic lights as a reminder to call and check on Granny, Papa, Mammie, Aunt Mary, or Nana, who is my mother. It's safe with hands-free calling, and I'm "stuck" in the car anyway. I can conveniently check on two or three people in one quick trip to town. Just a few short questions, and I can keep informed of how they sound, and it is an easy way to make their day go better.

Form a game plan for siblings to stop by at least once a month; once a week is ideal. The more people you can get on board, the better. I will caution you, though, that you may need a written plan for others to read so that the apple cart doesn't get toppled over. AD patients can get very agitated very quickly. That's not beneficial to the patient or to the caregiver. You may have to limit access to certain family members who just can't seem to get with the program.

—◦◦◦—

Granny with Elisabeth Edde, on one of their many visits

Another great resource is church family and neighbors. Depending upon your situation, this may not be an option for you. Fortunately, we live in a town similar to Mayberry.

Granny had spent all those years ministering to others, so when she became more homebound, I called in reinforcements. I let all of her brothers and sisters-in-law know that she would love to have a visit, if just for ten or fifteen minutes every now and then.

Whenever I see her childhood friends out in town, I encourage them to drop in. Many times, when I get there at night, Papa will tell me that so-and-so dropped by. Most times I don't have to even jar Granny's memory about if she had company or not. She's very quick to tell me about any visitors who may have stopped in.

Our church family is phenomenal. Dana Edde is the mother of four adorable children. She will probably be sainted when we get to heaven. (And not just for being married to Jeff Edde all these years!) She lives on the backside of nowhere, but once a month or so, I find out she has dragged all those young'uns over with a big plate of homemade chocolate chip cookies and paid my in-laws a visit. (By the way, most gruff people can be won over with food. It's kinda like at the zoo—feed that grumpy old bear, and you've made a friend for life.)

Dana's six-year-old son, Justus, has won Papa over. Justus is all boy. He is full of questions. "Whatcha watchin'?" "What are they doin' that for?" "Wanna wrestle?" You can't help but love the kid.

They visit for thirty minutes, and then they are on their way. They have no idea of the good they have done. Children are the greatest medicine for elderly people. No shot of B-12 could ever do as much good.

All those neighbors to whom Granny fed homemade cinnamon rolls all those years—well, they've not forgotten either. They were more than eager to lend a helping hand when I mentioned that I could use some help keeping an eye on my in-laws.

I encourage you to send a "form letter" to those people that you know wouldn't mind helping. Let it be short and to the point. Inform them of the situation at hand and what they should expect if they visit.

Example:

> Hello! As most of you know, Lois and Cordell are not able to get out and about as much as they use to. Lois has been diagnosed with Alzheimer's and Cordell has some slight dementia. It would be wonderful if you could stop in from time to time for a quick visit. Be forewarned that you will need to repeat yourself, but that's okay. Just don't be shocked if you get asked the same questions over and over. Feel free to bring them a treat if you so desire. They have no dietary restrictions. Thanks in advance for this unselfish act of kindness.

Networking isn't just for corporate gurus. It comes in very handy when caregiving too. Don't be afraid to call in favors. I have left town overnight only twice since I started on this caregiving journey. One of the things I have to do for Granny is give her a shot of Forteo every night. It is a medicine for osteoporosis.

I called two of my good friends who are nurses and asked them if they'd mind helping out. Gina Dillon came once and gave Granny the shot for me. The other time, Tina Tyree stopped in after her shift at the emergency room. Look outside your box. Help is usually just a phone call away.

When making this a "family affair," don't forget that not all "family" shares your DNA. Granny learned a long time ago, "Making a living is what you get. Making a life is what you give." She went about being the giver; it's only fair that now she should be on the receiving end of the giving.

What are *you* giving?

"I have shewed you all things, how that so labouring ye ought to support the weak, and to remember the words of the Lord Jesus, how he said, It is more blessed to give than to receive" (Acts 20:35).

Chapter 6

Over My Dead Body

"Intreat me not to leave thee, or to return from following after thee: for whither thou goest, I will go; and where thou lodgest, I will lodge: thy people shall be my people, and thy God my God" (Ruth 1:16).

How many of us have heard that verse quoted at weddings? It's a beautiful passage from the book of Ruth, but the truth is, it is not a woman talking to her future husband. It is Ruth speaking to her mother-in-law, Naomi.

Ruth's husband, Naomi's son, had passed away and now Naomi was leaving Moab and going back to her hometown, Bethlehem-Judah. Ruth tells Naomi that she knows her place in life is to take care of her mother-in-law, and that's just what she plans to do. The passage shows the devotion that Ruth has for her husband's mother. I admire that!

There is an amazing principle in the Bible that very few preachers touch on. It is the relationship between a mother and daughter-in-law. We have an amazing friend, Ray McCoy, who would definitely be my lifeline if I were ever on *Who Wants to Be a Millionaire*. He speaks seven languages, teaches Greek and Latin, and lived in Israel, where he studied to become a Jew. Now he is a born-again Christian who has taught my family a wealth of information about biblical customs. One of them is this role of a daughter-in-law in the Bible.

In biblical times, a woman prayed to have a son. It was considered a huge blessing to give birth to a baby boy. There were many reasons for this. First, the promise of the Messiah being born meant that perhaps your son would be the Christ child. Second, it had a lot to do with Middle Eastern custom. A woman did not work outside of the home. She married and became a wife and a mother. There was no social security fund, no retirement plan, no 401(k). A woman had to depend upon her husband to care for her until his death. At that time, one of her sons would take her in and her daughter-in-law would care for her.

If you gave birth to only girls, then you knew that someday, they would marry and leave with their husbands and take care of *his* mother. Your only hope for a future lay with your son's choosing a good, caring daughter-in-law. When Brother Ray explained that to me years ago, a light bulb went off in my head. *Aha!* I thought. *One of my jobs as David's wife is to care for Granny as she gets older.* Of course, at the time of that epiphany, Granny was still running circles around me.

To be perfectly honest, I never dreamed that when I purposed in my heart to take care of her as she aged that it would involve as much effort as it has. Nor did I ever dream that I would have to fight tooth and toenail to give her the care she deserved. Be forewarned! Some of the people who will oppose you will mean well, but you may have to go up against your own family members to do what you know is best for the patient.

I knew that Granny had spent her life and her health caring for her parents and her in-laws. She had worked tirelessly to keep them all *out* of the nursing home. It did not take a genius to understand that if Granny fought to keep *them* out of the nursing home, then *she* certainly didn't want to go there herself.

Granny at the pond, on one of our many family picnics

Granny's stubbornness has sometimes been her downfall—literally! Two separate events happened within a few months of each other that led to Granny's physical demise. The biggest obstacle we have faced in providing adequate care for her has been not only contending with mental issues (the AD) but also working around several physical factors. These could have been avoided if she had not been too stubborn for her own good. We never dreamed these two simple events would be the start of a horrible decline in her health, but they were.

The first one was when we were having a picnic down at the pond in the summer of 2007. Granny was sitting beside her good friend, Bobbye Jane Phillips, in stadium chairs. We had grilled burgers and enjoyed watching the kids fish. When it was time to go, Mrs. Bobbye yelled for David to come help his mother get up out of her chair. Humph! Nothing doing! Granny tried to jump up out of the chair without any assistance—and down she went. She lost her footing and plopped right back down in the chair—hard. I noticed she limped quite a bit after we got her up and headed to her car. She wouldn't admit it if she had hurt herself. She was too proud for that.

In the autumn of that same year, Granny's sister, Mary Nell Hight, came up to visit from Memphis. Granny and Aunt Mary owned a couple of rental properties together, and we had gone to one of them to try to collect some past-due rent.

Behind the house were some apple trees, and Granny had noticed that the man living in the house had not picked any of the apples, and those perfectly good apples were going to waste. Also going to "waist" was the grass—he had not mowed the yard in weeks, and it was actually up to our knees. Aunt Mary Nell warned Lois not to go back there; it was not safe. As Aunt Mary Nell and I were trying to get the rent, we heard a loud squeal from the backyard. It was Granny. She had just made contact with an apple. Her foot had found it, and she had slipped and landed soundly on her pride.

She was not to be out done, though. As she sat there on the ground, waiting for us to help her up, she frantically gathered all the apples she could reach into a pile for me to pick up and put in a bucket to take home for her to bake for David for supper. She knew how much he loved baked apples. That and carrots, of course.

What transpired over the next few weeks changed our lives forever. Granny couldn't quit limping. She kept complaining about her hip hurting, so David decided that we needed to take her to see Dr. Roy Terry, our family's personal orthopedic doctor.

(To be a true McDonald, there are at least two prerequisites: First, you are a die-hard Georgia "Bulldawg" fan. Second, you must have broken at least your arm. Other body parts are often broken just out of family loyalty. But the arm—preferably your dominant hand—that has to be broken and put in a cast to truly qualify you for the McDonald family crest. So we have become great friends with Dr. Roy Terry, who, by the way, is also a University of Georgia alumnus.)

When I took Granny to see him, he discovered she had degenerative arthritis and had fractured her hip. She was going to need bed rest and then very intensive physical therapy. Both would prove easier said than done. But by this point in my caregiving role, I had learned to expect the unexpected.

—⁂—

Not long after the phone call we received in Florida back in 2000 from Papa, we realized that Granny and Papa weren't going to be capable of running the golf course forever. We put it up for sale and sold it.

They had officially retired for the second time. They both were retired from teaching school, and now their career at the golf course was over. Granny retired to her kitchen, and Papa retired to his ugly green chair that he moved from the golf course to his den.

So at first, when we had to confine Granny to bed rest, it worked out okay. Papa was there to keep an eye on her. Well, more like an ear. He wasn't moving from in front of his television unless absolutely necessary. She did all right as long as she had her *Guidepost* magazines to read. Once she started feeling better and began physical therapy, however, it opened up a whole new can of worms.

The first person that home health sent to work with Granny was Mrs. Carolyn, an older lady and probably a retired nurse. Way too nice to be in home-health physical therapy, though.

Granny was started on injections of Forteo. It was something she would have to take every night for two years. I was given the in-service on how to administer the shot, and that began my nightly visits to her house. I worked out a schedule so that I would pop in around supper, bring them a bite to eat, and give her the shot. Then out the door I went. While I was there, though, I began to notice several things.

Granny and Papa could never remember if or when they had had their medicines. Marilyn brought pillboxes from the drugstore her husband owned, and I filled them up on Sunday afternoons with the following week's meds. Problem temporarily solved.

(An ongoing theme you may recognize when dealing with AD patients is that no matter how clever your solution to a problem may be, odds are that it will only work for a while, until they lose another ability, and then you will have to reinvent the wheel. Be patient. You will surprise yourself with how clever you can be when you need to be.)

I also noticed that Granny was not doing the physical therapy exercises she had been given to do. Mrs. Carolyn had given her a worksheet that plainly explained how to do some simple strengthening exercises. When I would go in, I would ask her to do them for me. She clearly did not know how to do them, because she had not been doing them.

We would begin on them, and when she would get bored or tired of them, she would squeal, "Oh-h-h! That hurt my back!" It scared me to death, the first dozen times or so—until I dropped the paper on the floor in front of her. Here was a woman who would squeal like she was being tortured if I asked her to lean forward (while sitting, mind you) and touch her toes. "My back! Oh! My aching back!" Then one evening, I accidentally dropped the sheet with the exercises on it.

"Oh, honey, let me get that," she exclaimed. And down she went—way farther than I had tried to get her to lean. *You ring-tailed tooter! You are faking it!* So, being sneakier than she was, I rigged several more clumsy episodes. Every time was the same. She would bend over and get whatever I needed. No problem! But for me to turn around and ask her to do the same thing in an exercise was excruciating—for her and me.

Just to be sure I was not oversimplifying things. I had another X-ray and MRI of her back scheduled. We went in, and they reassured me there was nothing new there. There were just some old vertebrae that were losing density but nothing that would cause this kind of pain. Plus, Dr. Terry did several in-office tests. He had her lie flat on her back and lift her legs. No problems in the office, but at home with Mrs. Carolyn … well, that, my friend, was a different story altogether. Hmmm, time for Plan B.

The next time Granny was due for physical therapy, I was there, waiting. I pulled Mrs. Carolyn aside to assure her that Granny was faking some of the squealing she was doing. Mrs. Carolyn looked at me like I was Hitler. Where I was concerned, she was clearly dealing with the most uncaring person she had ever encountered. This sweet little old lady was most definitely in pain, and she would not push her past her limits. No, ma'am!

So I watched. Mrs. Carolyn would get Granny to go into the front bedroom and lie down and then proceed to have her do exercises. Granny would do one or two just fine, and then Mrs. Carolyn, meaning well, I'm sure, would say something to the effect of, "Now, Mrs. Lois, that doesn't hurt does it? Is your back okay? Don't let me hurt your back."

"*Oh!* My aching back!" Granny would squeal.

Okay, I saw that coming. I tried on several visits to push Mrs. Carolyn to push Granny to do what she was supposed to do. Instead, Granny would have Mrs. Carolyn plop down on the bed and talk about grandchildren. She always had a great visit, but her back wasn't getting any stronger in these little gossip sessions. Only one thing to do …

"Mrs. Carolyn, you're fired."

I called the home health office and said, "Hello. This is Lorrie McDonald. I am Lois McDonald's caregiver. I have fired Mrs. Carolyn. She is too nice. Do you have someone there who would be more firm? Like, say, a Sergeant Carter type?" And with that, they sent me Rusty. Ex-marine? Perfect!

Yes! Score one for the caregiver!

Rusty showed up the next visit and was as sweet as Granny's iced tea—until it came time to do her therapy. That's when the rubber met the road. He told her to rise up out of the chair and then sit back down, strengthening her legs. After two, she started the squealing.

"Okay! We'll do ten instead of five, then," he said. "You need a lot of exercising to help you get strong again. Some pain will be normal because you are quite stiff." He used a very "Sergeant Carter" tone, I might add.

Granny looked at me in horror! Humph! This was supposed to be her visiting hour. She couldn't believe I actually was going to make her *do* her physical therapy.

Rusty told me something that changed the way I worked with Granny from then on out. He was actually a very loving man. He never pushed her past her limits, but he never caved into her manipulations either. He told me that most people "loved their family members right into the grave." I asked him to explain.

He said that we do too much for people as they get older, and once they have lost the ability to perform a task, they rarely ever regain it. We give them a walker when they really just need a hand to help steady them. We give them a lift-chair, when all we are doing is destroying their leg strength. We take them to the doctor, and instead of making them walk, we shove them into a wheelchair and roll them straight to the inability to be independent. He said, "We 'nice' them straight to the nursing home and then straight to the funeral home. Give them some work to do. Make them feel useful. Wear them out during the day, so they will sleep soundly at night."

He warned me that it goes against most people's grain to actually do what the patient needs. It comes off as gruff and uncaring, when in reality it is much more humane than nice-ing them to death. It takes a lot more work on the caregiver's part to maintain the patient's strength and independence, but that it is what the majority of them really want. He said it was refreshing to meet someone who actually wanted to improve the patient's life. He also said that most family members and paid caregivers are lazy. It takes work to do what I had planned to do with Granny. Most people would rather stick the patient in a comfy chair and hand her a remote control. A stationary patient is much less trouble for the caregiver. Rusty and I respected each other. Granny may have *enjoyed* "Aunt Bee" coming for her visits, but I realized "Sgt. Carter" was exactly what she *needed*. He and I would get along just fine.

So I have been the bad guy more times than I care to count. People at church sometimes look at me in shock when Granny gets up from the pew, and not only do I not help her up, but I discourage anyone else from doing so. Boy, do I get the looks. At first, I tried to explain myself, but it becomes too complicated too quickly. It boils down to asking myself what I want to give Granny—sympathy or independence? A wheelchair or capable legs? A remote control to keep her busy or a math worksheet to get those brain cells moving?

One of the first things I did was take away Granny's lift-chair. Rusty was right. She didn't need a lift-chair. She needed to strengthen her legs to be able to lift herself out of all the other chairs she sat in. She wasn't always going to be able to push a button to lift her butt. She needed to be able to lift her bottom up by having strong leg muscles. I know other family members didn't agree with what I did, but thankfully, it was orders straight from the top brass. Sgt. Carter told me to get it out of there, so I did. And guess what? Granny got stronger. The Marines will do that to you.

People often look at me as though I am disrespecting her. I'll admit it is a fine line. People on the outside looking in do not know the whole story. They don't know that those cries and whimpers stop immediately if I ask a question, such as, "Do you think Papa would like a milkshake from Sonic?" She always perks up, stands up, and says, "Well, I bet he would!" I know when she's hurting and when she's focusing more on the process than the task. I know because of the countless hours I spend with her every day. People in passing only assume they know what's going on.

Some people who are quick to judge me are members of our own family, and they have no idea of the nights I go home, cry myself to sleep, and beg God to give me wisdom to help Granny and not just perform for spectators. There are those who ooh and aah over her in front of a crowd but never spend an hour working with her on her exercises, as I do (while she's slapping at me and calling me every name in the book). It is more important for them that they appear to honor their elder than it is to honor Granny and encourage her to push herself.

I am sure there have been times when I didn't show as much compassion as I should have. I will have to answer for those times, but for the most part, I know my heart was right, and I am completely aware of Granny's capabilities. Those abilities change from day to day, even hour to hour on some days. So when we are out in public, and I insist that she walk the twenty steps to the car, as opposed to waiting for me to get the car, I think of an old saying: "Those that matter will understand, and those that don't understand just don't matter."

Rusty's tough-love approach has made Granny more vibrant and lively than she ever would have been, had he not come along. I took his suggestion of being firm, and it has worked. The other thing Rusty suggested, however, nearly started a war.

———◦◦◦———

Rusty told me about "swing bed," which basically is where a patient goes into the hospital for thirty days to receive around-the-clock supervision and intense physical therapy. I was reluctant. I didn't like the idea of Granny getting out of her house, out of her routine, out of her element. I had heard of so many people who went into the hospital then went to the nursing home and then to the funeral home. I knew Granny had more life in her yet to live. Unfortunately, I had to mention this to David and Marilyn. I told them both that this was *only* for thirty days, and then she would come back home.

The course of the next few months was an emotional roller coaster. The facility they placed Granny in was one street over from our house. By this time, we had sold our home in town and were living up the road in the same rental house that had been the scene of the apple incident. We were busy planning a new house, and life was rushing by. I still went in every night and gave Granny the Forteo shot. It was just easier than trying to make sure she got it every night and showing someone at the facility how it worked. Plus, Granny expected me to come "put her to bed." As I went in each night, I was not a happy camper.

She seemed to be getting worse, not better. She was definitely more confused, and her large motor skills were not improving at all. I went to several nurses, but no one ever seemed to know who was actually working with her or what her progress status was. They knew all about her grandkids but nothing about what she was *supposed* to be there for. They also mentioned that her charts clearly marked she was experiencing terrible back pain during her exercise sessions—here we go with *that* again.

So, being the sleuth I am, I showed up the next day during her "workout" session. Not good. She did exactly the same thing to these poor girls as she had done to poor Mrs. Carolyn, squealing, "Oh! My aching back!" She had even added tears to it now.

(If you are reading this and thinking, *Maybe Granny's back really was hurting her*, then you are thinking the same thing I thought a thousand times—until her doctors tested her to see if it was consistent. It was not. Not to the degree of her performance. MRIs, CT scans, X-rays, and physical exams all proved the same thing. As long as they kept her occupied and kept her from being bored or even focused on the task at hand, she would do her exercises perfectly—she'd fly through them! On numerous occasions, I would tell her that as soon as she got done, we would leave and go Christmas shopping. She would do each drill without as much as a grunt. You would have to have spent the hundreds of hours I spent with her to know when it was put on and when she really was having some pain. Just as a mother begins to recognize the different cries from her child, you will begin to tell what is real and what is worthy of an Oscar. This is another reason why it is so important to have one primary caregiver. You need to know your patient. Trust your instincts.)

Granny would not do the exercises with the nurses, so they would help her back to bed and then leave her for the next six to eight hours to lie in bed and read or watch television. This was *not* what we signed up for. Plan C. (Or are we up to Plan D by now?)

All this time, my sister-in-law and I were butting heads because she found out that there was an empty bed at the nursing home, where Granny could get around-the-clock care. Marilyn truly believed that the nursing home was the best place for Granny. But all I could think about were the stories Granny had shared with me, time and time again, when we went to and from the doctors. "*No!* We are *not* putting her in a nursing home,"

I insisted. "Granny fought tooth and toenail to keep everyone else out. I am *not* doing this to her." But life comes at you fast. Our thirty days at the facility would soon be up, and she was worse!

Day in and day out, we would go 'round and 'round. A family member told me how selfish I was being to not want what was best for Granny, and I told her that if the nursing home was so great, why had Granny worked so feverishly to keep her own mother and father out of it? David knew how busy we were as a family, and he wasn't sure we could give her the care she needed, even if we did bring her to our home. So I even butted heads with him. Every time I hinted at her moving into a family member's home, I was told that she needed around-the-clock care at the nursing home. *No.*

We were building a new home. I homeschooled our three younger children. I worked several hours a week at the dentist office, doing bookkeeping. And I took care of Granny and Papa on a daily basis. David suggested that maybe the nursing home *would* be best for Granny.

"*Over my dead body!*" I screamed. After all, was that what Ruth did with Naomi? I think not! She stuck by her side and offered to work to keep the two of them alive. And in the long run, boy, did it pay off for Ruth. She married that cutie, Boaz, and just happened to become the great-great-great—(you get the point)—grandmother to Jesus! I just couldn't help but feel an uncanny defensiveness for Granny. I really can't explain why this was so important to me, other than I just knew Granny deserved to be where she would be the happiest—at home!

And with that response, we began praying for God to work this out. I knew I was going to need full-time help to keep Granny at home. We just didn't know where to begin to find that kind of help. I reluctantly agreed to move Granny across town to the nursing home, just long enough for her to have some real physical therapy with a real therapist. That also gave me enough time to find someone trustworthy and stubborn enough to do the task at hand.

Every time I was with Marilyn, she would tell me how good they were to Granny at the nursing home. The truth is they *were* good to her. As good as one person can be to the ten people that person is assigned to look in on. The ladies up there did a wonderful job of making Granny feel at home, but no matter what, it was *not* home. I wondered why in the world you would want your mother anywhere other than at home, if she was well enough to be there and if you had the means to keep her there. We were blessed enough to have both.

Marilyn and I always have been close. The fact that we had two entirely different game plans for Granny really put a strain on our relationship during this time. I could not get her to see my reasoning, and I certainly couldn't understand hers. I explained to David that I felt Granny deserved better than "institutional care"; she deserved "individual care." He agreed and promised to talk to his sister to help her see that point. Marilyn honestly believed it was best for Granny to go to the nursing home. I did not.

I talked to dozens of people who are caring for an AD parent. Each and every one said they had a family member who butted heads with them about patient care. Each one said that it put a real strain on family relationships. It would be very deceitful of me to paint a rosy picture and say that everyone involved is going to agree with you. That's just not reality. So you have to decide whether you are in this for the patient or for peace? Because sometimes, you just can't have both.

Be aware that you might run into resistance from places you never dreamed you would. I think I would have handled it better if I had been forewarned that not everyone would agree with keeping Granny *out* of the nursing home. If the time came when she needed more care, then we would cross that bridge when we got to it. You may have crossed that bridge. I am well aware that there will come a time when we would have done all we could do. I just knew that we were not there … yet.

Granny may have been slipping, but she still had enough of her right mind that we had several conversations about this while she was still at the nursing home. She would tell me over and over that she didn't want to be a bother to any of us and that she was fine there. She didn't mind staying there. Each time, I would lean in close to her, look deeply in her baby-blue eyes, and take both her frail little hands in mine. I would speak straight to her soul.

"Granny, you listen to me, and you listen good. You are *not* staying in this nursing home. You are *not*! God is going to answer our prayer and work this out so I can get you home where you belong. You have to trust me! I am *not* leaving you here. You are not a bother. You have killed yourself for everybody else. You are not staying here. If I don't find someone to stay with you by Christmas, you are coming to live with us. You got that?"

She would always tear up, squeeze my hands, and say, "Lucy, you're the greatest! I just hate being such a bother."

She was never a bother. Oh, she drove me nutty every day. But she was never a bother. You might not understand that statement if you are not a caregiver. But if you are, you get it.

———ɷɷɷ———

I explained to Granny, in front of all the family members present, that her stay in the nursing home was just for some rehab and that I expected her to work hard so I could take her home.

As we left the nursing home that day, David looked at me and said, "I'm worried about you, sweetie. You are working too hard. You are taking care of the kids, me, Granny, Papa, and overseeing the building of the new house. It's just too much on you. Think of it this way: Momma's being here will give you a few nights' rest, okay? It will all work out. But enjoy having nurses to take care of her."

The first night Granny was up at the nursing home I decided it might be nice to get a little rest from my caregiving responsibilities. Then my phone rang:

"Mrs. McDonald?"

"Yes," I replied.

"Well, Mrs. McDonald, your mother-in-law won't take her medicine from any of us nurses. She *insists* that you give her medicine to her and that we are trying to overmedicate her. I hate to ask this, but—"

"I'm on my way." And with that, I darted out into the cold November air and began my trek to the nursing home to put Granny to bed … because after all, that's what I do.

Eventually, I "introduced" Granny to the nightshift nurse, and she allowed her to give her the meds, but I still went every night and gave her the shot of Forteo. And you know what? It never was a bother.

———ɷɷɷ———

With a title for this chapter of "Over My Dead Body," you may think that I am anti-nursing homes, period. That is not so. I just knew that *for us*, that was not an option. Granny deserved more out of life than feeling like she was a bother to us. I know that there are legitimate cases where a patient does need around-the-clock medical supervision, and you are just not equipped to do it.

I believe in too many cases, however, that the main reason people get placed in a nursing home facility is out of convenience. Often, there are family members who could take the loved one into their homes, but they don't want to put forth the commitment and effort that it involves. Families have gotten too busy, and their lives are too complicated to slow down to care for those who cared for them.

Sadly, there is a real pattern emerging that is so subtle, it almost goes undetected. A couple gets married, has children, sends those children to daycare, and spends very little time nurturing and caring for those children. Then those children grow up and get just as involved in life (sports, friends, hobbies, etc.) as their parents did, and still, little time is spent bonding with their parents. These children grow up, get married, and have children, and then when the parents of these grown children need care, they do just what was done to them when they were in need—they send the parents to "day care." It becomes a logical answer to let someone else care for my responsibility. Many parents are on a fast track, sending themselves straight to a nursing home without ever realizing it by pawning their children off on others to care for them.

If you have spent time with your children when they were growing up, playing with them in the backyard or taking them on walks—anything that says they have your undivided attention— then you are nurturing a relationship that will actually benefit not just your children but you also. I heard a quote once: "If you're children don't have to look for you when they are young, you won't have to look for them when you are old!" If you have been there—really been present for them—when they were growing up, they will be present for you as you age.

The book of Proverbs talks much about training up your children so that when you are old, they will honor you. Too many moms have their noses stuck in their smartphones and try to portray their "perfect" family on Facebook, while shooing their children away so they can update their status. All the while, those poor kids learn that if they act out or throw a big fit, then they at least can get a little attention from Momma for that.

Most of these children are being left to themselves. Ironically, *"The rod and reproof give wisdom: but a child left to himself bringeth his mother to shame." (Proverbs 29:15)* Funny how it doesn't say he brings his father to shame but rather his mother. I believe that is because God intended for the primary job of caregiver to be the mother. I know that in today's world, that is not always the norm. But that doesn't mean it wasn't God's plan.

There's more truth in this verse than today's modern parents want to admit. Whenever you see some urchin running around Walmart half dressed, acting a fool, you say to yourself, "Where's that kid's momma?" (Or in the vernacular of the Deep South, "That young'un ain't had no momma!") What's sad is that all too soon, that momma is going to need a place to go for her own nurturing, but that seed was never planted in her children's hearts. There is a sign I see in stores sometimes that is sad but true. It reads: "Be nice to your kids. They're the ones who pick out your nursing home!" Indeed, you do reap what you sow.

———◦/◦/◦———

There are times when the family has done all they can do, and there is a legitimate need for medical help. Our family had three such cases. The first was with my brother-in-law, Steve Wilmore's, stepfather. As I mentioned, Mr. Frank Hire had been a successful businessman who ran thirteen different businesses. His business partner, Mr. Delmer Jent, had been put in the nursing home in Lafayette, Tennessee, and on a visit back from there, Frank told Steve's mom he thought he had the same thing that Delmer had. What Mr. Jent had was Alzheimer's disease.

It wasn't long before Steve's mom, Beatrice, begin to notice some very strange behaviors in Mr. Hire. He was showing signs of delusions and bouts of anger. BB, as everyone called her, was a petite lady. I've mentioned the incident where he stood in the bathroom one night and started yelling at BB that she had another man in the house, when in reality he was looking at his reflection in the mirror. After that, she had to make a decision. She was not physically strong enough to take care of him—or to fight him off if he were to turn violent—so she placed him in the same nursing home where he had visited his partner.

Mr. Frank was in the nursing home for thirteen long, hard years. Steve's mom traveled at least once a week to visit him. As his AD grew worse and he no longer knew her, the family grew more and more concerned over BB's health. There came a time when some of the family suggested to her that the trip was somewhat dangerous for her because it was almost an hour away, and Mr. Frank didn't know she was his wife anyway. That's when she sweetly reminded her family that she knew him, and when she said, "I do … in <u>sickness</u> and in health," well, she meant it.

—⌁⌁⌁—

Uncle Tommy Hight, Aunt Ruth Jean, Granny, and Uncle Ray

Uncle Ray McCall was Granny's older brother. Our dear, sweet Aunt Helen cared for Uncle Ray for years as his health failed. She took him on sunny afternoon car rides. She took him out to watch the deer in the fields. She loved him and cared for him with everything she had in her.

But eventually, Uncle Ray began to fall more often. Uncle Ray was a big man, and Aunt Helen had lifted him more times than she probably should have by herself. The time came when it was no longer safe—for either of them—for him to be at home.

She was so devoted to him, that she continued to care for him, even when they had to move him to the nursing home. She set up "house" right there. And on the morning that he slipped from this shore to heaven's, she was feeding him his breakfast, one small bite at a time. One minute, she was gently placing the spoon to his lips, and the next, he smiled and was gone.

I would never fault her for doing what was best for Uncle Ray. I just know that in our case, we were not to that point. I was young and healthy enough to tend to Granny at home. Aunt Helen was a shining example of unselfish love and devotion. She will be greatly rewarded someday for being such a wonderful caregiver.

—◦◦◦—

The third person in our family that had to have nursing-home care was Uncle Tommy Hight. He was Aunt Mary Nell's husband. She was the sister who owned the rental properties with Granny. She, too, did what she could.

Uncle Tommy was a preacher for over sixty years. He was diagnosed with Alzheimer's disease several years ago. Aunt Mary covered up for him, as many spouses do. We went to visit them once in Clearwater, Florida, where they were spending the winter. I knew on that visit that Uncle Tommy had dementia. Aunt Mary just smiled, corrected him, and helped him finish his train of thought and bragged on him to all of us. Unless you were looking for it, you never would have noticed that he had a problem.

They eventually moved from their home in Memphis back to Carthage, where all of Aunt Mary's family is located. God's timing is always impeccable. Not long after they got here, his health began to deteriorate, and Aunt Mary devoted her days to caring for him. Several years passed, and all she did was care for Uncle Tommy.

She has one son, who is a pastor in Virginia, and another son, who is a doctor in Atlanta, Georgia. She did all she could do to keep them aware of what was going on but not alarmed. As both sons visited, it became obvious to them that their mother had done all she could do for their father. Uncle Tommy was sleeping twenty-two hours each day. He needed more care than Aunt Mary was capable of providing at home. She, too, was by his side when he passed from this life to the next.

I commend all three of these strong, devoted ladies for doing all they could to keep their husbands at home for as long as possible. I just know, however, that there are too many people in nursing homes because it was not convenient for a family member to take them in. It all boils down to your working that out with God. Someday, when I stand before Him, I hope He takes me by the hand and says, "There is someone I'd like you to meet." And with that, I hope to sit down with Ruth and Naomi and have a long conversation. After all, they were my inspiration for taking care of my mother-in-law.

—◦◦◦—

There are as many different situations as there are different people reading this book. The decision to put your loved one into a nursing home or assisted living is one you have to make, taking into account all the factors that are pertinent to your particular situation. For us, it was a matter of heart.

David and I prayed that God would somehow send us an angel to help us take care of Granny—and He did just that. I still visited Granny at the nursing home each day. I always told her to pray with me that we could find someone to help her out at home. She always adamantly reminded me she did not need help. She took care of herself and Cordell just fine. Then she would look around the nursing home room and ask, "By the way, where is Cordell, and who's moved my furniture?" I realized that her being there was only adding to her confusion. We needed a miracle—and soon!

—◦◦◦—

One of the saddest things that happened during this time was at our annual McCall Christmas party that we hold in the fellowship hall of First Baptist Church. I arrived at the nursing home to pick up Granny and was shocked to find her already gone. It didn't take me long to guess who had picked her up for me—Aunt Ruth and Uncle Gary Garrett. They had driven in from Hendersonville and were unaware that I was coming to get her, so they "stole her away" first. Aunt Ruth and I discussed at great lengths that night—and agreed—that Lois had no business being in a nursing home. I also told her and Uncle Gary that David and I were working feverishly to come up with a new Plan B.

Granny had a wonderful time at the party that night. She loved visiting with family and reminiscing about all the ghosts of Christmases past. The sad part came when all the gifts had been opened and the aluminum foil placed back on the casseroles. It was time to go *home*. Only Granny realized she wasn't going "home"; she was going back "up there."

Aunt Ruth offered to take Granny back so that she could visit with her a while longer. As Granny sat there crying, I hugged her and whispered to her, "You are coming home, Granny! You are! I promise!" I left that church fellowship hall that night with a renewed commitment to bringing her home, where she not only *wanted* to be but *deserved* to be. I knew we would get a Christmas miracle. But it was already December, and time was ticking away.

Granny's total time away from home was only from October 6 until December 22, 2007. I kept my promise because God was faithful and got her home just in time for Christmas.

Granny, *home* with her family for Christmas. God is good!

Chapter 7

Pray for an Angel

Everybody loves a good Christmas story. Christmas is Granny's favorite time of the year. I know of very few people who enjoy all that surrounds this holiday as much as my mother-in-law. It is only fitting that God would grant her very own Christmas miracle.

The whole time Granny was at the nursing home, working to get stronger, I was behind the scenes, working to get her home. If you are going to keep a loved one at home, then learn from my hours of labor! There are some critical things you need to know and consider.

Where do you find a capable person to help you with the caregiving? This is one of the largest growing job fields out there. The babies flooded the hospital baby wards back in the 1930s and '40s. Now that same group of individuals is flooding the hospital geriatric wards. As the population ages, there is a growing need for in-home caregivers.

(If you are the parent of a teenager who is not sure what he or she wants to do with his or her life, suggest caregiver. I have included a whole section on this occupation at the end of this chapter.)

The first thing I did was talk to Granny's doctors. They assured me that with some moderate supervision, she would do much better in her own home. This is the case with many people with AD. They are not animals to be kept in a cage like a zoo; they simply need to be in a safe environment. Safety should *always* be your number-one concern. There may come a time when it is no longer in the person's best interest to be at home, and that is something on which you will have to keep close tabs. I knew that I would still be bringing Granny and Papa their supper and give out nightly meds, so at this time, what I needed was someone who could come in Monday through Friday, 8:00 a.m. to 5:00 p.m.

I checked with the human resource person at the nursing home, who generally has a list of in-home help. I know that several companies specialize in in-home health care but not in our very small rural town. To be honest, I really wanted someone we knew. I was hoping for at least someone whose family we knew. The nursing home gave me the names and numbers of ladies who were supposedly "qualified" to be in-home caregivers.

I called several people on the list and actually interviewed a few of them. I was not impressed. Either they were too elderly to do the job well, or they were of very shady character. I knew I wanted nothing to do with any of them. Be forewarned! Just because someone has placed her name on a list does not make her qualified for this type of care. I checked every reference carefully. I did not want a "babysitter." I wanted someone who would help me to help Granny. I knew that with the proper structure and plan we could not only add years to Granny's life, but that they also would be productive years, full of actual "living." That's what I envisioned for her. Your situation may be different. Your patient may be too far gone—or so you think. I think most elderly people could improve the quality of life if just given the proper attention. Either way, the people I saw and interviewed were not what Granny needed.

I knew we needed a strong-willed person who could follow directions. She needed to be honest, hard-working, and capable of doing both light housework and implementing physical therapy sessions. I did not want someone who was going to be on a cell phone all day or sit and watch soap operas. I cannot tell you how hard it is to find a qualified and capable person. So I asked the one person that I knew wanted what was best for Granny, even more so than me. I asked God to send us the right help.

You may not be a Believer, but that has little to do with our story. I *know* the power of prayer. Let me assure you, prayer works! In miraculous ways.

"And whatsoever ye shall ask in my name, that will I do, that the Father may be glorified in the Son. If ye shall ask any thing in my name, I will do it" *(John 14:13).*

People may hear that verse and say, "Well, then, I'll ask for a million dollars." They miss the point of the verse. The point is, will what you are asking for glorify Jesus Christ? I knew that asking God to help me help Granny would bring Him glory. So He did it!

———ﻌﻌﻌ———

David and I began praying every night for God to show us who we needed to stay with Granny. As if my list of criteria wasn't long enough already, I also had my father-in-law to contend with. Gruff is a mild adjective when describing him. Whoever we got was going to have to be strong willed enough to undergo some daily verbal jabs.

Here is a list of the qualities we were looking for: young but mature, firm but kind, diligent, hard-working, dependable, prompt, honest, good-natured, respectful, neat, a good cook, a good housekeeper, trained in some medical knowledge, and—oh yeah, perhaps the most important thing for us at this point—available to start work immediately.

One morning, Jenna Green, a young lady with whom we used to attend church, crossed my mind. I had not seen her or heard from her in at least a couple of years, so I had no idea what she did for a living at the present time. But she crossed my mind several times that morning. I found her parents' phone number and from them I got her cell number. As fate (divine intervention!) would have it, she was staying with an elderly lady full time.

When I called Jenna, I told her that we desperately needed someone to stay with Mrs. Lois on a regular basis. She explained that she was committed to Mrs. Beatrice and had been working with her for several years. She actually lived in the home with Mrs. Beatrice and only left on the weekends. Mrs. Beatrice was ninety-two years old, and her health, although not good, had been stable for some time now. My heart sank. There was no way I wanted to "steal" her away from another family, but we were running out of time. Christmas was in just a few weeks, and I had promised Granny she'd be home by then.

Before I hung up the phone, I said what even I thought was the strangest thing. I thanked Jenna for her time and told her if she knew of someone else who could do the job to please give that person my name and number, we were desperate. Then I said, "I hope you don't take this the wrong way, but

Mrs. Beatrice is a born-again Christian, and at ninety-two years old, she has lived a long, full life. I know she sleeps away most of her days now, so if, by chance, she goes home to be with the Lord in … oh, let's say the next two weeks, well … you will know you are meant to work for us. Take care."

I made that phone call on December 3, 2007. Mrs. Beatrice passed away peacefully, with her family standing around her, singing hymns, on December 11, 2007, just nine days after my phone call. Granny had just received her Christmas miracle.

———ᴓᴓᴓ———

I knew Jenna loved Mrs. Beatrice, and she needed time to grieve. I also knew that Christmas was the following week. I asked Jenna if she could start on Friday, December 28. She agreed, and I told her that David and I would take turns staying with Granny from the twenty-second, when she was leaving the nursing home, until Jenna started.

I know God works in mysterious ways, but this one was just incredibly special to us. Jenna was everything on my list and then some. To be honest, I believe everything Jenna had done up until that time had prepared her to do all that I would ask of her with Granny. Jenna became my "partner in crime," except our only crime was robbing this horrid disease of its power to steal Granny's last few years from her. I was on cloud nine. Of course, reality would soon set in, and I would discover I had just undertaken the biggest task of my life. But for a few short winter days in 2007, I basked in the glow of knowing that I had asked for a Christmas angel and God Almighty had sent me Jenna Green.

Even after Jenna started working for us, David and I continued to spend the night with Granny and Papa. Because he worked in people's mouths all day and needed to be alert, it was better if I stayed during the week, and he pulled the weekend shift. Marilyn also stayed a few nights to help out. So many people with AD get what are referred to as "night frights." I am thankful that I was able to curb most of those by reading Granny bedtime stories. It is a really good idea to have someone in the house with the loved one during the adjustment time after coming home from the hospital or nursing home.

I gradually stayed there less and less. There were some nights that I would leave after she had been in the bed for an hour, and I knew she was sound asleep. All in all, I stayed for two months after she came home. I just wanted to do whatever it was going to take to make sure she was home, safe and sound. Thankfully, having Jenna coming in the daytime began a wonderful routine that helped us gain incredible ground at whipping this disease for as long as we could.

Our "angel" Jenna, sneaking Granny out the front door

I want to go on record as saying that I could not have accomplished all I have in improving Granny's and Papa's lives without the help of Jenna Green. I know that I was blessed to have been sent someone who was of a like mind. Jenna and I spent hours discussing the fate of older people. She and I both knew we could make a difference in their lives. It is a delicate equation. We had a rare situation in that both the family caregiver (me) and the hired caregiver (Jenna) were willing to work together for the good of the patient (Granny), who was still in good enough health to be given a chance at a fuller life. Although Mrs. Beatrice's family was willing to work with Jenna, Mrs. Beatrice was already so feeble that Jenna didn't make much of a difference for her. Jenna had spent the last two and a half years bringing joy and comfort to Mrs. Beatrice; that in and of itself is a wonderful ministry.

———⚬⚬⚬———

I have heard horror stories of caregivers who worked for families that did not have the best interests of the patient at heart, such as the family of an elderly woman who loved to visit folks. For years, she had been retired and had established a "trail" of sorts. She lived up the road from a quaint little store that served breakfast. A crowd gathered there each morning for a cup of coffee and an earful of gossip. She then made her way to town and stopped in at several of the local businesses to share what she had found out over breakfast. As she went from shop to shop, she felt a connection with people and most important, she felt alive.

When her health began to deteriorate to the point of needing in-home care, her family hired someone, who was more than qualified for the job, to sit with her. Only that was problem. The family wanted the caregiver to just *sit* with her. The caregiver knew of this sweet lady's daily excursions. She also had worked with enough people to know how good that interaction with the real world is. She assumed, upon taking the job, that she would become her chauffeur and take her around, offering a steady hand and being the designated driver.

The family told the caregiver, however, in no uncertain terms, that did they want their elderly loved one to leave the house. If she needed to go somewhere, her son would take her. The only problem was that the son never took her anywhere, other than necessary doctor visits. The caregiver's job would be to do light housework and cook the meals.

How was this lady supposed to survive without knowing the goings-on of her neighbors? She was a people-person, not a *Jeopardy*-watching person. Surely her family knew this much about her, right? It didn't matter. The sad truth was that she was being denied a simple pleasure that could have easily been afforded. The caregiver watched day by day as the woman's health slipped away and often wondered at the family's reasoning. Were they afraid that she and the elderly lady would get out and have an accident? Were they afraid the caregiver would shirk her responsibilities or would be out gallivanting around? Or were they perhaps afraid that their dear sweet mother just might say or do something to embarrass them?

We will never know, because the caregiver felt completely helpless to help and eventually quit. Then the family did what we expected. They put her in a "good" nursing home. "For Mother's benefit, don't ya know." What a pity this family did not understand the worth of a great caregiver and the difference it would have made in the quality of her life.

———✿✿✿———

You can use several resources to find the right fit for your family. Be sure you contact your loved one's doctor, and make sure that all safety issues are addressed. Next, consider checking with the following establishments for someone who can meet your family's needs:

- In-Home Health Care Providers
  Your area may be large enough to have more than one of these businesses. Be sure you compare cost and performance with references that you check out *personally*.
- Church or Civic Organization
  You may know of someone in your church who would make a great caregiver but who has never considered the field. Invite that person out to lunch and share your vision. Sometimes the perfect help is the person who has the most potential, not necessarily the most training.
- Family
  Someone in your immediate family may be currently out of work and may have all the right personality traits to bring exactly the type of care your patient needs.
  In my own family, my grandmother has always been very vivacious and has lived alone since my grandfather died suddenly of a heart attack in 1997. She has never had a driver's license, but that didn't concern her at all. She always had a son nearby to take her where she needed to go. Situations arose in one of my uncles' lives that left him looking for a new place to live. He decided it would make more sense to move in with Mammie and look after her. She is ninety years old and still going strong, so this arrangement has worked for her.
- Others in the Same Situation
  Countless people have called me to ask if I know someone else who does what Jenna does for us, or perhaps she could recommend

someone. Ask around for recommendations from those who are currently using a caregiver. Most of them know of others in their field who may be available.

No matter how you go about finding a caregiver, be cautious and thorough. You want to be sure to hire the caregiver on a trial period of at least sixty days. Give her a *written plan of action*, and go over it with her in detail. Make sure you are on the same page *before* she begins. Elderly people generally do not like change. It is best to do your homework beforehand and avoid any confusion by constantly changing caregivers. Your situation may call for daytime help *and* nighttime help. Get creative when you start looking for help. You may have different family members who would be more than happy to stay two or three nights a week. Just make sure these are dependable people who will be there on "their" night.

Be sure to pop in unannounced and often. Change the time of day in which you make these surprise inspections. Are the caregiver and your loved one engaged in a meaningful activity? Or is the television being a babysitter while your caregiver surfs the Web or being fabulous on Facebook? Be firm, and be completely clear about what you expect. You may need to hand the caregiver this book and point out chapter 8 to give her a better understanding of what can be accomplished. Do not be discouraged. You may need to be more creative in your search methods.

After Aunt Mary's husband, Uncle Tommy, passed away, we knew that she needed "someone" to be there, just to be an extra set of eyes and ears. (All McCall's end up having hearing loss, and that can be dangerous when living alone.) Fortunately, Becky, a lady who was in between jobs, went to church with her. Becky had been staying with Aunt Mary's pastor's family until her job became available. Pastor Tim asked if she would like to move in to help out Mrs. Mary. She gladly did.

She ended up staying for three years. It was a blessing to us that we knew Aunt Mary was not there alone at night. It was also a blessing to Becky because she received free room and board for three years. When the time came for Becky to take a new position, I found myself crying out to God again, "Help, Lord! We need another caregiver—by Monday!" It's amazing to me just how He works. It always seems to be at the last minute, but it is always exactly what we need. Amazing!

Remember how I told you to be creative in your thinking when looking for caregivers? Well, driving away from Aunt Mary's, I was talking to God as if He was in the car with me because, of course, He was. I was thinking about another younger widow lady in our church who might work, but she was very unsteady on her feet, and that would be like the blind leading the blind. So I quickly reminded Him that I would prefer someone younger. Then I thought of Lauren.

Lauren Yuresko is Audrey Hepburn reincarnated. She has to be. She is a tall, beautiful seventeen-year-old who is the picture of grace and elegance. And she just happened to be without a bedroom.

The Yuresko family moved to Carthage from Hilton Head Island, South Carolina. They bought a historical home and began to do a few updates. That was three years ago. Anyone who has been involved in a remodel knows the time, money, and energy that involves. So they decided the wisest thing to do was to live in a camper behind the house while the remodel took place.

Lauren had been living in the camper with her mom, dad, and brother, so technically she had not had her own room for quite some time. Although the completion date was getting closer, she was still the first person God brought to my mind. She would soon be eighteen and wasn't sure what she wanted to do, so this worked out great for everyone involved.

Lauren and Aunt Mary became fast friends—Lauren at almost eighteen and Aunt Mary at eighty-three. They are giddy girlfriends when they are together, and I love it. Once again, I had turned to God to ask for the right caregiver at the right time, and He was faithful again—as always.

Aunt Mary and Lauren—best buddies

———⟨ᴏⁿᴏ⟩———

Stop right here and think about the young people *you* know. Do you know of a teenage girl who has no certain plans for the future? You might start her on a very fulfilling career as a caregiver. Over the next few pages, I will give you some suggestions on getting a young lady headed on the right path.

(I am not being gender-biased when I use feminine pronouns to describe the caregiver. Girls *tend* to have more natural caregiving ability than boys. If you want to guide a young man into being a caregiver, help yourself! I'm sure that an older man might even prefer having a male caregiver. For all practical purposes, you could apply this information to any caregiver, male or female.)

———⟨ᴏⁿᴏ⟩———

Since hiring Jenna and going on this journey with her, I have been amazed at what a wide-open field in-home caregiving is. She gets regular phone calls, often as much as once a week, from someone who needs to find a caregiver. There is such a need for good, dependable people who want to make a difference in someone's life. I have begun what I consider a public relations campaign for the field.

Look for people who are compassionate and have a bubbly personality. Several young girls in our church come to mind who fit that description. I have talked to them from time to time to see where their vocational interests lie. I have mentioned the unique opportunity they could have, if they so desired.

That just seems to be the problem. Many young girls today have no desire to do *anything*. They have been raised in a Pinterest fairy-tale world. They think they are going to sit at home and make a summer retreat in their backyard using nothing but pipe cleaners and Nutella. Between Instagram, Facebook, and Google+, who could possibly expect them to look for a job or even take one with excellent on-the-job training? They may Tweet that they are looking for employment, but in reality, they are content being unemployed. You do not want them! Keep searching and praying the right girl is out there.

Jenna got so many phone calls each week that she began recruiting other girls to do what she does for us. Jenna has done a terrific job of mentoring young girls. Each situation will be unique, but below are some of the overall general requirements:

- Friendly
  Many older people tend to be hard to deal with. It helps to have someone who has a natural ability to lighten the mood and smile. Often, Granny's physical health affects her mental and emotional health. The same idea works in reverse. When we can brighten her day with friendly banter, she tends not to focus on her very real physical ailments.

  Is this person good with young children? That would be a good indication of how well she would work with the elderly. The old saying, "Once a man, twice a child" has proven true with us. Aging adults truly have the same needs as children being cared for. They benefit greatly from having someone read to them, sing with them, and let them take a nap. They need play dates and adventure every day and—quite possibly most important—a gentle touch or even a hug. AD patients, particularly in the beginning stages, know that they are not firing on all cylinders, so a reassuring attaboy, such as you would offer to a young child learning a new task, will go a long way in reaffirming their independence and dignity.

- Honest
This person will be in your loved one's home. You want to be sure you can trust her completely. Jenna was given full access to the house and on many occasions, she would clean up and come across loose money lying around. She always made sure to turn it into me. I will admit there were times in the beginning when I would leave money lying about on purpose, just to test her character. I am happy to say that she never let me down. We kept a money bag in a secure location in the house, and I kept petty cash in it for times when Jenna might need to run to the store for us or if the only thing that would defuse a situation that arose with Papa was a chocolate milkshake from Sonic. (Desperate times, desperate measures.)

- Dependable
Your situation may differ from ours. We needed daytime help because my husband and I were able to check on Granny and Papa in the afternoons and at bedtime. What we needed was someone who would be there when she was supposed to be there. Routine is key for AD patients. It was important to us that Jenna take this job seriously and thankfully, she did. The person you hire needs to understand the commitment to the patient.

- Reliable
When Dr. Lim diagnosed Granny with AD, I started my "Assault on Alzheimer's" campaign. I knew that to get any results, we needed to be consistent. I needed Jenna to follow my directions, even when she didn't understand why I was having her do what I asked her to do. This made all the difference in the world.

One of the most difficult things we encountered was when Granny got worse, and we had to look after her seven days a week. I picked her up for church twice on Sundays, so I had that day covered. We originally asked another family member to come in on Saturday to keep Granny on track, but I don't believe that person saw the importance of having a game plan and following those guidelines. Because that family member wasn't there very often during the rest of the week, she wasn't aware of how well the routines we established worked. She and I talked several times, and she said that just giving Granny something to do would be the same as the tasks Jenna did with her day in and day out. The problem is that AD patients desperately need *routine*.

Some people do not like to be told what to do, and others just won't understand the importance of the routine you establish. Either way, it makes for a frustrating experience. I don't believe that this family member ever fully comprehended the end result of allowing Granny just to sit and look at the paper or to watch television, as opposed to being actively engaged. Having reliable caregivers who can work together on the same game plan is key to improving the patient's health.

- Trained in First Aid
You need to insist that the caregiver is trained in basic first aid. This course can be taken at any number of places. Local hospitals and colleges offer classes on a regular basis. It is mandatory that any caregiver know simple CPR and how to deal with minor scrapes and injuries.

Each patient will have his or her own medical history, so be sure you go over all pertinent information with the caregiver periodically. Granny's orthopedic surgeon insisted that she stand up straight when she walked. I was always against her using a walker because of the damage I could see it was doing to her mobility. Jenna completely agreed (along with Granny's doctors and physical therapist), and so we worked at having Granny stand up straight and use her cane instead.

Many elderly people are on blood thinners. Although this does wonders for keeping heart attacks and strokes at bay, it wreaks havoc on skinned shins. Make sure your caregiver understands how to stop the flow of blood and knows proper wound care.

Be sure you train the caregiver on when and how medicine is given. Also, have a hiding place for medicine bottles—this is just like with small children. Keep all medicine out of reach. Consider the dangers of this scenario: Granny can't sleep, so she takes a 10 mg Ambien to help her fall asleep. She has Alzheimer's, so of course, in ten minutes, she can't remember that she took the Ambien, so she sees the bottle and takes another one. Another ten minutes pass. She still can't sleep. She knows what to do. She sees the bottle of Ambien and takes another one. See the danger? The same holds true for many medications.

Always keep the number to Poison Control by the phone, along with the number to the doctor. Go over scenarios with a written game plan as to how to handle any situation that may arise.

- Domestic Engineer

Doesn't that sound fancier than "knows how to do housework"? You will be shocked at how many young people have no clue how to wash dishes, much less wash clothes or make a bed. You may have to actually train this person how to clean a bathroom.

Part of my "Granny's Game Plan" was making her feel useful and productive. One of the reasons intuitional care is so harmful to so many elderly people is that it takes away their contribution to society. As long as people feel as though they are part of the solution, they won't feel as though they are the problem. Doing everything for them goes back to what Rusty called "nice-ing them to death."

Another aspect of Jenna's job was to keep the housework done. Her exact instructions were to give Granny jobs every day that she could complete and feel good about. I cannot tell you how many baskets of clothes Granny sat and folded after Jenna had washed and dried them and brought them to her. Jenna would hand Granny the broom and ask her to sweep out from under the table she was sitting at. She would bring Granny a drawer from a dresser or nightstand and have Granny clean it out. This not only kept Granny occupied so that Jenna could complete other chores, but it also was "work with a purpose" for Granny. She would get focused on the task at hand and forget that she was … well, forgetful.

Fixing meals is another piece of the puzzle. Your patient may have special dietary needs. Fortunately for us, this was never an issue. Your caregiver should be given adequate instruction on nutrition, and the two of you need to come up with a weekly meal plan. Another great job we gave Granny was weekly grocery shopping. Grocery-list making is a great activity! Each week, our local paper runs a circular ad for the local grocery store. We give this to Granny, along with a notepad and pen. I cannot tell you the hours she has spent in meal planning.

Along with making out the grocery list, Jenna has Granny do all the food prep she can while sitting at the table. They are engaged in meaningful conversation the whole time. If Granny were in some form of institutional care, she would have little or no choice in her meals. Here, she is still doing the job she has done for sixty-plus years. When she goes to bed at night, after chopping up all the veggies for a big, hearty pot of homemade soup, she feels she has accomplished something—because she has.

Make sure your caregiver is on the same page with you as far as household chores are concerned. I have talked with some caregivers who felt that cleaning house was an entirely separate job and was somewhat "beneath" them. Obviously, I would not hire them or recommend them to anyone. I explained to Jenna from the beginning that I was basically hiring her to help Granny do all the things around her home that Granny would be doing by herself, if she were able. That obviously was going to include household duties.

The role of the caregiver will be as diverse as the patient for whom she is caring. It is up to you, as the family caregiver/coordinator, to devise the best list of criteria for your family's needs.

If you have someone in mind that you believe has the makings of a good caregiver, I highly suggest you have him or her read the following two chapters. The things covered have been put into practice and have been found to make a significant difference in the life of more than one AD patient. It is a very challenging profession but one of the most rewarding fields out there. Caregivers change the life of another human being for the good. Who knows? Perhaps you will become the angel that some family has been praying for. What could possibly be better than that?

You may think that you don't need help, that you can take care of your loved one just fine by yourself. The truth is that AD is the most draining disease I know of, not necessarily for the patient—though perhaps in the beginning, when the patient is still cognitive enough to understand what looms ahead—but for the caregiver. This disease will suck the life right out of you. If you have undertaken the care of a loved one full time, at least recruit some part-time help. Have a backup person who can come in and is fully capable of filling in for you when you need a break. Ask for help. As the disease progresses, you are going to need someone who will offer you some relief from time to time. Take it! You will be surprised at what one night away from it all can do to recharge your battery. Even Jesus took time away from the multitudes He was helping to "set Himself apart" for a time. It is better to "pull apart" for a short time than to "fall apart." I don't see you walking on water, so if Jesus needed some time away, don't beat yourself up for needing a break, too.

—————

One of the things that any good caregiver has to consider is where her job ultimately leads. As Jenna has pointed out to me, when you are hired to be a caregiver, your job is to stay with that person and help her live a fuller life. Ultimately, however, the end will come. Your patient is going to pass away, and it will be time to be an angel for someone else. You will suffer loss each time you lose a patient, but take heart in knowing that by your being there, you brought great joy and dignity to someone else. Well done!

Jenna, Marilyn, me holding Ellie Beth, and Granny

"To every thing there is a season, and a time to every purpose under the heaven: A time to be born, and a time to die" (Ecclesiastes 3:1–2).

Chapter 8

Sunshine, Exercise, and Cracker Barrel

When was the last time you visited a nursing home and saw the rows and rows of lost-looking souls sitting strapped in wheelchairs, staring at one another with that "deer in the headlights" look? Most are usually in pajamas and a robe. Hair unkempt. Slippers on their feet. Skid-proof socks. The television is on TV Land with a rerun of *Gunsmoke* playing in the community room. It doesn't matter, because the majority of the "inmates" (that's what my oldest son calls them) aren't watching it anyway. Most of them are staring out the window, wondering how in the world they could have spent sixty to eighty years as a productive member of a family. Where was that family now? Perhaps at soccer? Gone on vacation? Surely there had to be some explanation as to why no one bothered to visit for a week— or was it two? Surely it's not been a month, has it?

I want to reiterate that there are some wonderful nursing homes out there. I have also visited assisted-living facilities that are incredible. It is not that I think having to put your loved one in one of these places is a death sentence. It's just that if these facilities are the next best thing to home, why not keep them home, when possible? Just because your loved has AD, you *do not* have to believe the experts when they tell you he or she needs institutional care. We worked (and boy, is it work) to keep Granny and Papa at home. Alive. Thriving. Involved. *At home!*

Our church goes to our local nursing home on the first Sunday of every month and holds a church service for the residents from two to two thirty. It's only thirty minutes out of our month, but it is something the elderly look forward to all week. During one of these monthly visits, I noticed how enamored the old folks were with the children we brought along with us.

They barely paid attention to the preaching, but oh, those children! *They* held their attention.

After the service on this particular day, my daughter, who was only five or six at the time, sat down at the piano and pecked out a song. She was a huge hit. And all those old people wanted to hear more. They didn't care that it was "Twinkle, Twinkle, Little Star" over and over again. Most of them probably couldn't even hear what she was playing. They just loved watching a child play the piano. They watched her, and I watched them. I sat there that day and felt a tugging of my heart. Aha! A family ministry had just been birthed.

Hope Hubbard, Faith Hubbard, Delanie McDonald, Grace
Hubbard, Collin McDonald, Connor McDonald

One night after a mission's conference service, a friend of ours walked up to me. Cherie Hubbard has three of the most gorgeous daughters I have ever laid eyes on. They are beautiful inside and out. She said, "Lorrie, I know you are going to think I'm crazy for telling you this, but for months now, I have felt like I should ask you about something."

"Okay, I won't think you're crazy," I responded. What she would have thought was crazy was that I knew what she was going to ask me, even before she did. She explained that for some time, she had felt the urging to take her three girls up to the nursing home and let them play music for the residents. Coincidence? Hardly.

We began taking our six children to the nursing home over twelve years ago on the fourth Saturday of every month. I believe all children should learn at least one musical instrument. While learning that instrument, they will need to practice. Old people are always happy to see young smiling faces. Plus, they have the added benefit of usually being hard of hearing. So it is of no consequence to them if the kids play a little off key. They are just thrilled to have them visit.

So, there they went. Collin and Faith brought their guitars. Connor and Grace brought banjos. Delanie and Hope serenaded with violins. These thirty-minute practice sessions did wonders for everyone involved. Our kids learned to perform in front of a crowd—an often sedated one but a crowd, nonetheless. They learned to work together on a musical piece or two. (You've not lived until you've heard a bluegrass version of "Silent Night.") It also had benefits that we may not fully comprehend for years to come.

It has been a huge encouragement to the nurses and staff to watch this group of young people come every month—for more than twelve years now—and give of themselves, to be a blessing to an often forgotten group of people. Recently, when my sons were filling out college entrance forms, they came across the "Community Service" section. They both looked a little confused when I told them to put down their nursing home ministry. Connor said, "That's not community service, is it? That's just what we do."

—◦◦◦—

Because of this and other ministries involving the nursing home, I have spent quite a bit of time there over the years. Ours is one of the cleanest, friendliest nursing homes I have ever stepped foot in. The nurses are top-notch. Residents are seen to immediately, and everyone always seems to be in the best care possible—for a nursing home.

We homeschool our children. One of the reasons we do so is because of the awesome teacher-to-student ratio. Three kids to one me. That is a pretty good classroom size ratio, according to anyone's standards. The same thought process went through my mind when considering leaving Granny at the nursing home. *Hm-m-m, I thought. There are anywhere from twenty to twenty-four patients per hallway, with one to two workers per hall. Even on the best days, that's ten to one. Not so good.* That might have been okay if my plan didn't involve actually improving Granny's physical condition. I never simply wanted her to be looked after and cared for. My goal—and we *have* succeeded—was for her to *thrive* during her last years here on earth.

I go in each month and look at those people sitting there, mostly just waiting. Waiting for the next dose of medicine. Waiting for the next visit from their children or grandchildren. Waiting on someone to come and push them back down to their "room." In general, just waiting to die. Not Granny! She's out having the time of her life.

Granny gets to hear the kids practice too. Most months, I have Jenna get her dressed, and I stop by and take her to the nursing home with us. Because of AD, she asks the same questions a dozen or more times in the five miles between her house and the nursing home.

"Where are we going, Lucy?" she asks with genuine interest.

"To the nursing home," I reply, intentionally vague.

"Why are you taking me up there?" she asks with genuine concern.

"The kiddos are playing for the residents today, and I thought you might enjoy hearing your grandkids play and sing."

"Oh, honey! You know it! Bless those old people's hearts. Just breaks mine every time we go up there to see those poor ol' dears just sitting there, all pitiful like. I am so glad I've never had to spend the first night up there … or have I?" She begins to be confused and have some faint memory of having been there.

"You were just up there for a few short months for rehab a while back. Do you remember that?" I ask.

"Now that you mention it, seems I do recall that." She sits quietly for a minute and a half. Then comes the question I've been waiting for.

"So … where are we going, Lucy?"

When Dr. Lim diagnosed Granny with AD, something inside of me came to life. I am one of the most stubborn people I know of—just ask my hubby. I cannot stand to be told something "can't" be done. I read a quote recently: "Most people stand around complaining it can't be done, until someone comes along and does it!" I want that person to be me when it comes to Alzheimer's. I proved that you can improve an AD patient's health—mentally, physically, and definitely emotionally. Do not get me wrong; I know there is not a cure for AD … yet. But I decided not to stand around and complain that improvement couldn't be done, as plenty of well-meaning people told me. Lots of them even had initials after their names. You know what they found out? It *can* be done.

Dr. Lim's note from September 22, 2008, clearly stated that Granny got *better*! He looked at me at that visit and said, "Perhaps I have misdiagnosed her." He had not. But I cannot tell you the excitement that I felt, knowing that all Jenna and I had implemented was paying off. I had already felt that God was laying it upon my heart to share our story, and then Dr. Lim suggested that I keep a journal, to write down all the things that we did with Granny and share that with others.

If you are just starting out on this journey, then you may not understand the magnitude of his words, "She's better." But in reality, you don't *ever* get told that about an AD patient. They do not improve and certainly not by eighteen months' worth, which is what he told me she had recovered.

This chapter is a summary of the years of trial and error that I had with my mother-in-law, Lois McDonald. What you, as a caregiver, should remember at all times while reading this book is this: if you chose to implement any of these methods, just know that this is what worked for us. Some days, everything we did had the Midas touch and worked beautifully. Other days, I felt as if we would have been better off to stick her in a wheelchair with fuzzy socks in front of TV Land. But that's not the norm.

You also may be very surprised that most of the things I mention are somewhat common sense ideas. The only problem with that thinking is that when you are dealing with another family member's health, you will get lots of advice from people who probably know less than you do about the situation, and they will encourage you not to be so radical. Smile, thank them for their concern, and then forge ahead. I have laid my head down many nights and just relished the thoughts of what Granny had accomplished that day. The joy I brought to her on those days made it all worthwhile.

So without any further delay let's begin the whole reason you bought this book.

——⟨𝒐𝒐𝒐⟩——

1. Sunshine

"Truly the light is sweet, and a pleasant thing it is for the eyes to behold the sun" (Ecclesiastes 11:7).

I guess this one was a no-brainer idea for me. I am a huge advocate of the outdoors. I had a saying when our children were little: "If the sun's out, the TV doesn't come on." Meaning that if it was a pretty day, we were going to be outside enjoying it. But our son Connor is one of the most literal people you will ever meet. Ever. So when he was about three and a half years old, we just happened to stop in to visit my mother on a very bright, sunny day.

We walked in, and Connor stared at the TV. Then he ran out on the front porch and stared up at the sky. Then he ran back in and stared at the television. Then he ran back out and stared up at the sky.

"Connor, honey, what are you doing?" I asked, clearly confused.

"Momma! Nana's television is working!" He was clearly thrilled.

"Yes. Why wouldn't her TV be working?" I replied, even more confused.

"Because the sun's shining," exclaimed Connor, beaming with joy.

"What on earth does the sun shining have to do with whether or not Nana's TV works?" I asked.

"Momma!" he insisted, completely put out with my obvious ignorance at this point. "You know how you always say, 'If the sun's out, the TV doesn't come on.' But Nana's does! Hers works, Momma, even with the sun shining."

Dear Lord! It was clearly a miracle!

Granny always has been a lover of the great outdoors too. There are days when she forgets that. You will have to *remember for them*. I get so angry when this disease causes Granny not to remember *who* she is. So what if she can't remember that she loves to be outside. I remember that, so I decided to remember *for her.*

One of the reason she loves me so much is because when I married David, she finally got someone who enjoyed riding horses with her. We spent so much time outside over the years, in all kinds of weather, fooling with those horses. I smile every time I think of the times that we fought those silly horses in ninety degree weather. It was never too hot and never too cold for Granny to ride horses. So if she could still remember what she would like to do today, she would remember she loves to be outside!

I told Jenna that we were going to start taking Granny outside every day for at least thirty minutes and have her sit directly in the sunshine. Their house was providentially built with a large front porch facing directly east. Therefore, right after breakfast was the perfect time to head outside. Granny has always had two huge black rocking chairs on her front porch. She had been on the go so much that she never truly got to enjoy them. Until now.

Jenna bundles her up. (Remember the ballpark story in chapter one?) Even on a sweltering day, Granny dons a sweatshirt. So being cold-natured was no excuse. We put her sweatshirt on, even a jacket if it is cool weather (say, in the low to mid 80s). We always tie a scarf around her gorgeous gray hair, and out they go.

I have been amazed at all the scientific data that is surfacing now on the importance of vitamin D to our bodies. It seems like everybody I talk to has been put on 50,000 units of vitamin D. But God gives us a healthy dose of that vitamin every time we step outside. He also invented a safety mechanism to tell us when we've had too much sun. It's called our skin. When we begin to sunburn, then that's His way of saying, "Okay, enough for now. Come back out tomorrow. The sun will still be here!"

Granny, Delanie, and me
Notice Delanie and I are in short sleeves, and
Granny is dressed for an Arctic blast.

Since we live right up the road, I steal her away almost every week on the Gator (our farm utility vehicle). I get so tickled because it may be 95 degrees, but she bundles up and off we go. We ride all over the farm. We go up to see the horses or down to look at the creek and the pond. She always tells me all the things she's going to do "next week" to the farm. I just drive, listen, and smile. It only takes thirty minutes out of my day, but I can't imagine the hours it is adding to her life.

When Jenna takes Granny out on the front porch, they do lots of activities. Jenna is learning to play the guitar, so she gives Granny the hymn book and lets her turn to different songs. Jenna plays guitar while they sing together. She gets guitar practice, and Granny couldn't care less how off key Jenna's playing is. She just loves to sing.

Jenna brings the newspaper out and has Granny read to her. Sometimes they sit and watch cars drive by. But one thing will happen for sure while they are out there. Granny will notice the birds sitting on the telephone wire that goes across the front of the yard. She loves to watch those birds.

We have cattle in the pasture in front of the house, so she always comments on those too, if they are grazing where she can see them. Marilyn placed a bird feeder right on the front porch, so between the birds and the cows, she has a good time enjoying God's creations.

What a small investment a bird feeder or two is. The dividend is huge. Granny sits there and talks to us about how pretty those birds are. She gets hours of enjoyment from watching them, all the while getting good, clean, fresh air. Plus, it only makes sense that if she is experiencing the pleasure of watching the birds, then she can't be experiencing pain.

I gave my very fit grandmother, Mammie, who is ninety years young, a bird feeder for her birthday last April. When I get to travel and see her, I refill it with bird feed for her. There is a large iron pole right outside her living room window where she likes to sit and read. She gets to be a part of the great outdoors vicariously, from her big comfy couch. If I lived closer, I would bring her outside every day for her daily dose of vitamin D, but since I only get to visit her occasionally, I make the most of my time when I do get to go.

Buy your loved ones a simple-to-use bird identification book. Depending on the progress of the disease, this may or may not "click" with them. They may enjoy looking through the book but not connect the fact that they are able to identify the birds outside by looking in the book. Either way, they will get the enjoyment of looking through the book.

Tons of studies have proved that just being outside in nature has healing powers. Many cutting-edge hospitals have implemented a "green area" outside so their patients can get out into creation and take in the fresh air and greenery. Just being outside has a calming effect. That trick works on fussy newborns and fidgety ninety-year-olds.

I list the sunshine first because of all the things we have done with Granny, I truly feel this one jump-started all her other progress. We take advantage of it almost every day. I recently heard a seminar given by Dr.

John Lee from back in 1997. He mentioned that vitamin D has numerous benefits and that the only way your body can truly absorb it is through exposed skin. As people get older, they tend to cover up their skin more and stay inside more. I knew nothing about his findings when I began taking Granny outside. I just knew that being in the sunshine always made me feel better, so it would probably help her too.

People repeatedly ask me, "You don't take her out there when it's actually cold, do you?" I always respond, "If the sun is out, so is Granny!" I have to admit that there have been exceptions to that but not many. Sometimes it has been in the thirties, and I've driven up to see Granny and Jenna sitting out there in those two rockers, sunbeams shining down on them. Jenna would have on her heavy coat, and Granny would be just a speck peeking out from a furry winter cap and an heirloom quilt that was tucked all the way up around her chin. What a wonderful sight those two are! Jenna always uses discretion and asks Granny to tell her when she's ready to go back in. Granny loves this morning routine.

I have known for years that I have a touch of SAD (seasonal affective disorder). When it's rainy and gloomy outside, I tend to get gloomy too. It got so bad one year that my sweet hubby bought a used tanning bed for me, just to use as "light therapy." It does wonders for me. Having that knowledge tucked away led me to believe the sunshine would do Granny good too. I was right.

I know that some people will argue about the fear of getting skin cancer from overexposure, but this is just not the case. First, your loved ones are not going to be outside long enough to get blistered from the sun. Second, if they are in their eighties or nineties, odds are you are not going to overexpose them to the sun to the point of getting skin cancer. I have seen firsthand that the benefits of Sunshine Therapy far exceed any danger from the sun.

We don't just expose Granny to the sunshine. We also do some deep breathing exercises with her. We get her to breathe in deeply and really fill up her lungs with fresh air. Deep, slow, methodical breathing. The kind used in meditation. We do this, and it has a medicinal effect on her. It steadies her breathing, lowers her blood pressure, calms her fears, and basically does a body good. Ten or fifteen slow, deep, cleansing breaths, and she is a whole new person. This can be done several times throughout the day, not just when in the sunshine, but the fresh air is key.

2. Exercise

A fit body makes for a fit mind—this is pure common sense, but how many older people do you know who are just rusting away? Remember Rusty (no pun intended), Granny's physical therapist? He used to say the elderly go from the job site, to the couch, to the bed, to the coffin. Keep them active!

Did you know that 25 percent of all elderly patients who enter the hospital with hip fractures die within two years? (Dr. John Lee, 1997 seminar). The more active and flexible you can get your patient, the less likely they are to break something if they take a tumble.

I bought a set of three-pound weights, and Jenna has Granny "work out" with them every day—once in the morning and again in the evening. Granny had a torn rotator cuff in the past that never properly healed, so we adapt the exercises somewhat, knowing that. She's not training for Mrs. Senior Universe; we are just keeping those old bones and muscles mobile.

You almost always will have to work around a physical drawback when dealing with the aging. "Parts" just start wearing out, but that is no reason not to adapt movements to their ability. Soon, they gain strength, and their ability improves.

A morning workout session for Granny includes lifting the weights ten times with her arms bent, ten times with her arms straight, and helping her lift them up to the sky. Then we add leg raises. She sits and raises the right leg ten times, then the left, and then both. Then we have her bend her knees together and lift them out together. (Much like the motion of sitting on a swing.) We have her twist from side to side and really stretch out that old aching back. Then there's the doozy that gets us yelled out more times than I care to count—we have her stand up (for no good reason, she often tells us) and sit back down ten times, without our help. She has to maneuver her bottom to the front of the chair, use her arms to push herself up, and then come to a complete upright position. Oh, don't get me wrong; we stay right there, within an arm's reach of her. But we have her work and work and work to stand on her own. We are building muscles, building stamina, and most important, we are building confidence.

But she cheats—I swear she does! She'll hunker over, plop down, and say, "One …" Then, being the meanies that we are, we say, "No, ma'am, we can't count them if you don't do them right. Now, all the way, up straight."

She always complains about how stupid this is. She always complains how bad her back hurts. She always complains that we can't make her do this. She always complains.

I keep saying "we do" this or that because even though only one of us is there with her at a time, Jenna and I do it exactly the same way. Neither one of us cave in to Granny. It's a huge hassle for us. It's time-consuming, aggravating, and exhausting for us. But we both realize it is not about us and what's best for us. This is about Granny, and we know this works. Unfortunately, not everybody who helps us from time to time understands this, and she can get away with slacking with a few well-meaning people. Then it actually makes our job much harder than it has to be. So it is very important that you try to get all involved on board. (By the way, good luck with that.)

Walking is the greatest activity in the world for anyone of any age. On pretty days, Jenna takes Granny out to the double carport. The only problem with that is that we have to go past Billy Goat Gruff to get her out there. Papa doesn't necessarily understand our game plan. He thinks its "dangerous" for Lois to be outside, "gallivanting" around. He fusses at us that she's too unsteady on her feet to do so much walking. I know he means well, but he's wrong. So when we can't appease him with some chocolate, we just have her walk laps through the house.

Jenna and I both have become adept at distracting the "guard dog" with a "bone"—Papa prefers chocolate or ice cream, or even better, chocolate ice cream. So that is what we do. If we are headed out to walk around the carport, and Papa is guarding the door from his ugly green chair, then we fix him a little snack. He never leaves his chair. It would be lovely to get him to go into the kitchen and eat at the table, but how could we be that lucky? Fortunately for us, if we fix him a snack and have him come into the kitchen to get it, by the time we have snatched up Granny and have her shuffling to the door, he is preoccupied with his treat. We just casually call over our shoulders, "It's such a pretty day that we are going to go out back for a little while." He mumbles through his chewing, "Lois ain't got no business out there." But because he's busy spooning up his prize, he rarely bothers us, more than a verbal snap. Thankfully, his bark is worse than his bite.

10/30/2008

Our biggest challenge with the AD was Granny's poor posture.
She couldn't "remember" to stand up straight.

Because of Granny's poor posture and osteoporosis, one of our biggest challenges with her, every single day, is our "stand up straight!" regimen. She starts out walking upright, but by the time she's made one lap through, she's slumping over like a cavemen. So we work on posture all the time. This one area is a deal-breaker for many of the people who "help" us with her. Some very well-meaning individuals just do not understand the importance of posture. They allow her to slump over and unfortunately, many times they give her the walker, thinking that is somehow safer and will steady her more on her feet.

In reality, all of her doctors and physical therapists have adamantly explained that the walker is her biggest detriment. But since these people do not normally make it to her doctor visits with us, they assume they are helping, when in fact they would help more if they would just follow the program we have implemented and not try to do what they think is best. Instead of helping her posture, using her walker worsens it, to the point that

Jenna and I have both caught Granny leaning completely over on the bar of the walker. My fear is that because people keep handing her the walker, and she insists on leaning over it, she really *is* going to fall someday when one of us is not around. The best thing would be to throw the walker out the back door. But we can't get everyone else to understand that, so Jenna and I just hide it.

Because getting Granny to correct her posture irritates her, it is just easier for some people to leave her alone and assume she can't do any better. This is when it helps to know your patient. Jenna and I are both aware that the slouching is nothing more than a horrible habit Granny falls into when she is allowed to do so. It also is a result of muscle mass being lost due to constant slouching. A strong trunk area of the body is the key to good posture, good balance, and good health. So pull those shoulders back, and quit that slouching.

Most days, getting Granny to walk for just ten minutes at a time can be quite the ordeal. She complains, slumps, huffs and puffs, and some days, just flat out refuses. Do Jenna and I skip it for that day? No! That is the lazy way out. It will not help Granny, nor will it help us in the long run. Old people are stubborn. This is when we use the AD to our advantage.

Because Granny's short-term memory is so bad, if she puts up much of a fight, we just outsmart her. Here is how this scene has played out dozens of times:

"Granny, let's stand up and do our walking." Jenna says.

"Jenna, my back hurts. Where are we walking to anyway?" huffs Granny.

"We walk all the time, Granny. It's good for us! Hop up, Lucy, let's get a move on," Jenna coaxes.

"*You* get a move on. I'm not going anywhere." Her tone is more hateful now.

"Yes, ma'am, we are. Come on. You'll feel better." Jenna smiles all the while.

"I'm not walking, and that is that!"

And with that, Jenna knows it's time to implement a little cleverness. "Fine. I'm going into the kitchen. I'll be back in a few minutes. Here—look over the *Carthage Courier*." She hands Granny the local paper, which she has looked at dozens of times, and Jenna steps out of the room.

This is the point when most of our helpers give up. They don't want a fight on their hands, so they just leave her sitting there, thinking that reading is a good activity too. Yes, it is, but she *has* to keep moving. She needs to keep her routine. If they allow her to protest and get out of the activity, then it is horrible for Jenna and me the next day.

Jenna and I have learned that there is a sort of preset default button somewhere inside an Alzheimer patient's mind. Jenna goes out of the room for anywhere from ten to fifteen minutes. and then when she walks back in the room, she goes about it a different way.

"Granny, I'm *so* sorry it took me so long. I apologize! Good grief, you're being patient. Bless your heart. Here you are, all ready to walk to the mailbox, and I can't seem to get my act together this morning! I am so sorry to keep you waiting this long!" Jenna says, all in a flutter.

"Well, honey, don't you worry about that. You can't help that! Granny was just sitting here reading the paper. Just give me a second, Lucy. These old bones get stiff when I've been sitting for too long." And up, up, up she comes out of her reading chair.

I cannot tell you how many times we have pulled this trick. I used it numerous times when we first started giving her medicine to her at night. She wanted to sit there and look at each pill. She wanted to wait to take it. She'd say she'd take it later. So I learned to take the medicine back out of the room with me and come back with maybe a half of a banana, and I'd say something along the lines of this: "Okay, here's that banana you needed to take your meds with. You know you are *so smart* to want to take your medicine with food. I'll bet that helps. I never thought about doing it that way. Do you think that would help me?" Or if I'm being really sly and need her to concede to the good of the team, I'll say something along the lines of, "Here you go. I'm going to tell Delanie the next time I can't get her to take her medicine that you like to take yours with a half a banana. Granny, you are a genius! I'll bet that will work, don't you? I'll bet if she knows that's how you take your medicine, I'll be able to get her to take hers. Here you go. Go ahead and swallow these down." Problem solved.

And what do you do when all the tricks in your carpetbag fail? You very sweetly say, "Okay, well, you don't have a choice. Up. We've got to get you some exercise before you grow roots." Prayer, too, works wonders.

Not all AD patients will have other physical ailments. Your may have the opposite problem—your patient may be a go-getter with whom you have trouble keeping up. You can buy a monitoring device to literally keep track of your patient. You want to ensure his or her safety at all times. Since Granny has so many physical drawbacks, we could keep an eye on her. If your patient is still physically fit, then get him or her out and active.

———⋙⋘———

Don't be afraid to think outside your box—or outside your house for that matter. The more you can incorporate these activities together, the better for everyone involved. You're saving some time and offering multiple stimulations to your patient. There are times when AD will be a monster you can't control, and you just have to do the best you can on those days. Don't forget that every single activity may be met with resistance. Not a single day goes by that Granny doesn't tell Jenna or me that she doesn't want to do one of the activities. We gently urge her on, and we almost always have a successful attempt.

Some activities, no matter how great an idea, are just going to be a flop. Aunt Mary moved back to Carthage from Memphis a few years ago. (Just in time, if you ask me.) As I have mentioned before, she could convince Granny of just about anything. She and Uncle Tommy moved into a beautiful home just across town that happened to have an in-ground swimming pool. David and I were in the process of building a new home with our own pool, but at the time, Aunt Mary's seemed like the perfect destination for some summer fun. If only I could have gotten Granny to see it that way.

When we owned the golf course with Granny and Papa, she and I taught swimming every June. We did that for years and years. I taught the beginners, and Granny taught the advanced swimmers. On the last day of the swim camp, Granny would teach them to dive. I knew how much she loved to swim, so what a wonderful opportunity. Or so I thought.

I explained to Granny that one of Aunt Mary's and Uncle Tommy's favorite forms of exercise was swimming. I dressed her in her bathing suit, along with a cover-up and her flip-flops. She wouldn't make the cover of *Sports Illustrated,* but it would work.

Shortly after we got to Aunt Mary's house, we headed out back to the gated pool. Once inside the door, she headed over to a very lovely lounge chair, where, she said, she would "watch you all swim." Well, no, ma'am, that ain't the plan!

"No, Granny, we are here to swim with *you*. We are just going to do a few laps, enjoy some sunshine, and do a few water aerobics, and then Aunt Mary has made us a lovely lunch." (Sunshine, exercise, socialization, adventure—man was this a good idea!)

"*I'm* not getting into *that* water. I can't swim," she declared.

"What? Of course you can swim! You and I taught swimming, for heaven's sakes! We'll just do a few laps." Aunt Mary and I led her to the steps of the pool.

Let's just say that not only did we *not* do laps, but I couldn't get her to let go of the side of the pool. Not to be out done, Aunt Mary and I held onto the side also, one of us on each side of Granny, and did several water aerobics. Granny would do the weakest version possible of each one, and I was not a happy camper. There was absolutely no reason why she shouldn't love this. It was a beautiful summer day, the water was just the right temperature, and she was here with three of her favorite people. (Delanie had come along and was swimming like a fish in the deep end while we were in the shallow end, doing the equivalent of trying to coerce a cat to swim.)

Never one to admit defeat, we stayed in the water about forty-five minutes, moving Granny's arms back and forth. Kicking her legs in and out. Squatting up and down. Clinging to the side of the pool like a lifeline.

We got her out, dried off, went inside to change, and had a lovely lunch. AD is so unpredictable, and what works today may not work tomorrow, but I've learned the opposite also is true. Just because you can't get your patient to complete an activity today does not mean that tomorrow it will not be a whole new experience. So the following week, we tried it again, and the next week. We did this off and on all summer. It just never clicked.

Granny constantly told me she felt like she was going to fall. No matter how much I explained that she was in water, so she could "fall" all she wanted, and it wouldn't hurt her, since she would float, she convinced herself if she fell, she would drown. Since I have never wanted to scare or frighten Granny, I just chalked it up to a great idea but lousy execution.

Ironically, a year or so later, Dr. Lim had another CAT scan of her brain. He found out that she had atypical Alzheimer's. Well, that figures! How could I possibly believe that anything about this experience could be "typical"? But what that meant was that typically, the cerebral cortex (frontal lobe) of the brain begins shrinking. The cerebral cortex is broken up into lobes that each control different body functions.

The frontal lobe is in control of our emotions, sequencing events, humor, sarcasm, irony, and our ability to have a fixed persistence of a single thought, mood swings, and memory. So you can see how all the symptoms of AD are affected in this area. Granny's MRI showed that she did have some shrinking of the gyri (brain substance in folds) and some swelling of the sulci (spaces in the folds of the brain), but there was a greater shrinking of the cerebellum—which is in charge balance and equilibrium. She really *did* feel like she was falling.

Knowing this, Jenna and I worked overtime with helping her to stand up straighter and to walk without the aid of the walker, which she tended to almost tip over. I realized that being in the swimming pool just added to that swooning feeling she has on dry ground. This information caused me to withdraw our pool time.

So try an activity, but if your patient truly has difficulty with it, you may have to switch gears. Many able-bodied elderly thoroughly enjoy swimming, hiking, biking, and lots of outdoor activities. If you have a patient whose mind refuses to keep up with his or her body, put forth the effort to keep your patient active. The greatest way to know if your patient is capable of performing a task is to discuss it with his or her doctor and then give it a try.

—⊙⊙⊙—

"A body in motion tends to stay in motion, while a body at rest tends to stay at rest." I wonder if Sir Isaac Newton had a mother-in-law he was dealing with when he stated his law of motion. Regardless, I have quoted him a thousand times.

We did a ton of different exercises with Granny. You can use any of the movements I have listed here, or you can come up with your own. You can also visit any website on exercise for the aging and get a list of wonderful movements. But the key is that you actually have to do them! Most of us don't like the idea of exercising, but once we've completed the exercise, we feel better. I recently saw a Pinterest post that read, "Food is the most abused anxiety drug. Exercise is the most underutilized antidepressant." I couldn't agree more.

You don't need fancy equipment. You don't need equipment, period. Instead of the dumbbells we use with Granny, you could just as easily use two cans of peas or corn or whatever is in your cabinet. Get your patient to make loops in the air with her arms and tilt her head forward, backward, and side to side. Think of any exercise you have ever done in gym class and just adapt it to the capability of your patient.

Your patient has no excuse for not exercising some body part every day. Is your patient an amputee? Ever seen the Special Olympics? He can move the body parts he does have. Get him active. And by all means have him breathe in deeply and exhale deeply. You want him to get the oxygen flowing and the blood circulating.

I want to share a story that happened to us. Connor, Delanie, and I were sitting in the living room, relaxing after a long day of yard work. We were going out to eat with some other family members, so we turned the television on for a few minutes to wait for David and Collin to finish getting showered and dressed. The TV channel was tuned to a triathlon, and a reporter was interviewing several different participants. One was a very fit-looking middle-aged woman. She stood beside an older gentleman, gently patting him on the shoulder, while a paramedic tended to his lower leg. The caption below him read: "Mr. Smith, age 78." I was blown away that a seventy-eight-year-old man was participating in a triathlon, but the woman's next words shamed me forever.

When the interviewer asked her how was her dad feeling, she said, "He's really been in a lot of pain the last twenty miles or so." *What?* Twenty miles or so? Apparently, he had completed the umpteen miles of biking and swimming, but here, on the last leg of the race—a twenty-seven–mile trot—he had been running in pain the last "twenty miles or so"! My sixteen-year-old son, who was sprawled across the couch, looked up and stated to no one in particular, "Okay, I'm a total slug. If that old man has just done all that, I'm buying a gym membership tomorrow! Wow!"

Kudos to you, sir. Seriously, what an inspiration. I wouldn't buy your patient a Speedo just yet, but as you can see from this story, the more active you can keep him, the better his quality of life will be.

⸻ ◦၇◦ ⸻

Aunt Helen on her new toy

I have included a picture of Granny's sister-in-law, Aunt Helen McCall. (You might recall that this is the Aunt Helen named after the state.) At the spry young age of eighty-seven, her family bought her a bicycle for her birthday. Good for you, Phillips family; good for you! Aunt Helen is vivacious and as sharp as a tack. I believe there is a direct link between staying active and staying sharp mentally. My maternal grandmother is an example of this.

At ninety years old, Mammie has slowed down a bit in the last year, but she has been an inspiration to me for years. She lives on a rural road that dead-ends into a state highway. It is exactly two miles from her driveway to the dead-end. For years, she would take a stroll in the morning to the end and back. (For those of you slow in math, that would be four miles.) Since she lives alone and doesn't have much else going on, on some afternoons she would make that trek again (that would be eight miles).

I used to get into fights with my mom and some of her brothers, who raised Cain about Mammie taking those walks. They fussed and fussed

123

about her doing that. Didn't she know there were dogs up and down the road? They could chase her. They could bite her. She could fall. She could get mugged.

Well, all of that was true. And you could get abducted by aliens on your way into the grocery store, too. Odds are that none of that is going to happen. Other than a couple of the dogs following her down the road, she remained safe for all the years she walked that road.

I remember one winter morning when it started snowing, and my mother called, wanting to know if I had Mammie with me. I did not. She said she had called all morning and had not reached her. Since Mammie has never had a driver's license, we assumed she should be at home. I suggested that perhaps she was walking. The snow wasn't that bad, and maybe she decided to get her walk in before the snow became serious. My mother thought that was ridiculous. But when I finally got through to Mammie that afternoon, that is exactly what she had done. "Good for you, Mammie!"

She chuckled and told me she had "gotten in trouble" with her children. I reminded her that they would all die early of heart disease if they didn't get active and that she should keep on walking, and I'd drive *her* to *their* funerals. Oh, I know that doesn't sound very kind, but they all tend to take after my grandfather, Mammie's late husband, who would rather sit than move. He died seventeen years ago, and Mammie is still sashaying down the lane. There is just something to staying active.

Exercise really is a close second to getting sunshine. Just get your patient moving. Break up their Olympic training into little segments throughout the day. We do about thirty minutes every morning, then ten to fifteen after lunch, and another ten to fifteen in the early afternoon. Start out slowly and continue to add more movements as she gains her strength back. Never underestimate the benefit of simple movements while lying on the bed, sitting in a chair, or driving her down the road. Anywhere can be your gym, and your membership is free.

3. Routine

Every night before we turn in to bed, we have a short family devotion with our kids. For as long as I can remember, David has asked each child, "So, what did you do today?" And for as long as I can remember, Connor, our very literal child, has answered, "I got up. I came downstairs. I had breakfast ..." Same answer every time. Oh, he eventually gets to the good stuff. "We played golf and I shot three under." "We went bowling with the teens from church." "I saw Big Foot traipsing through the hay pasture." No matter how exciting his day may have been, it always starts the same. "I got up. I came downstairs. I had breakfast ..."

You need to establish that sort of regimen with your patient. Jenna and I do tons of fun and exciting things with Granny—it's very important to bring adventure to her daily life, when possible. Most of the day-to-day activities, however, need to be very methodical. Let me explain.

—⟨⟨⟨⟩⟩⟩—

When Granny wakes up in the morning, she eventually looks over to her left, where there is a dry erase board on the wall.

It reads: "*Today is:* _____"

Each night when I put her to bed, I fill in the details like so:

Today is: Tuesday
Put on the clothes in the bathroom.
Jenna will be here at 9:00

We have found that a visual reminder often helps alleviate some of the confusion. If you have ever been hospitalized for any length of time, you know the days can quickly run together. Is it Monday or Wednesday? As many people age, they retire. One day begins to resemble the next, and it does get a bit confusing. I have found that if I fill in on the board what Granny is to do, then most days we can get her up and get her started without too much complication. That is, however, *most* days. Some days are real doozies.

For some reason, Granny is stuck on Sunday. This is the case with many AD patients; they just assume that every day is a certain day of the week. It's like it is their own personal *Groundhog Day*. It seems to be Sunday for many of them.

Melanie Smith, who works for us at the dentist office, told us that her daddy, whom everyone calls "Uncle Bob," did the same thing. There is a little tire store at the end of the road from their church, and one Tuesday morning, Uncle Bob pulled in and rolled down the window of his pickup truck.

"Well, boys! Something happened today that ain't never happened before!" he hollered over to the men working, clearly puzzled.

"Yeah? What's that Uncle Bob?" they asked in curiosity.

"Well, I got to church early and nobody showed up but me. Not even the preacher! How about that?" he said, shaking his head, still confused.

Uncle Bob Dillehay

Now, living in a small town, everybody knew Uncle Bob's mind wasn't as sharp as it used to be. But they also knew that they wouldn't embarrass him for anything. So, they just nodded in agreement, and he drove on down the road to his house. None of them dared mention to him that the reason no one showed up was because it was Tuesday, not Sunday. Mel said that happened dozens of times. But she never panicked and worried that she should move him into a nursing home. No, sir.

She just figured it did him some good to get up and get dressed. No harm. No foul. Of course, the time came when she did get him some in-home care. As a matter of fact, she had an angel or two sent to her also.

—◦/◦/◦—

Apparently, Sundays happen to be a very popular day in the memories of the forgetful. That is the day that Granny is stuck on too. I started putting the date on the board for one very irritating reason. It didn't matter if it was Monday or Saturday, when Jenna or I showed up in the mornings at Granny's, she was either fully dressed or in the process of dressing for church—every morning.

Why would that be irritating? Well, because of the mess she would drag out on her bed. One morning she got out three dresses, four skirts, eight blouses, and four blazers. There were more stockings laid out on her bed than in the Rockettes' dressing room. You never saw such a mess. She was sitting there in a slip, with one foot in her stockings, completely flustered.

I must admit, my tone was not dripping with patience that morning. "Granny! What on earth are you doing?" I asked, sounding shrill.

"What do you mean, what am I doing? I'm getting dressed for church. What does it look like?" she shouted back at me.

"Granny, today is Tuesday. We don't have church on Tuesday."

She sat there for a minute and then, with all the sincerity in the world, she looked up at me and said, "Then why in this world did you get all these Sunday clothes out?"

Silly me.

—◦/◦/◦—

Here is a journal entry from Sunday, August 3, 2008:

She had on a blazer with a bra and slip but no blouse. So I explained to her that might be okay for a Madonna concert but not for church. She started in with, "Where are we going?"

Papa came in and yelled at her, "Lois, you know good and well where you're going! Stop asking!" Then Granny shot back at him, "Cordell, if I knew, I wouldn't be asking! Just go back in yonder and watch television."

So on the twelfth time she asks, "But, where are we going?" I sarcastically answered her back, "Golfing! Now grab your clubs!"

To which she huffed, "You're kidding me. I thought we were going to church."

Just shoot me now.

Granny and my "secret weapon," Aunt Mary Nell

So we started the routine of my putting on her board what the day was and what she should wear. I always lay her clothes right beside the sink in the bathroom and have (for a lack of a better word) "trained" her to get up, go to the bathroom, take off her Pull-Up, and then put on her clean clothes. Some days, this works like a charm; other days, she gets more clothes out to try on than a fashion model headed for the runway.

I feel I should share a word here about Pull-Ups. "I'm a big kid now!" Well, that's a great catchy phrase for a two-year-old graduating from diapers to Pull-Ups, but when I tried to talk my (at the time) seventy-eight-year-old mother-in-law into wearing them, that was a different story.

Because Granny's back bothers her so much, she took forever getting into and out of bed. Strangely enough, this like, many other ailments and issues we have worked through, only lasted for a short while, and then, like magic, she was getting in and out of bed just fine, with very little fanfare. For months, though, it was an epic struggle.

Very few family members experienced this the way I did. It was one of the most difficult things I ever dealt with. Another of our routines is that I stop in around 8:00 p.m. to put Granny to bed. In reality, I get there at eight and start herding her to the bathroom. I don't actually get out of there until close to ten many nights. Here's the deal with AD patients: some nights (very few) there is no fuss, and Granny just hops up (relatively speaking) and heads to the bathroom. Jenna's or Marilyn's routine is to always lay Granny's gown and clean Pull-Up on the bathroom sink.

I get her in the bathroom, bring her the nighttime meds, and encourage her to take off her clothes and put on her gown. I try to give her as much privacy as she needs, so after making sure she's well on her way to getting dressed for bed, I step across the hallway to "my chair" beside her bed.

For months, Jenna would come in at eight o'clock the next morning to find a huge puddle of pee all over Granny's hardwood floors—it would take Granny so long to get up from bed that she would stand up and just pee all over her and the floor. We never fussed at her for this, because it was clear why it happened. So after Jenna and I brainstormed with each other, we came up a couple of solutions.

First, we brought a potty chair into her bedroom and placed it right beside the bed. (We had one from when David's grandmother was alive.) Logic would dictate that this would solve the problem. But Alzheimer's does not play by logical rules.

This solution was short-lived—just for a few months—because we never could get her to get out of bed and on the potty chair without her continuing to wet the side of the bed and herself. Okay. If at first you don't succeed …

I bought a pack of Pull-Ups. I had put off this tactic for several reasons.

One was that I know my mother-in-law so well, and so I knew this would go over like ants at a picnic. The night I introduced her Pull-Ups was fit for an episode of *American's Funniest Home Videos*.

"Granny, you know how you always pee on yourself in the mornings when you first wake up?"

"I *do not*! Why, I've never peed on myself! Why would you think that?"

I don't know. Maybe the two loads of towels Jenna washes in bleach every day. Back to the point.

"Well, actually, you do. But that's okay. It's not your fault. But it *is* dangerous for you to pee on the floor and then walk through it to the bathroom. First, it's nasty. Second, it's a wonder you don't slip and fall. So … to take care of that problem, your doctor suggested you wear Pull-Ups to bed." I smiled sheepishly and hoped with all hope that this went well. Humph! Did I mention how well I know my mother-in-law?

"*Which* doctor? And why in the world would you tell him I pee on myself when I most certainly *do not*?"

Pretty much as I expected. "Okay, well, here's the deal. It's not fair to Jenna to have to come in every day and clean up that mess. It's just nasty. So for lots of reasons, we are just going to get you to sleep in this disposable underwear from now on." *Please, oh, please, oh, please let this work.*

"Disposable underwear, my foot! That thing's a diaper, and I *am not* wearing a diaper!" With that, this poor frail woman, who can barely hobble to bed, blew past me and marched to her bed, where she promptly threw herself down on the bed and gave me death looks. Okay. Plan B. (You will get *good* at coming up with Plan B's.)

"That's fine. I'll just call Aunt Mary and tell her you thought her idea was stupid. I'll just give these back to her." I said in my most dejected tone possible.

"Mary Nell? What do you mean it was Mary Nell's idea?"

Ha! Got her! Aunt Mary Nell has always been my ace in the hole when it comes to Granny. She is the one of her three sisters who has always been extremely close to Granny. "Desperate diseases call for desperate cures."—Hippocrates

"Sure, Granny. Aunt Mary doesn't want you peeing on the floor, just like she doesn't want to pee on her floor. So, every now and then, if she's not feeling well, she will wear a Pull-Up to bed. But I can tell her that you think the idea is stupid. No biggie." This, by the way, was not a lie. Aunt Mary and I did have this conversation to some extent. I had told her my plan beforehand, and she thought it an excellent idea. She also said that once when she had not been well, she had used one. With that statement, I knew I'd eventually win this war. If all else failed, I knew I could just call Aunt Mary and let her talk to Granny over the phone.

"Well, you say Mary Nell uses these diapers? I mean, disposable underwear? Well, I guess it couldn't hurt anything. It's not like anybody would have to know."

"Of course not!" And with that, I slipped them on her with a sigh of relief. She thought they were the strangest things in the world for the first couple of nights, and then, as time passed, if Jenna forgot to lay one out with her gown, she would yell for me to fetch her one. After all, if they were good enough for Aunt Mary, then they'd be just fine for her.

———

When working with AD patients, nothing works smoothly all the time. Remember, what works today won't always work tomorrow. Another one of my routines started because of the Pull-Ups. But this one involved Papa, not Granny.

On the second or third night when I tried to get Granny to put on the Pull-Ups, she had completely forgotten anything about Mary Nell. And rarely does a technique work more than a time or two. As I got Granny into bed, I basically told her she *had* to wear it. It was not up for discussion.

As I was leaving, she mumbled, "That's fine because as soon as you leave, I'm getting up and taking it off!"

I hung out in the hallway for a few minutes, waiting to see if she would be good to her word or if she would not remember what she had threatened. I walked into the den to see what Papa was doing, and he had just opened a package of peanut butter and crackers and popped the top of a Coke. I knew he should not have caffeine right before bed, but I could only slay so many dragons in a day.

"Hey, Papa. I'm gonna hang out here with you for a few minutes to make sure Granny doesn't get up. You really don't need to drink that Coke right before bed. It will keep you from falling asleep."

"I'm not going to drink it all. I'm only gonna drink half of it. Would you like the other half? No sense in throwing it away."

"Yeah, I actually need a good stiff drink. Half a Coke would hit the spot."

"Here, take half of these eat-a-snacks, too. There's six in here. I won't eat but three of them. You ever seen this show? That Barney is something else." He turned his attention back to Mayberry.

"Yes, he is." I sat there and visited with him for just fifteen minutes or so, but we laughed as we watched *Andy Griffith Show* reruns, and my snack had just hit the spot. Then I checked on our patient, and she was already sound asleep. Since I didn't see any sign of a Pull-Up slung on the floor, I knew she hadn't followed through with her threat before falling asleep. Sometimes AD works to our advantage. She had probably forgotten her threat as soon as I walked out of the room. Either way, the mattress would be safe one more night.

The very next night when I walked out to the den about 10:00 p.m., dog-tired and ready to hit the hay myself, I saw what Papa had done. There on the ottoman in front of the couch was a napkin with three little crackers and a glass filled with about half a can of Coke. I was *so* tired, but anybody who knows my father-in-law knows this was one of the most loving things he had ever done. So, what did I do? I plopped down and told him, "Thank you! This will just hit the spot." And with that, he smiled a satisfied smile and said, "That Barney sure is funny!"

—⌇∅∅∅⌇—

The best of routines will work only if executed correctly. Here is another journal entry to show you what you may have to deal with:

October 1, 2008

Note to self: Fire David McDonald as a caregiver! He dropped Granny off tonight for me. He said he would put her to bed because it would be late before I could get here. He dropped her off and *told* her to head to bed. Well, why not tell her to do some brain surgery on her way because she's not doing either! He *assured me* when I called him on my cell phone on the way home that Granny *assured him* that she was headed straight to bed. He was gullible enough to believe her! Not me! I know better. I decided to "pop in" just to be sure. Just as I expected! When I got here, she was sitting in her chair with only her slip on. Hey, she started to get ready for bed. I give her that much. Instead of getting ready for bed—by now it's almost eleven—she was sitting there shelling peas!

You just can't find good help.

———

As I mentioned earlier, each night I leave Granny on the potty and walk across the hall and sit in my chair beside her bed. I do this for several reasons. First, this gives her some privacy, but I can still keep an eye on her safety. Second, I review what Jenna has written in the journal to know what needs to be addressed. I bought a journal, and every day, Jenna writes in it what they did that day and how everything went. At night I give her specific instructions for the next day and let her know what time Granny got into bed.

Third, this allows Granny to keep her independence. She doesn't need me to dress her. As long as she is capable of dressing and undressing, I'm not about to take that ability away from her. Beware of helping your patient to death. Literally.

One night as I was sitting there, I noticed Granny was "stuck" halfway up from the toilet. She had both hands on her pants about midway up her thighs. She just stood there for the longest time in that position. Finally, I hollered to her, "Lucy, are you stuck? What are you doing, standing there like that?"

"I can't remember if I'm pulling *down* my pants so I can use the bathroom, or if I'm pulling them *up* because I just did!" she shouted across the hall to me, clearly in a quandary.

I don't remember the last time I laughed so hard! I assured her that she could go ahead and sit down and try to use it one more time; it couldn't hurt. This is a woman that we have to remind to go to the bathroom during the day, but let me need to get her into bed and suddenly, she needs to go every ten minutes.

You can either laugh at this disease or cry. Thankfully, that day we could laugh.

—⟨⟨⟨⟩⟩⟩—

Another routine I do with Granny that has worked wonders for her mental and emotional wellbeing is to read to her at bedtime. When dealing with AD patients, it will help to remember the saying, "Once a man, twice a child." My children always loved for me to read to them before bedtime. It is a great way to wind down Granny's day and get her relaxed and in a good frame of mind before bedtime.

Nighttime can bring about fears and cause delusions. For some reason, many AD patients have a fear of nighttime and darkness, much as young children do. To combat this fear, I make bedtime a calming time for us. I keep a nightlight on in the bathroom across the hall and near the floor of Granny's bed to give a small glow, so she's not in complete darkness. Using a nightlight has been extremely helpful for us.

Every night when I sit down in my chair beside her bed, I keep the lamp on beside us. This gives her a chance to get use to the dark with me sitting there, but it also gives me enough light to read by. I pick up one of the same three books and read her a short story every night.

One of our family members, Jack McCall, also is an author. He is one of five children born to Frank McCall, Granny's oldest brother. He is a humorist and has written a series of books about his childhood, a collection of short stories that always have a good moral meaning to them. You can get the series by visiting his website: www.jackmccall.com. The names of the books in the series thus far are: *Daffodils in Autumn, Falling Leaves & Spring Time*, and *Fireflies in Winter*.

I highly recommend them for you to read to your loved one; I recommend them for several reasons. They are written about the time in history that most AD patients can remember just fine. Most AD patients can recall the 1940s and '50s as though they were there this morning. It's just remembering the past forty or fifty minutes that gives them fits.

The books are full of good, clean humor. *"A merry heart doeth good like a medicine." (Proverbs 17:22)* A good chuckle before bed will help your patient relax without drugs. (Unfortunately, most doctors tend to prescribe more medicine than they do practicality.)

To date, there are three books in his series, so I start in the first book and read a short story, and the next night I move on to the next story. We have gone through all three books dozens of times over the years. But Granny still loves them and gets a kick out of hearing these stories. She actually remembers many of these stories taking place or hearing Jack's mom, Aunt Mary Helen, relate them to her.

One night, because I was tired of reading the same stories over and over, I picked up another book by someone we didn't know. It was a book of stories written about older people and was filled with humor. Oh, Granny got a big enough laugh out of it, but the whole time I was reading it to her, she'd stop me and say, "Now, who'd that happen to? Whose family is she a part of? Funny, I don't remember this ever happening. I think Jack has flat out made that up! I know Mary Helen would have told me about that if that had really have happened. Now, who'd that happen to?" If it ain't broke, don't fix it. So, back to Jack's books we went.

If Jack ever gets laryngitis and can't speak at one of his engagements, he should call me—I have his stories memorized. I'm quite sure I could relate them to the crowd just fine.

Reading to Granny only takes an extra fifteen minutes of my night, but she is usually relaxed and ready to stay in bed—very important to me—and drift off to sleep. Plus, it is a mental exercise when I ask her about some activity Jack mentions in the book, and if I'm not familiar with it, she's always eager to explain it to me. This is definitely one of our best routines. You should try it.

We have found that the more routines we can incorporate into Granny's life, the better we and she will be. We get her up at the same time each day. All meals are at the same time, served at the same place. Exercise and fresh air are scheduled at the same time every day. You may think this sounds incredibly mundane and rigid, but nothing could be farther from the truth. We "schedule" fun things every week—outings also are important—although some days she is up to it, and other days are a total waste of makeup.

4. Purpose

It has long been said that most people die within three years of retiring. If that's not enough reason to keep busy, I don't know what is! Everyone needs to wake up with a purpose every day.

About the time we found out that Granny had dementia, I began reading books by someone who has become one of my favorite authors. Karen Kingsbury is an unbelievably talented Christian fiction author. In one of her books, *Remember*, Ashley Baxter, the main character, works with AD patients at a group home. At the time, Granny was just forgetful, but I after reading the book, I stored away in my memory bank something that Ashley did for one of the residents.

One of the characters was a grumpy old Gus who sat and randomly moved his hands in circles. Over and over and over. He was not a social butterfly, and other people just assumed he was a little crazy because of the antics with his hands. Not Ashley. With a little detective work, she soon found out that he used to do saddle-repair work. He had done it for decades. How was this productive man supposed to just sit all day? She bought him an old, worn saddle off eBay, along with some polishing cream, and he blossomed. He spent hours a day restoring the old saddle into something show-worthy. He regained his self-worth and began to function with those in the home with him. He just needed a purpose.

I realize this is a fiction book, but I applaud Karen Kingsbury for delving into the world of Alzheimer's disease enough to make very valid points. I can relate to so many of the scenes she plays out for our imagination. Instead of asking me, "Has anyone ever told you that you have the most lovely hair?" (as one of the characters in the book did to Ashley), I get, "So, Lucy, where are we headed?"

I filed this information away and when Granny started needing more and more attention, it was brought back to the forefront of my mind. This woman had been busy for more than eighty years of her life. She never enjoyed sitting and watching television for very long, so that bored her quickly. So, one day, my epiphany came when I asked myself, "If she had her choice and her full mind, what would *she* be busy doing today?"

—⌒⌒⌒—

A game plan was born. I sat down with Jenna and brainstormed a list of activities that would be good for Granny. Knowing your patient makes this easy. It will still work if you are caring for someone who is not a family member or even one you don't know very well. Experiment with different activities until you find something that engages the patient's imagination. You can also simply ask what she used to do in her twenties, thirties, or forties for fun. What were her hobbies? You will be surprised what you find out.

Granny loves to cook for people. Although it isn't safe for her to cook without supervision, it's perfectly safe with Jenna or me there. Here are some of the things we do with Granny to allow her to continue her love of cooking and the ministry of feeding the masses:

- Jenna will give her the flyer from the newspaper and have her make out the menu for the week and the grocery list. This eventually causes some confusion because she goes over and over and over it, but for a while, it engages her mind.
- Granny chops up all the vegetables for all the meals. She sits at the table, and Jenna brings everything to her. It hurts Granny's back to stand for too long, so it is perfectly fine for her to sit and just chop away. Therefore, she feels as though *she* is still doing the cooking for her family.
- Granny washes all the dishes. She actually complains sometimes to Jenna that she is paying her to do that, but Jenna gently reminds her that it is actually part of Granny's therapy, and she can do it just fine. We are only talking about three plates, three forks, and three glasses, but it is good for Granny to walk to the sink and to be involved in this way.
- Jenna keeps Granny up-to-date on all the neighbors that she has fed over the years. If Mr. Sloan has been in the hospital, then they make cookies and take them over for Mrs. Gladys, just as Granny would have done before—even though Jenna has to continually remind her who they're cooking for and why.
- When the church asks for volunteers to bring finger foods for an after-church event, we always volunteer Granny. Jenna helps me keep her involved.

- Granny goes through her own cookbooks and especially her own recipe box and "plans" meals. This almost always sparks a trip not only to the grocery store but, more important, down memory lane. She will go on and on about who she got this recipe from and who she has made it for. Even if we end up not making the dish, she feels like she has accomplished something—because she has.

Here is a journal entry from August 10, 2008:

When we brought Granny home from church, I sat a loaf of bread and some peanut butter and jelly in front of her. I let her make us all a sandwich and I got everything else together. When we left, we all thanked *her* for fixing us lunch, and she just beamed and said she should have made us more than just a sandwich. Bingo! She actually remembered what we had for lunch! Wow! She can never tell me what she had! It must have mattered more to her because *she* was doing it for *us*. It had just become memorable because she had a sense of purpose.

Granny's garden.

Granny and Delanie breaking beans and shucking corn.
Dolly and Dooley are keeping them company.

One of the things I enjoy most is gardening. Granny has always been so busy, buzzing back and forth from the golf course and home that she never truly got to have a decent garden. She had a sad little plot out by the barn every year, but it produced more rocks and weeds than it did tomatoes and okra.

When the kids and I planted the garden, we took Granny down there on the John Deere Gator and let her hand us the next seedling or seed packet. When we would drive by the garden, I would slow down and tell her that *her* garden sure was looking good. She'd say cute things like, "I need to get out there and weed it. I'll do that tomorrow." Of course, the kids and I tended to it, but she didn't know that. I would sometimes pull her up right to the edge and give her a hoe, and she would whack away for thirty minutes or so right in one spot. When we would leave, she would just be exhausted from working in *her* garden.

When we started harvesting, I really did put her to work. We used a wheelchair when we had to go somewhere that would be too much walking for her, so I pulled her down by the garden in the wheelchair and put her under the big oak tree with Delanie to shuck corn while I picked it. We did this for days on end. I would take her big bags of green beans, and she and

Jenna would sit on the front porch and break them. The day I made salsa, she chopped tomatoes until she had had her fill of them.

But every single night when we had worked, she was more than ready for bed. No fights on those nights! She had put in a long day's work. She had a *purpose*.

"The sleep of a labouring man is sweet" (*Ecclesiastes 5:12*).

Another thing I did to give her a purpose was plant a garden on her porch. I have to admit there are times when I feel like I have had these great epiphanies from God. Because this one turned out to be rather ingenious, and I don't think I am smart enough to have thought of it myself.

On one of our trips to Walmart, Granny smelled the tomato seedlings and remarked how much she missed growing her own tomatoes. Never mind that I took her up the hill every week to the "big" garden; she couldn't be expected to remember that. But what if I planted a garden on her front porch? After all, she and Jenna were out there every morning anyway. This gave them more reason to be there and gave Granny another purpose.

I bought eight matching pots and lined them up along her front porch. I purchased tomato plants, okra, squash, and bell pepper plants. When everything was on the porch, we pulled everything within reach of Granny. She planted her own garden. She had the job of watering it each morning. Of course, Jenna would go back and forth to the faucet, filling up the silver coffee pot Granny used to water her plants. But it was Granny who was tending her "garden."

Because the front of the house was only in the morning sun, we never reaped a huge harvest of vegetables. But the benefits we reaped from that little venture were priceless. She had a garden. She had a project. She had a purpose!

It was the process, not the produce, we were after. I brought in plenty of veggies from the real garden, and she was none the wiser.

Did your patient like to garden? Let him get his hands dirty in the comfort of his wheelchair, and watch him bloom, blossom, and grow!

—◦◦◦—

I remember years ago, when my grandfather was alive. He had retired years earlier and sat outside under an oak tree all day. Just sat out there! It would drive Mammie crazy.

My family moved into a new house, and he and Mammie just happened to ride up the day we were moving in. He was well into his seventies then. He'd had open heart surgery several years before, and my momma babied him to death. He was perfectly healthy. The doctors said so. He just was a boat adrift on the sea.

As soon as I saw him come upstairs to my bedroom, I put him to work. "Hey, Pa, do me a favor and put my bed together for me," I said.

"I better not. I'll leave that for your daddy to do," he said in his normal gruffness.

"No, Pa, *you* do it, please! Daddy's going to be tied up moving the rest of the stuff in. Please!" I begged. Even as a young teenager, I knew that it was better to burn out than to rust away.

I was right. All the man needed was a little purpose and a screwdriver. He put my bed together and began to unthaw. I repeatedly told him what a great job he was doing and how much I appreciated it. Once or twice, my mom came in the room, fussing at me and him both, but we *both* shooed her away. The difference I saw on his face when they left to go home will stay with me forever. He just needed to be needed.

———⟨⟩———

When my brother-in-law, Steve's stepdad, was first put in the nursing home, he did what he had done for years. He sold shoes! Steve said that Mr. Frank would go up and down the halls, stop by all the little old ladies lined up in their wheelchairs, get down and take their shoes off, and have them try them back on. He had been a successful business owner with thirteen different stores. He knew a good clientele when he saw it. I wasn't around then, but I hope the nurses didn't shoo him away.

Not only did it probably do him good to feel productive, but I'm sure it made the women in the home feel great. Have you ever known a woman who didn't feel better after buying a new pair of shoes?

———⟨⟩———

Melanie, from the dentist office, told me that one day she walked into her daddy's house to find him "slap dab wore out," as he put it. She could see that he was actually a little sweaty and asked him what on earth had he been doing that had him so tuckered out.

"Brenda Gail (that's what he called his caregiver, Pat) has had me spreading mulch all day long! She's a slave driver, I tell you. But we got her done. And it looks great, I tell ya," he explained to Mel.

Pat looked at Mel and winked and replied, "Yes, ma'am. Uncle Bob really worked hard today. We're both gonna sleep well tonight!"

Mel said that when they walked out of earshot of Uncle Bob, Pat explained. "Actually, *I* shoveled mulch all day, but I set your daddy up with a shovel to hold onto. *He's* only swatted at flies all day. But he thinks he has helped me put out mulch. When I got here today, he was a fidgety mess. He was restless and just looked like he needed to do something. Of course, he didn't know what he needed to do, but he was definitely getting more and more agitated as the morning wore on. So, we loaded up and went and got mulch. Then we headed over to my house, and he 'helped' me spread mulch!"

"Pat, my dear, you are a genius!" And with that, Mel went back to where her daddy sat and asked him to tell her all about his busy day.

—◦◦◦—

When my dear hubby decided to build us a cabana out by the swimming pool, I suggested he go get his daddy to "help" him. At first, David bucked, afraid it might be "too much for him," being out in the heat for so long. With one "you have *got* to be kidding me" look from me, he agreed that it would do them both some good.

Papa, bottom left, "supervising" the construction of our cabana

Every day during David's vacation, he ran down and picked up Papa, and told him he needed his help on this little project. David had a crew of friends help him because this is no ordinary cabana. It is like most projects my husband begins   an elaborate architectural sight to behold. Hindsight is 20/20 and thousands of dollars cheaper, usually. But David decided to build it in the same triangular shape of the concrete slab it was going to be sitting on. Now that we have taken out a second mortgage and sold a kidney, we realize he could have made it a huge rectangle that crossed over the driveway and saved tons of money, hassle, and headache. But it would not bring any of the bragging rights that the current cabana brings. Plus, because it was so intricate to build, Papa really used his brain to think through several aspects of it.

Every night when I went in to do my nighttime routine, Papa would rehash all the day's progress, and being Papa, he really enjoyed sharing all David's little mishaps. He slept like a baby during that project and was dressed and ready to head out the door when David pulled in to get him.

One morning, one of David's patients lost a cap off a tooth, so David went to the dentist office and dealt with that before he picked up Papa. A few minutes after eight, my phone rang—Papa wanted to know where David was. The day was wasting away and he (Papa) had a lot *he* needed to get done on that building today. Priceless, I tell you. Expensive ... but priceless.

———— ❧ ————

Papa working the concrete chute at the pond

Another one of the projects that Papa helped David with was building a picnic shelter on our pond. David had Papa hold the concrete chute as it came out. Did David *need* him to hold the shoot? Of course not! Did Papa *need* to hold the chute? Of course! He "worked" hard that day. David, who would rather work construction than be a dentist, does all the projects on our farm or at willing neighbors' homes, for that matter. Our boys know how to wire a building, pour concrete, build a building—you name it, they can do it. David always calls Papa and asks him to come along, just "in case" David doesn't know how to do the job. I'm not the only one in our family who knows the importance of having a purpose. My father-in-law is a man who won't do it at all if he can't do it well. We just have to coax him out of that.

I know of some very ingenious people who ask AD patients to work on old appliances. Others give them yarn and ask for a baby blanket. Figure out some type of "work" for them to do each day. Be forewarned—they probably will butt heads with you and tell you they don't want to. Keep pushing them until something finally clicks. You both will be better for it.

Ideas

Gardening, photography, needlework, yard work, painting, mending, cooking, folding laundry, babysitting (supervised, of course), small engine repair, woodworking, sewing, scrapbooking, sight-seeing (with you), canning, sweeping, dusting—be creative! Was he an accountant? A church treasurer? Give him a list of numbers to add and an adding machine. Let him think he is still doing his job. An occupied mind is an active mind, and an active mind is a sound mind.

"For God hath not given us the spirit of fear; but of power, and of love, and of a sound mind" (2 Timothy 1:7).

—⟋⟋⟋—

Do not assume that just because your patient has never done an activity before that he/she would not enjoy it. Try to introduce a new activity as though you need help with it. Remember, you are giving your patient a purpose.

AD is a horrid monster. Any activity will only work for a short while, until it causes more confusion than stimulation. At that time, "change the channel," and move on to a different activity. You may even need to move the activity out of sight to eliminate frustration. But don't write it off completely. You may be able to do the exact same task tomorrow with stellar results. You just need to be flexible and patient.

When frustration does set it, try a "change of scenery." Head outside for some fresh air. It will take her mind off the activity, and will do you and the patient a world of good.

—⟋⟋⟋—

How about getting your patient a pet: a bird, a fish, a lap dog, a cat—or perhaps three horses? That's what we did for Papa.

We brought the horses that Granny is so crazy about down close to their house and fenced in a paddock for them. Our hope was that Granny would walk out there every day with Jenna, to accomplish exercise plus purpose. We did not plan on getting Papa's interest.

He has never helped Granny with her horses. He thought they were a waste of time and money, so he refused to be a part of her nonsense. But as grumpy as he could be, when he knew she wasn't up to walking out there, he started going. Little by little, he began to care for them every day. Now he feeds them, pats them, and—much to my surprise when I caught him—talks to them! Wow!

When the farrier comes to shoe them, Papa takes great pride in holding onto the reins to keep them still while the farrier works. Of course, the farrier is wonderful and praises Papa for the great job he is doing with *his* horses. Papa is always quick to correct him that they are Lois's horses, but she wasn't able to fool with them as much as he could. But I believe that somewhere along the line, they indeed became *his* horses. His purpose.

5. Appearance

In the words of comedian Billy Crystal, "You look *mar-ve-lous*! It is better to *look* good than to *feel* good, darling!"

I didn't gather research on this, but I bet there is a field called, "Make-up Therapy." One of the things Jenna found when working with patients, either at home or in assisted living, is when they look good, they tend to feel good.

When she was working with Mrs. Beatrice, Jenna would fix her hair and put a little makeup on her. Even if Mrs. Beatrice stayed in a gown and robe, she'd put her stockings on with her shoes. Jenna said she could see the transformation right before her eyes. Mrs. Beatrice would perk up in her chair, cross her frail legs, and tell Jenna, "Well, I guess we're ready for some company to drop by."

Even if company didn't drop by, it still gave her something to look forward to all day. Jenna has used that tactic a lot with everybody she has stayed with. To older people, "folks dropping by" was a more formal occasion than it is to our generation. Back in the 1940s and '50s, most families only had one car, if they had that. Most of them stayed at home all week and "went to town" on Saturday and then church on Sunday. Now, we sometimes "run to town" three or four times a day. Thinking someone might drop by just doesn't mean as much to us, but it still works to coax the elderly.

Jenna learned this trick while staying with Mrs. Beatrice and later on found out it worked just as well with Granny. Jenna goes in some mornings to find Granny all slumped over, barely keeping her eyes open. She gets her up and into the bathroom, and she begins the makeover.

"Honey, I don't feel like getting dressed today," Granny would often complain to Jenna or me. "I think I'll just keep on my gown today. Why don't you just leave me alone and go fix breakfast."

"Oh, I just figured you'd want to be dressed in case Mike or Jay stop by." Jenna would dangle that idea out there, knowing that the thought of seeing a grandson or two was perfect bait.

"Mike or Jay? What makes you think Mike or Jay might stop by?" Granny would ask, finding more life already.

"Well, they've got spring break this week, so you just never know when they'll decide to pop in for a visit." Jenna would be undressing Granny out of her gown as she spoke and getting her dressed for the day. Always remember, an AD patient *has a hard time thinking about two different tasks at one time.* Although this can be irritating for the caregiver at times, we have found it works greatly to our advantage to get her talking on one subject while completing the task at hand.

I think I should address lying. When Jenna and I deal with Granny and Papa, there are times when we have to be in the "truth of their minds". We don't have to lie to them to get them to do what we need them to do. If Mike and Jay had not been on spring break that week, Jenna would have picked someone else to lure Granny. Perhaps Jenna would have said something along the lines of, "Mrs. Dana hasn't been by in a few weeks. You know it's getting about time for her and those sweet, sweet kiddos of hers to stop by. We wouldn't want them to catch you in your gown, now would we?"

You can be clever without being dishonest. Contrary to popular conception, AD patients are *not* stupid. They tend to know if you are lying. Just because they can't remember from hour to hour doesn't make them ignorant, so don't act as though they are.

I have mentioned before that nothing irritates me more than to hear someone say, "Oh, she doesn't know the difference anyway." Maybe not, but *you* do. A little character and a lot of imagination will take you a long way in life.

God did send us an angel when he sent us Jenna. I will never forget the first few months of Jenna staying with Granny. I made Granny a hair appointment with my dear friend and hair dresser Stefanie Green. As Providence would have it, you could nearly throw a stone and hit her shop from Granny's front porch. I thought, what a wonderful plan! How could this possibly not run smooth as silk?

Welcome to Alzheimer's! The first time Jenna took Granny, I got a phone call within fifteen minutes of the appointment time.

"Mrs. Lorrie! You've got to get to the beauty shop, now! Mrs. Lois has lost her mind!" Came a panicked Jenna's voice over my cell phone. Yes, sir, smooth as silk.

When I walked in the door, I witnessed indescribable mayhem. Stefanie and Jenna were standing over the sink where Granny was literally sliding out of the chair. No matter how many times, they pulled her back up into the chair she'd squeal her theme song, "Oh! My back! My back is killing me! Oh-h-h! Stop! You're killing me!" And then she'd throw herself down the chair until at times her bottom was hanging over the end of it.

Poor Stef had a room full of other clients who looked on in horror, as we were obviously torturing this suffering, feeble woman. This was one of those times when I wanted to spank Granny. Her back was not killing her, and if it had been, it would have been because of the gymnastics she was doing in that chair.

"Granny, what in this world are you doing?" I hissed into her ear.

"They're killing my back!" she hissed back.

"Then stop throwing yourself down out of the chair. Sit still, and let Stefanie finish washing your hair, for goodness sakes! I cannot believe you are throwing such a fit." I was clearly the embarrassed mother of a toddler throwing a tantrum in the grocery store.

With that, she fussed back and forth for the next ten minutes or so, as Jenna and I helped her to sit back and let Stefanie finish. I had to make a split second decision. Was this for real? Remember, one, I know Granny—I know when she is putting on a show for attention, and this was one of those times; and two, I have had the orthopedic surgeon and physical therapist show me which positions stress her back and which do not. This one was just a slight incline in a padded chair. She sometimes sits back farther in my vehicle than this chair had her tilted back. This behavior was for show.

I get into more arguments with my family over this one subject than any other thing. Here is a small tutorial on doing things for attention:

"Once a man, twice a child." That idiom bears repeating. I have found that just as a small child will often "show off" in front of people for attention, so do the elderly. I don't know why that is so hard for family members to understand, but it is a sore spot.

Sometimes people will get mad at me and think I'm being cruel. What I have wanted to say on many occasions is that when they spend as much time with Granny on any given day as I do, consistently, then they can be the judge of her actions. I know when she's putting on a show. So does Jenna. We are with her day in and day out. We have learned all the patterns—the way she looks around to see if anyone is paying attention to her. The way she gets louder and more intense as soon as people start noticing her and trying to help her.

I cannot tell you how many times we have been headed to our seat at church when some very well-meaning people offer to "help" Granny to her seat. I try to shoo them away as politely as I can without being rude, but sometimes it's just too late. Once she has drawn an audience, she tends to moan and groan and squeal. I know Lois McDonald well enough to know that if she were in her right mind, she would never do such a thing, but she's *not* in her right mind. It's not Granny putting on this show; it's the dreaded demon Alzheimer's.

One Sunday morning Granny sneezed. The first couple sneezes were probably real. But then someone giggled at her. The next six or seven sneezes were performed for the crowd. Delanie, our daughter, was eight years old at the time, and she leaned in and whispered, "Momma! Granny's faking those!" Yes, indeed she was.

I ignored it for another few "ah-choos," and then I leaned over and said, "Granny, stop sneezing. You're disrupting the service."

David was mad as a hornet at me. "Why did you fuss at Momma? She can't help it that she's sneezing! Good grief."

Hm-m-m, well, I guess it was just a total coincidence that after a dozen or so outbursts, she didn't sneeze again. She gave me a smirk that said, "Phooey on you!" She was a little kid whose hand had been caught in the cookie jar.

Jenna and I have recorded dozens of times when she puts on a show for people when we are out in public or have visitors over. It is something we are aware of, but we choose our battles wisely. If you work with an AD patient for any length of time, you, too, will notice these performances. My advice is to try to keep the antics to a minimum, and remember, the average person probably will not believe you. That's okay. Just know that you are neither crazy nor cruel for trying to keep the situation under control.

These people who want to offer assistance mean well; they just don't know what a can of worms they open up by offering too much help. I am much more aware of this now whenever I see a caregiver out with someone. I offer assistance when I think it might be needed, but I am not offended at all if he or she adamantly refuses. I get it. Believe me, I get it.

Back to the salon story. Stefanie finished up Granny's hair that day, and I don't recall what she charged her, but it certainly was not enough. The next time we called to make Granny's appointment, Stef hesitated and then said sure and put her down for early one morning. Jenna reported that things went much smoother after that first incident.

After a few times of this, I happened to be in the salon getting my hair done one day and asked how Granny was behaving now. Stef said that as long as she had her come in when no one else was in the shop, she did fine. I found out that she was not booking any other clients at the time Granny was there. I couldn't believe it. I told her that she couldn't do that, because that was costing her money. She explained that she thought Granny did much better without an audience. Indeed.

Jenna and I discussed this and came up with the most ingenious plan ever. Jenna said that she had often cut Mrs. Beatrice's hair for her and that she would be happy to cut Granny's. So we gave it a shot. Bingo! No more Oscar-worthy performances at the hair salon for Granny. Jenna reported back that not one single time did Granny so much as grunt when Jenna was washing her hair or cutting it. Granny would have to save her theatrics for church and the grocery store.

—◦◦◦—

Have you ever walked into an elderly person's home and smelled body odor? Not a pleasant visiting environment. For some reason, most older people do not want to bathe. I don't know if it is because of a fear of falling or because of their past experiences.

Remember that Granny and Papa grew up during the Depression. Most families didn't have what we refer to as "city water." Most families had a well. A well from deep within the earth. A well that had ice-cold water, even in July. To take a bath meant drawing buckets and buckets of that frigid water, hauling it to the house, warming it on the stove, and then dumping it into a huge tub that they usually hauled into the kitchen, where it was typically warmer. It was very common for people from that generation to only bathe once a week, typically on Saturday night. And it was not uncommon for the whole family to bathe in that same tub of water!

Our generation has it easy. Hot and sweaty from working out in the yard during the summer? Jump into the shower. Freezing cold from playing in the snow? Jump into the shower. There have been days when I've had two or three showers in one day, depending on what I had going on that day. I will admit that when I found out that Granny, in her right mind, typically bathed only once a week, I was a little disgusted. Then she exclaimed to her poor ignorant daughter-in-law that she always washed off in the sink every day. What kind of Neanderthal did I think she was?

When the AD began to sink in, she simply couldn't remember to take a bath. One week slipped into two and pretty soon, I realized this too was going to have to become part of her routine. Since we took her to Wednesday-night Bible study at church, we decided that that would be a good day for a bath.

We purchased a bath chair that has half the bench in the tub and the other half over the edge of the tub, so we knew we could bathe her safely. Because she is so unsteady on her feet, we thought this was the best route to take with her. Papa, on the other hand, refuses to sit on the chair, so when we can coerce him into taking a shower, he throws it out in the hallway and just stands up to take a normal shower.

On Tuesday nights, I write on the memo board on the wall beside her bed:

Today is: Wednesday.
Do *not* get dressed!
Jenna will help you bathe.

Sometimes that works, and sometimes, Jenna has to come in and get her undressed from whatever couture she has put together. But Jenna always makes sure her hair is well kept, and she has on makeup and a cute outfit. We never take her out of the house without her being "put together." People notice. People often stop us and talk to us while we are running errands, and they almost always mention how good Granny looks.

Jenna's keeping Granny in a neat, clean appearance gives Granny self-worth and shows the world that we care about her and take the time to make her beautiful, because, after all, she is. I could never thank Jenna enough for taking such pride in her job, especially since her *job*, just happened to be my mother-in-law.

I recently went to visit Mammie. I couldn't believe how long her hair had gotten. She never wore her hair long. Never. I decided that since I don't live close to her that I would take matters into my own hands, literally. My uncle said she didn't want him to take her to the "beauty parlor," so she had just let it go. I was shocked at how unkempt she looked; not at all like Mammie typically looked. So, the next time I paid her a visit, I did so with scissors, comb, and curling iron in hand. I gave her the salon treatment. She and I both loved the way it turned out, and we were able to spend quality time together in the process. It was a win/win situation.

Remember how Pigpen in the *Peanuts* cartoon strip walked around with a cloud of dust and stench hovering around him? Well, with all due respect, that's my father-in-law. He has some slight dementia but is still in control of his faculties. Sometimes that works at a disadvantage for us.

He doesn't see the need to take a shower every week—or sometimes even once a month, for that matter. I don't tell you this to shame him but to be honest in trying to help caregivers understand what they will deal with. My father-in-law is a man very set in his ways. He is also very set in his ugly green chair. He is not the social butterfly that Granny is, and it is very rare that we can drag him away from the house. And if we do rouse him from his chair to take him somewhere, he seems to think a quick once over with a damp cloth does the trick. Trust me. It does not!

Jenna and I have talked to David and Marilyn dozens of times about this. Jenna suggested that Marilyn have him hop in the shower on the one day a week that she is there. My sister-in-law is too nice. She suggests it to him, she even lays out the soap, washcloth, towel, and most important, a clean change of clothes, but he blows her off most of the time and simply refuses.

Then we wrangled the help of my husband, whose idea of "getting Granny to bed" was sitting down to watch the Golf Channel and suggesting to her that she get into bed. He is a wonderful husband but fails miserably in the caregiving department.

Finally, after almost a month of Jenna's realizing that Papa had not given her any dirty clothes to wash—because he was still *in* them—I confronted Papa myself. Perhaps you should take notes on my tact here:

"Papa, you stink."

Ironically, this worked. I followed up that very blunt statement by telling him that it had been several weeks since he had changed clothes and that the den was really beginning to smell bad. David was coming and was going to help him take a really good shower. He didn't put up too much of a fight, and then we worked like a well-oiled machine.

David came in and herded him back to the shower, where a clean wardrobe was awaiting him. David stood outside the shower, calling out instructions: "Papa, use the soap and washcloth and scrub all over. Be sure you wash your hair too."

I popped my head in the door of the bathroom and motioned for David to come out into the hallway so I could share something with him.

"You need to pull the curtain back and make sure he's actually washing," I whispered.

"I will not! My daddy would die if I looked in on him," David retorted.

"You're gonna have to. He won't wash if you don't! Trust me!"

"You just go help bleach the floor out there in the den and clean up his little bathroom, and leave Papa to me." And with that arrogance, he pranced back into the bathroom. "Daddy, are you almost done?" he called into the shower. "If you are, just dry off and use that towel hanging over the rod."

I was still in the hallway when I heard the water turn off and some shuffling around. Then I heard what I had been all too certain of.

"*Daddy!* What on earth have you been doing in there! The washcloth is not wet, and the bar of soap hasn't even been opened! Good grief! Get back in there and let me help you. Good grief, Daddy!"

And with that bit of satisfaction, I headed to the den to help Jenna fumigate the joint.

Several minutes passed, and then David and Papa walked past us, headed out the door. "I'm taking Papa to town to get his hair cut. Don't fix him any lunch. I'll get us a burger and shake at Sonic."

Hey, you gotta' strike while the iron's hot!

——*◌◌◌*——

I don't know where your patient will fall on the personal hygiene scale, but you will have to work out a routine with him. He really does need a full-body bath at least once a week. If you are a woman caring for a man, you may want to enlist the help of a male family member once a week. I will mention here that in the very beginning, Jenna helped Papa with his bath, but he reached for her arm once as she handed him the shampoo, and it made her feel very uncomfortable. She and I both know that he's not fully "there" and never would have done something like that in his right mind. Nevertheless, she was uncomfortable, and I did not want that, so we decided it was best for his children to see to that task.

There is no reason you can't work around any awkwardness and get your patient the hygiene care he needs. In working with Granny over the years and talking to others who are in the same situation, I have noticed that the elderly seem to get to a state that is much like a young child when it comes to their inhibitions. A young child will hop out of the shower and run stark naked through the house to her bedroom and never think a thing about it. No matter who's in the house, children have an innocence about them. I have been shocked to walk into the bathroom and found Granny without a stitch of clothing on. It never fazed her. She just continued to talk to me while I handed her the undergarments and instructed her to get dressed. I never read about that in those thick books

I bought to understand AD. It would have been nice if I had been given a little heads-up. So there. Now you know.

David often said that it bothered him to help Granny to the bathroom because he didn't want to invade her privacy, and I understand that, but I think God provides for that by taking away the "shame" of having to have help. There was a time when it *would* have embarrassed her to death to have someone wipe her bottom after she finished in the bathroom, but some days she just can't do it by herself. It seems to bother us more than it bothers her. It is just another facet of caregiving that you need to be aware of.

If you do nothing else mentioned in this book, I encourage you to take the time to improve the appearance of your patient. You will bring dignity back to a person who may not even be cognitive enough to appreciate what you are doing for her. I have seen with my own eyes the difference a good haircut and a little tender loving care can do for a person's demeanor. Paint her fingernails. Get him a good shave. It's just another way to take pride in your work and show your loved one respect.

Do not allow her to sit around in her gown or pajamas all day. Yes, there will be times when you can have a lazy day, but on the average, get her up and dressed, and fill her with a little anticipation of what the day may bring. If she looks better, she truly will feel better.

6. Social Butterfly

If you don't think having a social life is important, just look at Cinderella. Going to just one ball changed her life forever! Being a caregiver allows you to be someone's fairy godmother.

Part of your weekly routine should include as many social events as your patient is up to attending. This would include going to church, weddings, funerals, bridal teas, wedding showers, taking her to your kid's ball games and soccer practices. For a man, maybe just take him down to the local Hardee's or wherever all the able-bodied men go for a cup of coffee. If you do a little research, you will be able to come up with a list of places to go and people to see.

David's assistant, Melanie, has an angel working for her too. This caregiver's name is Pat. To Uncle Bob, Mel's daddy, she is "Brenda Gail." Apparently from the first day Mrs. Pat walked through the door, he dubbed her Brenda Gail. So that's who she has been to him. I don't know how a man with AD, who has trouble remembering his own name from time to time, can remember such a moniker. But that was his term of endearment for her.

Mel said that her ninety-year-old daddy just loves the sweet tea from McDonald's. Some weeks, Pat would load him in the car every day if he got the "hankerin'" to get out, and they would head the eight or nine miles to the closest McDonald's, where she would get him a sweet tea. They might cruise through town a time or two, just to see if anything was going on there. Believe me, in a small rural town like Carthage, Tennessee, nothing is. Then she'd head back to his farm. They'd look at every herd of cattle the whole way back, and see who had tobacco out and whose hay needed cutting. Mel said when they would get back into the hollows (pronounced *hollers* in these here parts); Pat would drive 15 or 20 mph to let him soak it all up. To him, this was better than Cinderella's ball.

There would be days when Mel's daddy was convinced the hay needed to be gotten in. AD patients can be like a "broken record"—they are just "stuck" on whatever is eating at them. Pat would patiently drive him around and look at the farms nearby and explain to him that all the hay was indeed cut. Everything was perfectly fine on the farm. Most important, he could see it with his own two eyes. That outing would be enough to console him, and they'd head to the house—or perhaps to McDonald's for a glass of sweet tea.

This method of dealing with the confusion that comes with AD is so much more humane than a nurse at a nursing home who needs to check on three or four other patients, so she gives him a pill to sedate him and calm him down.

Granny loves the attention she gets at church.
Lydia and Elisabeth Edde are her chauffeurs.

Granny loves to go. It doesn't matter where or when. She's usually up for the task. But I will let you in on a secret. Probably 90–95 percent of the time when I tell her we are headed somewhere; she tells me she doesn't feel up to it, that she would just as soon stay home. She even tells me she's not going. But I know Granny well enough to know that's not her talking; that's the AD talking. The lazy way out for me would be to say, "Well, okay. I'll check on you later," and leave her sitting there.

This has never been about what is *easiest for me*. It's about what is *best for her*. The trick, as I've mentioned, is getting her focused on one thing and then helping her to do the task I need done. I distract her and get her ready to go.

I go in every Sunday morning an hour before church and get her up and fed. The entire time she is eating breakfast, she will tell me that she didn't sleep well last night and she thinks she'll just skip church today. I could say okay. I'll turn on a preaching program on the television and check on you after church. That, however, is not going to happen. She would miss out on the socialization that she experiences every time we go. Therefore, she goes to every service. I take her on Sunday morning, Sunday night, Wednesday night, and any special services that we have.

What if it's raining? We still go. I pull up under the carport and shuffle her into the car. Then I pull up under the breezeway at church and hand her off to a friend until I can get the car parked. Same thing is true when it's snowing. I've been caring for her for almost seven years, and she's never once slipped on ice or caught a cold from being out and about.

We've gone on a vacation only once in the past several years where I needed backup assistance in taking her somewhere. David and I took the kids to Kill Devil Hills, North Carolina, to see Kitty Hawk. We were only going to be there Friday through Sunday. I made sure I had taken care of their daily medicines. This was before Granny had the full diagnosis of AD. At that time, she was very cognitive and alert. I explained to her that someone else would be coming to take her to church on Sunday, and she was fine with that.

What wasn't fine was Sunday night, when I called to talk to Papa to make sure he was doing okay with Granny being gone to church. When the phone rang, imagine my surprise when Granny answered. She wasn't supposed to be there answering the phone. She was supposed to be at church. When I asked her why she hadn't gone, she told me that the person I had sent to take her had called her that morning and said it "looked rainy and windy," and she wasn't going to come get her in that. The person had brought them lunch and stayed for about thirty minutes and then left.

I asked to speak to Papa. Granny was still in her gown and had been *all* day. When I asked what she'd done that day, he said she hadn't moved from her chair, other than to go to the bathroom. I was furious! She would be absolutely stir-crazy for the next few days because her routine had been completely thrown off kilter.

I called my helper and asked her why in the world she hadn't taken Granny to church like I'd asked. She made several excuses about it "looking" rainy. Are you kidding me? I take her out in deluges! David assured me that the problem was that it takes a lot more work than most people want to put forth to get Granny dressed and out the door. It's just easier to make excuses that ease your conscience than it is to admit you just don't want to fool with her.

Sure enough, Granny dressed for church every day that week and was way more confused than she had been in a long time because her routine had been changed. Jenna said that it made the following week terrible!

Granny's routine had been changed, and although she couldn't remember what was different, she knew that it was. I wish that everyone involved could understand it is not a power struggle. Nor do I think my way is the only way. But the truth is, my way does work. We have seen Granny improve. There is a saying David often reminds me of to keep doing what I'm doing: "I like the way I *am doing it* better than the way *you are not doing* it!"

What really ticked me off was how much I hated it for Granny. She loves going to church. She always tells me how much she enjoyed it, and I quiz her on our way home about people who spoke to her and what Brother Ron preached. David normally takes our family out to eat on Sundays. We take Granny with us every time. Since Papa refuses to go anywhere, I definitely cannot get him out the door to church. His mind is not as far gone as Granny's; plus, she loves to go, and he does not. It's just who they are. I always bring him a to-go plate lunch, and that satisfies him.

We have the most amazing church family anywhere. Every week, different people come up and visit with Granny before and after the service. One person always gives Granny a big hug—our pastor's youngest daughter, Amie Grace Ralph. She has been doing this for as long as I can remember. She is a teenager now and continues to do what I have jokingly and lovingly dubbed her "old people ministry." One hug can change a person's day. She makes her way around the sanctuary and tells the elderly how nice they look, or "Good to see you. You're looking well"—any word of encouragement. She will never know the impact that has had on Granny. Recently, she leaned in and hugged me before bending down to love on Granny. I looked at her, cocked my head, and said, "So, Amie Lou, does this mean I'm officially old?"

Since we have a large, growing church, we often have bridal teas or baby showers following the Sunday morning service. I always get a gift for the recipient from Granny and have Granny sign the card. She may not know the person, but that would never have stopped the "real" Granny, so why not keep her socially involved by doing it *for* her?

She always tells me what a wonderful time she had as we head home so she can lie down and rest before the evening service. She gets a great sense of belonging, and it costs me nothing more than a modest gift and a little of my time.

You may be thinking, "Yes, he loves church, but his delusions have gotten so bad on some days that he might say or do something that will embarrass him." That crosses my mind every time I head out the door with Granny. But so what? Almost every family is dealing with AD—we all know someone who has it. If you don't, you will. Most people are incredibly understanding.

I recently spoke to someone whose father has been diagnosed with AD. He is experiencing delusions almost on a daily basis. She said her mom was afraid that he might say something out of line at church, as he always has been an outspoken leader of our church. I gently smiled at her and told her, "Jennifer, we love Brother Bob so much that if he were to get into the pulpit and yell 'At-ten-tion!' I truly believe our whole church would stand and salute. We love him that much."

We are all in this together. Don't let your fear of what might happen keep you from taking him out and adding to the enjoyment of his day. The world is becoming more and more aware of the challenges the caregivers of AD patients are facing. So dress up your patient and continue taking her to the places they are accustomed to going. It will not only do them good, but it will do you a world of good also. And the rest of us just might learn a little humility in the process. "At ease."

—◦◦◦—

There is no end to the places you can take your loved one if you use your imagination. The end result is you get her up, dressed, and out into the world for stimulation. One of the first things I told Jenna was that when she went to the grocery store for Granny and Papa, I wanted Granny to feel like *she* was doing the shopping for them. I also told Jenna that if she had errands to run, she should take Granny with her.

Granny goes a couple of places every week, other than church activities. She goes to SavWay Grocery and to Walmart—mainly just these two places because there are not many more choices in our small town.

Granny loves to shop. Anytime I am heading to the outlet mall in the next town over, I take Granny with me. We make a day of it. Is it a lot of work? Absolutely! Does it wear me out? Absolutely! Does she remember it the next day? Maybe and maybe not. But she sure enjoys it while it's happening. Does that matter? Absolutely!

Granny is such a bargain-hunter that once we were in a large mall in Nashville, and as I rolled her past one store in particular, she kept reading their signs out loud to me.

"Storewide Sale. Thirty percent off. Everything in the store 30 percent off! Wow! I think we should go in there. Look at that. Everything in the store is marked 30 percent off! Let's go in there!"

"Granny, you don't need anything from that store. It's okay. We'll go on to the next one," I assured her.

"Humph! How do *you* know I don't need anything from that store?" she asked, practically turning around backwards in her wheelchair to read the big pink signs.

"Because that's Victoria's Secret. They sale sexy panties in there. That's why!" I told her in hushed tones.

"Humph! Well for 30 percent off, I could have used some of their sexy panties!" She clearly was put out with her chauffeur.

"Indeed you could have, Lucy, indeed!" I said as I envisioned Granny in one of their hot pink get-ups. I picked up the pace to change our scenery as quickly as possible.

Although our rule is that Granny walks everywhere we go, when we take her shopping, she rides in a wheelchair. We back off the walking rule because the purpose of the shopping trips is not exercise; it is socializing.

When Granny can sit in a wheelchair and wheel herself from aisle to aisle, she does not wear herself out. She takes her time and looks at all the products. Then when we see someone we know she gets to sit and visit for a while. Living in a small town means we always see someone we know. Jenna and I both make a note in the daily journal so the other one can quiz Granny to see if she remembers seeing someone and talking to that person. That's always a good memory exercise for later in the day.

Because Granny is often childlike, we never pass up a chance to get her a treat. What child doesn't enjoy a milkshake or an ice cream cone? So when we finish running errands, we usually pop into Sonic for a little snack, and we always take Papa a chocolate milkshake. His nature is to fuss when we head out with Granny, going anywhere. We always ask if he'd like a milkshake before we leave on shopping day and that tends to appease him somewhat.

—⁓⁓⁓—

I hate Alzheimer's with a passion! I don't hate that Granny forgets who certain people are as much as I hate that she forgets who *she* is. Our pastor's wife, Rhonda, has a senior ladies breakfast every year in the month of December. Granny has always enjoyed it and has been the life of the party for years. She would laugh and tell tales; even if they were the same ones over and over. She loved it! This past year was different.

Usually Marilyn takes Granny, but this past year, Jenna offered to take her, and she stayed with Granny during the meal. Jenna filled page after page in the journal, noting that Granny just sat there with what we call the "deer in the headlight" look. She answered questions when asked but didn't engage in the conversations like she normally did. Jenna remarked that Granny didn't quite understand where she was or who all these ladies were talking about.

That night as I read the journal entry, I asked Granny about it. It took her a little while, but she finally remembered going and told me she'd had a lovely time and that Mrs. Rhonda was an excellent cook. I'm glad she went; I just wish she could have "been there."

It would be easy to see her lack of interaction on a day like today and say it's not worth it. But I would be wrong! These days are when we are either making progress or digressing. So, I put forth the effort, and leave the outcome up to God.

—⁓⁓⁓—

Family and friends are another great source of socialization. Since Jenna takes Granny out once a week and runs the errands, and I take her to church every Sunday and every Wednesday night, I thought it would be wonderful if Marilyn took her around to a different family member's house on Thursday when she was with Granny.

Because these people were relatives of Marilyn's, I thought she would enjoy getting Granny up and dressed and going to a different place each week. Our family and friend base is so large that she could visit a different place each Thursday for almost three months before she would be revisiting them. Jenna agreed that this would be a wonderful activity for Granny. When I ran the idea past Dr. Lim, he couldn't have agreed more. So that was that … or so I thought.

As I have mentioned, you really need to get everyone involved on the same page. Marilyn has taken Granny to Aunt Mary's and to Aunt Mary Helen's. When I have mentioned to Marilyn that we'd like for her to take Granny visiting more, she has never fully explained to me why she doesn't want to do that. Marilyn is happy to come and clean out Granny's drawers and cabinets, but she's not really on board with the exercises or routines. Marilyn felt like just being there was enough. Everyone helping needs to understand how AD works, and since she and I had a different view, I chose to let it go.

This is just how it is. I love Marilyn, but I don't think she fully understands our game plan, just as David never puts Granny to bed the way I ask him to. He doesn't understand that the extra fifteen minutes will reap huge benefits the next day. I mention this issue because I don't want to paint a rosy picture, leading you to believe that all well-thought-out plans are carried out because that is just not true. That doesn't mean that one way is right and the other is wrong; that's just the way it is.

I do encourage you to implement visiting family and friends into your plan. I would suggest you call the people you will be visiting each week to let them know you will be dropping in for a short visit. Anytime I took Granny over to see Aunt Mary Nell, she always fixed us a bite of lunch, and we would stay an hour or two. It did all of us a world of good, and we would be on our way. Think of some old family and friends, and then pay them a visit. Some of them may even be at a nursing facility. You know *they* would love a visit from someone. You would be killing two birds with one stone of kindness.

Granny *loves* to visit with her sisters.
Then and now.

As I have mentioned, each patient and her circumstances are unique. Granny loves to *go*, and Papa loves to *stay*. Just because he says he doesn't want to go, however, doesn't mean that it's the truth. Because of Papa's personality, he comes across as very harsh at times. People get tired of asking him if he would like to go when they know he will fuss at them. Just as with me and Granny, when David can get Papa to join him, he always has a good time.

We are all golfers. When Papa couldn't play well anymore, then he didn't want to play at all. He never understood that his grandkids needed him to play with them, not because he was good but because he was their grandfather. When David gets up a match with our three sons and Steve, our brother-in-law, and his three sons, he always invites Papa along. Nine times out of ten, Papa makes an excuse as to why he can't go. When he does go, even if he just rides in the cart, it does him a world of good.

We also try to get Papa to go to football games. Once again, when we are successful, Papa has the time of his life. He use to coach high school football, and dozens of past players stop by his seat to shake his hand and say hello. It's almost like he transforms into a whole different Cordell we don't even recognize. So excited! So full of life! He talks to David all the way home about the people we saw. When we get him home, David always tells him, "See there, Daddy? You had a great time tonight. You need to go more places with us."

"We'll see, son. I'm probably going to catch pneumonia from being out in that night air. And I probably won't sleep a wink tonight either, after all that excitement," he complained as he plopped down into the ugly, green chair.

Ah! *There's* the Papa we know and love!

Papa and Ellie Beth, his great-granddaughter, and his ugly green chair.

—ᴏ/ᴏ/ᴏ—

Complaints or not, it's well worth it for you to make the effort to get your patient out and about. It is vital to his or her overall well-being. One of the reasons Granny improved so much was because we kept her active socially. When she was at the nursing home during her time of therapy, she was surrounded by people whose minds were worse than hers. As in any situation, you tend to rise or fall to the level of ability around you.

When she was surrounded by the other men and women in the nursing home, there was not a single time when I overheard her have a coherent conversation. The few times I sat in on her conversations, the poor souls she was talking to wanted to know when so-and-so was coming to take them home, or they talked about imaginary people in the room. I witnessed firsthand what a state of confusion that put Granny it. She couldn't make sense out of their conversation, because it didn't make sense.

When she is surrounded by alert, sharp-thinking individuals, it causes her to bring her A game. She doesn't want to appear foolish in front of them, so she tends to listen more intently and makes more of an effort to think clearly. Will she remember any of that conversation four hours later? Probably not, but *at the time* she engages her social skills, and that has done wonders for keeping her mind from deteriorating any faster. The question is, are you going to put forth the effort that it takes to engage them in socialization?

Is your patient going to ask the same question fifty times while you are out together? Yes. Is he going to do something that embarrasses you? Probably. Is it going to be work to get her dressed and out the door? Yes. Will he complain and say he doesn't even want to go? Probably. Should you make the effort anyway? Yes. Will there be days when it seemed disastrous? Probably. When you lay your head on your pillow at night, will you know you did the right thing? Yes!

7. Mental Workouts

Leonardo da Vinci said, "Iron rusts from disuse; water loses its purity from stagnation ... even so does inaction sap the vigor of the mind."

Remember Dr. Lim's "blue, baseball, Virginia" test? Granny always aced the counting part of the test. ("Start at 100 and subtract by sevens.")

She flew through it. One of the first abilities to go with AD patients is math skills. I talked to Dr. Lim about this because it made sense to me that if you can slow down the deterioration of a person's math skills, then perhaps you could slow down the progress of the demon disease.

With that bit of deductive reasoning, Granny, the teacher, became Granny, the student. Marilyn took a plain spiral notebook and wrote page after page of simple math problems, about twenty to a page. Every day, Granny does a page or two of them. I also got simple workbooks at sixth-grade to eighth-grade levels. You can pick those up at Walmart or Sam's. We didn't just do math. Those workbooks come in a ton of different subjects—any mental stimulation is a good thing. Math skills are processed on the left side of the brain. Doing math problems every day keeps the left side of the brain stimulated.

Doing "homework" is another great way to keep an eye on your patient's cognitive abilities. You will know instantly when she is losing the ability to perform certain tasks. Since we homeschool our three younger children, we often would have Granny "help" them with some of their schoolwork. I would make copies of their work, and she would do it with them to "show" them how to do it. And when she got them all correct, we praised her as if she was a third-grader! She often fussed at how "stupid" it was that we had her do this, but that's okay, Lucy! Just like we ignored her when she complained about doing physical exercise, we also ignored her when she bucked at doing mental exercise.

———*◦/◦/◦*———

Coloring is another great skill for the aging. Mammie colors every day. She taught herself to draw when she was in her late seventies. She loves nothing better than sitting with blank paper and coloring pencils. For someone who never had an art lesson in her life, I am very impressed with her ability. She recently gave my mom and dad a whole stack of drawings—more than one hundred—that she had done that she was going to throw away. They are incredible. Some of them were on the back of junk mail because she had run out of drawing paper. So with that knowledge, I made a quick trip to an office store, purchased a ream of paper, and made a trip to see this incredible woman.

Mammie, age ninety, sitting with some of her drawings.

Some of Mammie's drawings that she taught herself to do.

Drawing and coloring are good for the mind. It engages the right side of the brain, which is the creative side. It encourages small motor skills and keeps them engaged in a carefree activity, as opposed to a logical activity such as math. Most people tend to be dominant on one side ("right-brained" or "left-brained") and will enjoy doing one type of activity more than the other. Both are important, however, so I encourage you to buy coloring books and crayons or print coloring sheets off the Internet. You can find coloring books with a more adult feel to them, but there's nothing wrong with coloring Hello Kitty, either.

Painting and drawing also are great activities for working out the right side of the brain. I own an art studio called The Paint Pail. I pre-draw an image on a canvas and then in classes, once or twice a week, I instruct people in how to paint it. The great thing about these classes is that there have been times when a three-year-old has sat across from a ninety-year-old, and they both end up with a masterpiece to take home. These types of studios have become wildly popular in the last few years. Do a Google search for "art studio" in your city. What pops up may surprise you.

I recently did a painting class at a nursing home. I was quite impressed with this particular nursing home. The staff does something adventurous with the residents every month, and each day there is an activity that stimulates their minds. I took in canvases, and then each resident painted. I helped with finishing touches, but they all were so proud of what they had accomplished.

One lady there, very fittingly known as "Granny," was deep in the stages of AD. She was painting a snowman, and every time the assistant who was helping her would walk away, she would completely cover the canvas with paint. I finally just told her to paint it anyway she liked. She didn't fully comprehend what I was telling her, but she did paint. In the end, I took my puff paint and "helped" her painting look like a snowman. She held onto it proudly for the photograph the coordinator took, feeling as though she had accomplished something meaningful that day ... because she had.

When Granny's brother Ray McCall was alive, he took art lessons from Mr. Bill Reece. Our three younger children took lessons from him also. It made perfect sense that Granny should sign up. She never produced a piece worthy of a gallery display (although Uncle Ray did!), but she was getting socialization, family bonding, and mental stimulation, and we got her all dressed up to go. We were killing lots of AD birds with one simple art class.

One of my most prized gifts I ever received was stationery that was made from some of Uncle Ray's artwork. I have since taken my children's artwork to a graphic studio and had them turned into note cards. Granny received a set of these last Christmas and thinks they are too pretty to write on and send out. At least she enjoys looking through them!

—❧❧❧—

Readers are leaders! I have known that for years, so when I started our mental rehab program, I knew the benefits that a person of any age receives from reading. Something jumped from the crevices of my mind, and I did a little delving into it. I recalled several Scriptures from the Bible that speak about God's word and health. I found this very interesting.

"My son, attend to my words; incline thine ear unto my sayings. Let them not depart from thine eyes; keep them in the midst of thine heart. For they are life unto those that find them, and health to all their flesh" (Proverbs 4:20–22).

I have heard dozens of stories through the years of someone being in a coma, or on his deathbed, or suffering from serious illness. When a loved one held a Scripture-reading vigil, the patient miraculously recovered. There are enough of these stories that I knew there had to be something to it.

I also know that God is not a liar, and that His words are true. Proverbs 4:20–22 was enough for me to come up with a plan. Since Granny and Jenna would be outside every morning anyway, they would start their day off with Scripture reading. *"I love them that love me; and those that seek me early shall find me." (Proverbs 8:17).* They took turns reading aloud. Where else did they begin? Genesis 1:1. They are stimulating brain cells—brain cells that He created.

I need to stress that you should use the King James Version of the Bible. This is the version that has been used since 1611. Granny grew up hearing this version. If an elderly patient ever memorized verses as a child, it was from this version. It was the *only* version available for hundreds of years.

The King James Version is the only one that has stood the test of time. Even if you or your patient is not a believer that does not change the promise of "health to all their flesh" mentioned above. Reading a chapter or more out loud each day will certainly not harm them in any way. If all those miraculous stories of healing are true, what could it hurt?

Reading aloud does something amazing that you may have not considered: it uses your eyes (left side of the brain) by reading the page. It uses your mouth (right side of the brain) by speaking the words. It involves your ears (right and left side), which hear the words being spoken, and it involves your hands (left side), with which you are holding the book. This one simple activity stimulates your brain in so many wonderful and powerful ways that it is a no-brainer! (Pun intended.)

⟞ ⟋⟋⟋ ⟝

I love to read Karen Kingsbury. Other favorite authors are Nicholas Sparks and Jan Karon. When I read a fiction book, I am transported in time to a little house on a prairie or to a forest with a lion, a witch, and a wardrobe. I can have a steamy date or run from the FBI. Reading fiction allows amazing things to occur in the brain. I have discovered, it's not just a good form of relaxation, but it also apparently fights off AD.

Many years ago, I was having some much needed "mommy time" while the kids were napping, when Granny appeared at our back door. As she came in, I was dying with laughter, laughing out loud at what I was reading—Jan Karon's *At Home in Mitford*. Granny smiled and asked me what was so funny. When I explained what was happening in the book, she asked if it was fiction. I told her it was and offered to let her borrow it.

What she said next just struck me as odd. It was so odd, in fact, that I have never forgotten it. She said, "I don't have time to read anything that isn't real and factual."

"I assure you, I'm not wasting time," I said, "but I do try to take thirty minutes each day to read something just for enjoyment."

Three years ago, as I was waiting in Dr. Lim's office for Granny's appointment, the title of an article in *Neurology Today* caught my eye: "How Reading Fiction Can Fight Off Alzheimer's Disease." I grabbed the magazine and began reading what I had often theorized. When your brain reads fiction, you involve the left side of the brain in the actual process of reading, but because your imagination gets carried away in a good book, you simultaneously involve the right side of the brain. Basically, you get "two for the price of one."

My grandmother reads everything from Trixie Belden to Dee Henderson. She loves anything set in a historical setting, so she also enjoys Janette Oke. This Christmas, I bought her several historical fiction books off the clearance rack of the Lifeway Bookstore. She squealed like a little girl when she pulled out the tissue paper and saw her fourteen new books.

That's how she spends her day. On the couch, under a lap blanket that I gave her for Christmas a couple of years ago, with a good book in her hands. That makes me happy.

Perhaps your patient is a man. Try Louis L'Amour, or the Hardy Boys books, or *Little House on the Prairie*. Magazines are good, too—*Sports Illustrated, This Old House, Guideposts*, or *Good Old Days*. Just know that reading is medicine for the brain at any age.

Now I finally have the argument I've always needed when David catches me curled up on the couch with Nicholas Sparks—"But honey, I'm fighting off AD as we speak!"

That is why we do Bible reading in the mornings with Granny, and I read to her from Jack's books or other fiction books at night. We are getting as many parts of her brain moving as possible.

Go ahead and reach for that book—it's good for you. Who knows when that "Once upon a time" might lead to "and they lived happily ever after."

—◦/◦/◦—

Crossword puzzles, seek-a-words, or better yet, the mathematics-based Sudoku are wonderful forms of mental stimulants that we all should find time for each day. Remember: "Inaction saps the mind." That is true for any age.

Make a list—of anything! Remember that the left side of the brain gets involved in sequential order; in other words, lists. When we get the grocery-store circular, Granny goes through the flyer and makes a list of all the things we need. A typical session might go something like this:

"Granny, we need to make our grocery list for Friday. Sit down here and go through the sale paper and make us a list. Okay, Lucy?"

She beams. "Okey-dokey, Lucy! Easy enough. I can do that." Then she queries, "Did you say *today* is Friday?"

"No, ma'am, today is Tuesday," I tell her as I begin getting lunch on the table. "But we go grocery shopping on Friday. So go ahead and make a list."

"Look a-here, would ya? SavWay has got chicken breasts on sale for $1.39 a pound. Wow! We ought to get some of those, don't you think?" She scribbles "chicken breasts" on her list. Productive. Mental stimulation. Good deal.

She flips to the next page. "Frozen waffles are on sale. You know how Cordell loves those." She scribbles "frozen waffles" on the pad. She looks over the next page. "Juicy Juices. We definitely need to get those for when the kids stop by." She scribbles on the pad.

And so this goes on and on until she goes through the entire flyer. She feels as though she has accomplished something worthwhile. She sets it aside and asks me, "Do you need any help getting lunch?"

"No, ma'am, I've just about got it finished," I assure her.

Then she glances over on the table and something new catches her eye. "Hmmm, what do we have here? Here's the grocery flyer. Well, look a-here, would ya? SavWay has got chicken breasts on sale for $1.39 a pound. Wow! We ought to get some of those, don't you think? Why don't you give me a pen and paper, and I'll make us a grocery list for Friday. Wait—what day is it today? Is today Friday? Oh, here's a pen and paper right here. I'll use this." And with that, she tears off the list she just wrote and begins again.

Those of you who work with AD patients are probably chuckling and shaking your head, saying, "Yes! That's exactly what Momma does"—or what Daddy does, or Uncle Bob. Some of you may think that's a waste of time. She doesn't even remember what she just wrote. But that's not the point. You don't need to be concerned as much with the end product as with the process.

Make it pertinent to the patient. Was he a mechanic? Have him make a parts list for fixing an imaginary problem with your car. Does he like sports? Have him make a list of the teams playing on television today. Talk to him about the players, or have your son or daughter engage him in meaningful conversation. Was he the church treasurer? Give him an adding machine and some old checks. Just get the patient to feel useful and to use that brain.

—⁂—

Just as in physical exercise, if you work out one side of your body, you need to work out the opposite side. Now that we've made a list and stirred up the left side, let's do another exercise to wake up that right side.

Swimming is often considered the perfect exercise. It works out practically every muscle in your body without putting a lot of strain on your joints. That's why I was so discouraged when I realized Granny was not going to get into the water and do water aerobics with me. If swimming is the perfect exercise for the body, however, then music is the perfect exercise for the brain.

A bazillion studies have been done on the effects of music. There are volumes and volumes of books written on the subject. I'm just going to list several facts that I considered when I chose to incorporate music into our game plan with Granny.

- Music is mathematics-based. Granny is good at math, and she's also a piano player. Music is based on mathematical sequences.
- The left side of the brain deals with sequences and math.
- Music is also a creative art form.
- The right side of the brain deals with creativity and emotional expressions.
- Music involves memorization.
- The temporal sides of the brain are involved in memory and hearing, which are both used in performing and listening to music.
- Music gets all lobes of the brain involved, thus offering a complete mental workout.

We use music in Granny's daily routines in several ways.

After she and Jenna finish reading Scripture aloud as they sit on the front porch in the morning sunshine, they get out a hymnal we use at church. Jenna lets Granny thumb through the book, and when she comes across one that was long ago committed to memory, they sing as Jenna plucks along on her guitar.

Sometimes when the kids and I stop by for our nightly visit, Delanie will sit down at the piano and ask Granny to play for her. At times, she struggles to remember all the notes, but it's not long before she breaks into the boogie-woogie song she so often played for the residents of the nursing home. It doesn't last long, but every little bit stirs the embers of her mind.

Our church does not sing 7/11 songs—those are the praise and worship songs that consist of seven words sung eleven times. Our church still sings out of the old hymnal. One of the great things about this is that these are the same songs that have been sung for centuries. The words to "How Great Thou Art" are still the same today as they were sixty years ago, when

Granny sang them as a young adult. Once again, this stirs those coals in the furnace of the brain. This is another reason that attending church regularly has such benefits for her. She stands during congregational singing and belts out the same songs she has known for eighty years.

I witnessed an amazing feat last year as we were singing. Our church hosts a yearly music camp each summer. From that week, we learn several new songs from a new songbook that has been compiled from up-and-coming writers from other music camps held the previous year. It is typical for our church to favor a couple of these songs and thus, we sing them several times over the following months.

During one particular Sunday morning as we were singing one of those songs, I turned around to see Granny, who was too tired to stand, sitting and singing along. She was singing this new song word for word ... without a book. She had learned and committed to memory a new song! That goes against everything I have been told about AD–that once the patient loses an ability, she can't regain it. Yet here sat Granny, singing with her whole heart and mind. She had only heard this song a dozen times at most, but she clearly knew it from memory.

I believe there is such a link between music and memory that we should implement it more. This is the reason that when my children were younger and needed to learn the presidents or states and capitals, we set it to music. Be creative. Set all kinds of information to simple tunes that your patient has known for decades. Use the tune to "Twinkle, Twinkle Little Star," or "Happy Birthday"—whatever you can come up with.

Here is one of my favorites: "Stay in bed 'til Jenna comes, doo-dah, doo-dah. Stay in bed 'til Jenna comes, oh, doo-dah day!"

Another wonderful way to use music is for its calming effect. It says in the Bible, *"And it came to pass, when the evil spirit from God was upon Saul, that David took a harp, and played with his hand: so Saul was refreshed, and was well, and the evil spirit departed from him." (I Samuel 16:23).* Anyone who has spent any time around AD patients knows that as politically incorrect and cruel as it may sound, an "evil spirit" exactly describes this horrid disease at times. When I was coming up with our game Plan for Granny, I remembered this verse.

There was a ridiculous song that was popular when I was in my teens, and one of the lines was, "The freaks come out at night." If you are an AD caregiver, you can relate to that. When the sun starts setting, it is as though a switch has been flipped. Your patient may have been lucid all day, and then, as if on cue, when it gets dark outside, a darkness seems to come across him or her. Perhaps the following suggestion will work for you:

Get a few classical CDs—I suggest classical harp music or soothing piano hymns—and play them very softly in the background, just before dusk. This seems to help many patients. I played classical instrumental hymns, and it completely changed the mood of the room. Studies have proven that classical music causes plants to grow, it calms antsy babies, and it soothes the soul.

With today's advanced technology, you can easily download thousands of soothing pieces on an iPod to play softly in the background. You will need, however, to hide the source of the music behind something; otherwise, curiosity will kill the cat—the patient will find the source and begin pushing buttons.

———

Is it any wonder that our elderly typically wither away when they are placed in an institutional setting? Again, I know that not all nursing homes are a picture of gloom and doom; neither are many assisted-living facilities. I am talking about the type of nursing home that was intended for just "nursing someone" who is too far gone to be cared for at home. Unfortunately, too many able-bodied souls are locked away because no one wants to take the time or pay for the help involved to get AD patients the help they need.

Too many people assume that AD patients can't function any longer. As our days progress, I see that we *may* come to that someday. At that point, we may have to give up on our daily worksheets, but until then, I plan on teaching the teacher.

8. Adventure

Zora Leigh Enzor McDonald was Granny's mother-in-law. She was one of a very elite group, doing what very few people outside of biblical times have done. She lived in three different centuries! She was born on August 12, 1899, and died at the glorious age of one hundred on January 2, 2000. She lived in the nineteenth, twentieth, and twenty-first centuries!

She was widowed in 1985 and lived alone until—get this—she was ninety-eight years old. You cannot imagine the irritation I felt when I heard that her three surviving children, all in their seventies, felt she needed to be in a nursing home. Are you kidding me? She was ninety-eight. What were they afraid would happen? That she'd die at home in her sleep? She *had* fallen but didn't break anything. She was vacuuming her house the week they packed her up and took her to the nursing home.

Celebrating Granny Mac's ninety-ninth birthday

I had only been in the family about seven or eight years at this time, so I voiced my concern, but I didn't push the issue. This is one of the biggest regrets that David and I have. I was due to have our only daughter, Delanie, at any time and when we offered to bring Granny Mac into our home, I was met with quite a bit of opposition. None of her children took her into their homes, although Granny said she had tried to talk Papa into it. He was all for it, but his sisters insisted that she go to the nursing home. They each had their own reasons, but I regret that David and I didn't just make it happen.

So if I couldn't keep her at home, I did the next best thing. At least once a week, I would load up our three little ones and steal her from the nursing home. Collin was three, Connor was one, and Delanie still had the drive-out tag on her! Still, I couldn't stand the thought of Granny Mac being stuck up there when she had a mind better than all of us put together.

It all started the first week she was there. Aunt Ruby lived in Donelson, an hour away. Aunt Betty lived in Hartsville, which was nearly thirty minutes away. Papa lived at the golf course, so he wouldn't show up until dark. After she had been there three or four days, she remembered something at home she needed to get. Easy enough. I checked her out at the desk, and off we went. Her home, only a few blocks away, was still just as she had left it.

I had been given a key to the house years earlier, so we pulled up and all went in. Well, it was mid-morning, and she was concerned the boys might need a snack, so she high-tailed it into the kitchen and whipped up something for them from things left in the freezer and cabinet.

While we were there, we might as well watch her favorite game show on TV. The kids took a nap in the front bedroom, and I cleaned up the kitchen. Before we knew it, several hours had passed, and I realized I needed to get her back before they missed us. She had such a great time, she kept going on and on about how fun that was, and most important, she asked when are we going to do that again.

As time went on, I would get her and we would go "home" for several hours each week. Granny Mac loved it. I was with her the whole time. It really was perfectly safe. But that is not how her children saw it. We would have been in the clear if she hadn't told everybody what a good time she had and all that we did each time we went out.

I got a phone call from Granny one day, who said that said Betty, Ruby, and Cordell thought it was hard on Granny Mac to take her out of her environment and back to her home. As far as I could see, the only problem was that I had to take her *back* to the nursing home. But I listened politely, never promised anything, and then had a talk with Granny Mac.

I tried my best to get her to stay on the down-low and not let anyone know, but she had been stubborn for nearly a century, and she wasn't about to change now. So, the next time we headed "home," we had a rude awakening—they had changed the lock on her house! They also informed the people at the desk at the nursing home that she didn't need to leave the facility unless it was for a doctor appointment. They felt that it was what *they* needed to do. So that was that. Now I knew what *I* needed to do.

For the rest of her stay there, she frequently had "doctor appointments." Since David—my hubby, her grandson—was her dentist, I just had him call the workstation and talk to a different nurse each week, and he always told the truth.

"Hello, this is Dr. Mac at the dentist office. My wife is coming up there in a little while to check out my grandmother, Zora McDonald. I am her dentist, and I need to see her." And he did.

I would pull up in the parking lot at his office, run inside and tell him to come say hello, and then we were off on our adventure of the day. Locking us out of the house opened up a whole new world for us. We drove to Sonic and got a treat for all of the kiddos, the one-year-old and the one-hundred-year-old. We would drive up to the area she and Pa Mac had first lived when they married. That is known as the Maggart community. We would look at her old home, the one they had shared back in the 1920s.

I wouldn't take a million bucks for those days of living on the wild side. She told me so many wonderful stories. Imagine all that she witnessed from 1899 until 2000. She remembered vividly the horse-and-buggy days. She told me once that the only thing she and her family went without during the Depression was coffee and sugar. As soon as he was able to, her husband, Wayne, bought a fifty-pound bag of white sugar. She said she gasped when he brought in that much sugar.

"Wayne! What in the world will we ever do with that much sugar?" she asked him, wide-eyed as he carried it to the cellar.

"Well, I'll tell you what we won't do—we won't do without!" was his reply.

You and I probably go through fifty pounds of sugar in just a couple of months, but not back then. Times were different. People just thought differently than we do now. For instance, take the arrival of a baby.

When we bring a newborn home, it is usually to a beautiful nursery decorated with an elaborately thought-out theme. The new bundle of joy is brought home lovingly wrapped in a monogrammed blanket with his or her name emblazoned with colors that match that nursery. When we get the baby home, if he so much as sneezes, we reach for the 800 number to the hospitals nursery or their neonatal unit and the cell phone of the delivering ob-gyn and a holistic lactation nurse. Not so back then.

When Granny Mac had Cordell, February 9, 1927, she had him at home with help from a few knowledgeable neighbors. Granny Mac's parents had died when she was young, and she had been raised from "pillar to post," as she once told me. The way they did it back then, she said, was to have the baby, be surprised by the gender, and then wait for their first doctor appointment before giving the baby a name. That first visit usually wasn't until around the third month. No sense wasting the money for a doctor if the baby didn't survive, and many did not.

When Cordell was around three months old, Granny Mac rode to town with Pa Mac on a horse and buggy because Pa didn't get his first car until much later. They had one of those older neighbor ladies with them. As they were headed across the bridge, the aged midwife asked Granny Mac, "Zora, whatcha gonna name the young'un? He's gettin' too old to keep callin' him the baby. He's a strong little fellar. He's gonna make it just fine. You and Wayne need to name him."

"I don't know. We haven't given it much thought," Granny Mac said, staring into his little cherub face.

Granny Mac said about that time, they were crossing the bridge that was named for a Congressman from Smith County, Mr. Cordell Hull.

"Well, it's high time you name him! I'd name him Cordell Hull if I couldn't come up with something more proper," suggested the older lady.

So that is how I came to have a father-in-law named Cordell Hull McDonald.

I am so glad I took just a few hours out of my week to make Granny Mac's day. I guess that was when I really realized that the elderly have lived incredible lives to which ours can't hold a candle. How demeaning to stick them in a recliner somewhere with *The Price Is Right* on TV and think you are doing them a favor. The elderly need adventure in their lives. That's why I broke Granny Mac out of the joint as often as I could. It wasn't just good for her; it was an amazing adventure for me and my children. We experienced a living history museum. I remembered that, years later, when I began caring for Granny.

—⌒∾∾⌒—

A little adventure is a good thing, but sometimes it's a trip to the emergency room. When dealing with aging people there is that really tricky time, usually in their mid- to late seventies, when you have to realize they are independent. The problem arises when *you* know that they are slipping and aren't quite up to the speed they are accustomed to. They tend to attempt things that their minds say, "Sure! No problem! I've got this!" Their bodies say, "What? You've got to be kidding me! We don't function like that anymore."

As a caregiver, you have to decide when to intervene and offer words of caution and when to throw a hissy fit and let them know ain't nobody got time for a broken hip. I have experienced both situations with my in-laws.

—⌒∾∾⌒—

Look closely! That is my seventy-eight-year-old father-in-law *up on the roof*!

Up on the housetop reindeers pause—apparently, so does Papa.

One bright autumn day, I had the children and Granny down at the pond, fishing, when I happened to glance up at Granny's house—and let out the biggest scream you ever heard.

"What in the world is wrong, honey?" asked a very startled Granny, looking around for the snake I must have spotted in the tall weeds.

"Papa's walking around on your *roof*!" I gasped, pointing over to the house.

"Oh, is that all?" she said, clearly relieved. "I thought something was wrong."

"Um, there *is* something wrong! What in the world would my seventy-eight-year-old father-in-law be doing, traipsing around on your roof, with what appears to be a blower in his hands?"

"He's just cleaning out the gutters. That's the way he has always cleaned out the gutters. He's fine." She apparently was dumbfounded at my ignorance. After all, didn't everyone shinny up to his roof with power tools in tow?

"Granny, that's just not safe. He should have asked David to do that for him."

"What in the world for? Cordell's always cleaned out the gutters that way. He says it's much faster than moving a ladder from place to place and climbing up and down fifty times. He swears this is much safer. He climbs up once and walks around the perimeter, carrying the blower, and just blows them all out. He's fine. Really!" And with that declaration, she cast her fishing pole out again.

Two wonderful things occurred at that moment. First, I happened to have my camera with me to snap pictures of the kids "big catches," so I snapped a priceless picture of my father-in-law in action. Second, David McDonald called Sammy Oldham and had him out there the next day, and Papa got an early Christmas present—installation of gutter guards.

———⟐⟐⟐———

Granny loves horses. She loved them in her prime, and she still loves them in her twilight years. Over time, Granny slowly began selling off what had originally been her daddy's prized Tennessee walking horse stock.

She had close to a dozen horses when David and I first married. She and I loved nothing better than to saddle up the same two of her horses and go for a ride over the farm. Princess was her horse, and Peanut was mine. Peanut had been what we call barn-soured. She had been ridden so much in the hallway of the horse barn by the grandkids that when anyone tried to ride her out of the barn onto the trail, she had other plans.

When Granny was in charge of taking care of the farm, the pastures pretty much took charge. She never had the time and never took the resources to invest in weed control or proper fencing. There was wild bramble and briars everywhere. The trail was overgrown, and the two ponds look menacing and foreboding. Granny never minded; she just saddled up and forged ahead on Princess. Peanut was actually Princess's foal. Looking back, I realize Granny was a smart cookie back then. She needed someone to break Peanut's bad habit, and she felt I was younger and better equipped for that fight than she.

Out we would go, just the four of us. Granny and sweet, demure Princess; me and demon-possessed Peanut! We would get fifty yards away from the barn, and Peanut, as if led by a honing beacon, would abruptly halt, turn, and charge back to the barn as if leading the fight at Bunker Hill.

I would rein her in, screaming, "Whoa!" at the top of my lungs, while Granny was sashaying on up the path, whistling "Happy Trails to You" and calling over her shoulder for me to show Peanut who was boss. Well, apparently, that 1,500-pound monster was calling the shots. I would yank, rein, kick, and pray her back around, and the farther we got from the barn, the safer I felt.

I always enjoyed riding with Granny, but let's just say it was more aerobic than trail riding was meant to be. I always needed a first-aid kit when we got back to Granny's house because Peanut felt sure if she ran me through enough blackberry bushes and wild rose bushes, she would win, and I would lead her back to the barn. I did not. She had more brute force, but I definitely was more stubborn. But what are minor lacerations up and down your body when you're making memories?

—ᴓᴓᴓ—

One of the reasons I hate AD is that it alters the patient's personality. Help your loved one enjoy the things that she would enjoy if she remembered that she enjoyed them. Here is a perfect example: Jenna will tell Granny that it is such a pretty day that they should go out back and see the horses. Sometimes that's met with a "great idea, Lucy!" But just as often, she'll say, "That's okay. I just don't feel up to it," or on a particularly bad day she might say, "*What* horses?"

We take her out anyway. Why? Because

- she's getting exercise,
- she's getting fresh air and sunshine, and
- once she gets out there, it gives her mind an opportunity to "reboot," and she can remember how much she loves her horses.

It would be easier to concede and turn on the tube, but that's not how we got Granny to improve cognitively by eighteen months. Put effort into planning weekly adventures for your patient. While you are at it, snap pictures of her having her adventure. You can use the photos for brain stimulation, and it makes for great memories later. Granny loves nothing better to than to look back at the pictures of her "adventures," especially those that involved grandkids and horses or fishing.

———⁂———

Before Granny got to the later stages of AD, we went on what I now look back and see was the greatest adventure we ever took. Granny began selling off horses when she realized she just couldn't properly care for that many animals.

Terry and Beth Patty were so sweet to bring the horses
Granny had sold them through the years.
Here, on Thanksgiving Day 2006, Collin, Connor,
and Delanie all got a chance to ride.

I was shocked on the day she told me she had sold Doc. He was her stud horse that was worth a small mint. He was grandson and great-grandson, as she was always so proud to tell people, of world champions Merry-Go Boy and Midnight Son, both of which were of great fame in Tennessee walking horse history. All I knew was that he was the most beautiful and gentle old soul I had ever seen. He was big, strong, and very dignified. All seven of the grandchildren had ridden on him at one time or another, even when there were ten or twelve fillies. He was truly that gentle. So I was blown away when she sold him. He *was* the other man in her life.

As the years passed, Beth Patty, the precious lady to whom Granny sold many of her horses, would send photographs of her showing Doc and winning blue ribbons with him. Granny treasured those pictures and blew them up to eight-by-tens and hung them on the wall, along with her grandchildren's pictures.

One day I called Beth and asked her if I could surprise Granny by bringing her up for a visit. It was a two-hour drive, and we would bring the kids and make a day of it. Beth was thrilled. She and her husband, Terry, had often been so sweet and thoughtful by putting two or three of Granny's horses or colts from her horses into a horse trailer and bringing them down to show Granny. They knew how much her horses meant to her, especially Doc.

I told Granny the plan, and she squealed like a school girl. We had been to her orthopedic doctor a few weeks prior, and he said that with her osteoporosis, she needed to take precautions and not do anything that could cause a fall and damage her back. I told him we completely understood. All the way to Knoxville, I reminded her of his warnings.

She had mentioned maybe two dozen times how nice it would be to ride Doc just one more time. I gently reined in her imagination and told her she wouldn't be able to do that, because if she were to fall or even mount incorrectly, she could damage her back. She completely understood. But said, "Wouldn't it be nice to ride Doc just one more time?"

The closer we got to their farm, the more excited she got. The more excited she got, the more excited Collin, Connor, and Delanie got. By now, they had joined the campaign with Granny. "Momma! Why can't Granny ride Doc just *one* more time? Wouldn't that be nice? Nobody would have to know."

I wasn't caving. I was being level-headed and responsible. I was taking all the necessary precautions. Besides that, Cordell and David both would kill me if I let Granny hurt herself. Nope, not happening. Showing Doc her love would just have to be enough for Granny.

When we got there, we saw that Beth and Terry had a nicer barn than some people's homes. I'd never seen anything so nice for animals. They showed Granny all the colts they had gotten out of Doc and the mares on the farm. (Doc's social calendar had indeed been full.) They all were beautiful. And then we had a Walt Disney movie moment.

I actually tear up every time I remember what happened. We entered the barn on the end open to the driveway and visited all the stalls until we finally reached the two back stalls that just happened to be empty. I immediately recognized the name on one of those empty stalls: "Doc." I looked at Beth with a worried look and a nod toward the empty quarters.

"Oh, don't worry," she said. "The old man's fine. He's just enjoying some fresh air." She led our excited group out the other side of the barn that opened into several sectioned-off paddocks. That's when Granny saw him. She stopped in her tracks and squinted across the gorgeous green field.

"There he is. There's my ol' boy," she said in a hushed tone.

I teared up as I looked at her staring out at him, and I could hardly believe my eyes. Delanie, who was only five at the time, squealed and pointed at Doc.

"Momma! Granny! Look!"

As I looked up at Doc, I saw that he had spotted Granny. I swear he was staring intently at her, and all of a sudden, he recognized her. He reared up on his back legs and kicked his front hooves up in the air, like something from *Black Beauty*. He was breathtaking. He was definitely showing off for Granny! And with that, she was off. Granny scurried over to the fence and pulled out the gift she had brought for this man she still dreamed about. Doc got one look at Granny and one whiff of the apple she was holding, and he shot over to us like a stallion out of the gate.

Terry and Beth led him into the barn hallway, and we all just stood back and watched the way they nuzzled each other, all the while, hearing that familiar chorus, "Oh, what I wouldn't give to ride him just one more time."

So at that moment, I made an executive decision that I still am thankful for today. "Okay, you can't ride him, but you can sit on him. That's it.

Okay? Do you have any idea how much trouble I would be in if David or Papa knew I was letting you do this? No one can know—*no one* ... ever. Kids? Do you hear me? You aren't to tell anybody that I let Granny do this. Understood?" Head shakes, and "yes ma'ams" all around. "Good! I mean it. This will be our little secret."

Terry was already in action. He had gotten a step ladder with handles along the sides. Doc stood statue still. Granny and Delanie both shook with excitement and the boys beamed as they looked on. I prayed. Oh, how I prayed. "Please, Lord, help her be safe."

Granny walked up that ladder as though she did it every day. Then, with Terry steadying Doc, and Beth and me steadying Granny, Granny sat atop the only possession she had ever truly loved. As she sat there rubbing him and speaking the sweet words of true love, I kept reminding her, "Granny, remember, no one can know you did this. No one. Not ever. No one." She sat lost in her youth, and I asked, "Granny, are you listening to me?"

"Yes, honey, I heard every word. Now, do you have your camera? I would love to have a picture of me riding Doc just one last time," Granny replied in a faraway, dreamy tone.

"Granny! How can I keep it a secret if we have a picture of it? And you're not really *riding*. You're just *sitting*, remember?" I retorted, feeling I was losing ground.

"Momma! Take Granny's picture ... *please!*" came the hallelujah chorus from my three stooges.

"Oh, good grief." So I ran to the Suburban and grabbed my camera.

I swear Doc posed for that picture.

I realized that I had lost the battle but won the war, and Granny did what I knew, deep down, she was going to do since we had left Carthage four hours earlier. She patted Doc gently and then smiled at Beth and Terry, who had stood back with the children and me so I could snap her picture, and said, "You know, since I'm already up here, I sure would love to ride ol' Doc just one more time." And with that, she nudged him and clicked her cheek, and off they went, ever so gently sauntering down the path of the barn. My kids clapped and jumped up and down, and Terry and Beth held hands and let the tears run down their cheeks. I did the only thing I knew to do. I prayed.

Her last ride only lasted as long as a gentle trip to the end of the barn and back. She and Doc both understood what it was. He parked her gently up beside the ladder and stood statue-still for her to dismount.

Could she have made her back worse? Absolutely. Could she have really gotten hurt if she had fallen? Absolutely. Would it make David and Cordell furious with me if they had found out? Absolutely. Will that one single picture be worth a mint some day when Granny and Doc are both just sweet memories? Absolutely.

Granny and her last ride on Doc

———✺✺✺———

Not all our adventures are borderline dangerous. But Granny has always been a live wire. Why would I think that a silly thing like Alzheimer's would slow her down?

Another great memory we made was one day when she was seventy-six years young, and we had six inches of snow on the ground. Because Granny has always loved snow days, I wasn't about to leave her in the house to stare out the window at this treasure from God. I bundled her up. I had the Tahoe blazing hot, and I pulled up to the door of the house with just enough room to open the car door, and we swept her away.

We drove up the hill, where David and the kids were already waiting in his truck. I drove Granny up to the top of the farm, where she could watch them sled. They had the pink plastic kind of sled that kind of cradled around them. We left the Tahoe running and had planned on letting Granny watch as the kids zoomed down the hill. It was a perfect snow for sledding.

"What I wouldn't give to sled just one more time ..." came the plea from the cracked window.

Hm, where had I heard that before? This time, I just made life simpler from the start.

"Okay, Granny. But you have to stay in the vehicle until one of the boys brings the sled back up to the top of the hill. Then, I'll help you sit down on it, and then you *slowly* sled down to the hill where David's waiting, okay?"

"Sure thing, Lucy! Whatever you say."

Here we go again. "Lord ..."

So when the kids ran back to the top of the hill with their sleds, I hollered down to the bottom of the hill, "Sweetie, your momma wants to have her picture taken with the kids in the snow." Which she did.

"Honey, are sure about that? It may be too cold for her," he hollered back up the hill.

"The sun's shining, and there's no wind. I think it will be okay."

"Okay, if you think it's okay. Just make it quick. And whatever you do, don't let her fall down in the snow!" David warned.

"Oh, don't worry, we have this all *planned* out," I said, feeling that same queasy feeling I get when I've spent too much money while shopping.

And with that, Granny posed for a precious picture with the kiddos. Then, with a twinkle in her eyes, she turned to her three miniature partners in crime and said, "Here, boys, help me sit down in your toboggan."

As they looked up at me, excited and quizzical, I nodded. In for a penny, in for a pound. "Go ahead; just be careful."

"Honey, is everything okay?" David asked from the base of the hill. "Is Granny sitting back in the car?" He tried to peer up over the snowcapped hill.

"She's fine. She's sitting ..." I replied, as I snapped the picture of the cat who just ate the canary. "See for yourself!" I yelled as the kids all gave Granny a gentle nudge that sent her over the crest of the sledding hill. They all jumped up and down and ran along beside her as their almost eighty-year-old grandmother felt eight years old all over again.

"Honey! Have you lost your mind? Is that *Granny?* Granny, hang on! Look at you, Granny! Ain't you something!" David's yelling had turned from shouts of anger to cheers of joy.

I jumped in the Tahoe and drove down to the bottom of the hill, to my dear hubby and *four* of the most excited kids I believe I have ever seen. What an adventure!

Not all adventures have to involve nerves of steel and bungee cords. Thankfully, one of the things Granny loves is fishing. We try to allow her to enjoy that as often as possible. Jenna will take her at least once a week, sometimes twice a week, if our schedule allows it. During the summer, when the days are longer, David and the kids and I pull up in the Gator, pick her up at the door, and off we go. I try to always have a metal chair for her to sit while she's fishing, to help support her back. But even a good stadium chair suits her just fine. She loves it and literally would stay all day. And some days, that is just what she and Jenna do.

One particularly beautiful day, Jenna took Granny down to the pond to fish. When Jenna suggested leaving to go home to fix supper, Granny bucked. "No, the fish are biting great. Just five more minutes."

Jenna realized they had enough leftovers from the night before, so it would be okay to stay a while longer. Jenna, who had been engrossed in practicing her guitar, began to pay closer attention to Granny. She knew that Granny had been whooping and hollering about how great the fish had been biting, but she just smiled and asked if she needed any help getting the fish off the line. Granny had reassured her that she did not. So Jenna turned her attention back to her music.

After a while, even Jenna couldn't believe how many fish Granny was catching. So she put down her guitar and walked over to Granny's chair. "Whatcha doin', Lucy?" Jenna asked.

"Honey, I'm catching one fish after another. Wait … wait … I think I've just felt another one! Wow! Can you believe it?" exclaimed Granny as she reeled in what Jenna later described as the most shell-shocked fish she had ever seen.

"I wish you'd just look-a here. Ain't he a beaut? There's dozens of fish just like that one. Same size and everything. Amazing. What a great day for fishing!" marveled Granny. And then Jenna watched in amazement as Granny looked off, and her line slowly released back down into the water right in front of her … fish still attached.

Jenna chuckled and was about to tell Granny she'd forgotten to take the fish off the hook, and that's when it happened …

"I wish you'd just look-a here. Ain't he a beaut? There's dozens of fish just like that one. Same size and everything. Amazing. What a great day for fishing!"

That's when it hit Jenna that for the last thirty minutes or so, Granny had been catching the same fish, over and over and over. Jenna said she laughed so hard she could hardly breathe. She had to sit down beside Granny to get control of herself. As she did, Granny looked at her and asked, "What in the world is so funny?" And now Granny, who loves a good joke, was laughing too, as her line (and fish) slipped back into the water.

Jenna later told me, "Mrs. Lorrie, I thought I was going to need a paramedic to revive me when I saw Granny's big blue eyes grow as large as silver dollars as she looked at me and said, 'Lucy, you're not going to believe this, but I just caught *another* one!' I literally beat the ground, I was laughing so hard. And then to see the look on that poor fish's face when, for the hundredth time, he came out of that water. Priceless, Mrs. Lorrie, priceless."

What a great day for fishing.

Granny, doing what she loves

Take your loved ones fishing, take them shopping—just take them on an adventure every day. Granny loves to go Christmas shopping … in

June. Even on days when she has no clue what Christmas "is," or who we are buying this stuff for, or even what this "stuff" is, we are still engaging her in a meaningful adventure.

Granny has always loved yard sales. Always. So what if she doesn't fully understand what we are talking about some of the time when we tell her we might stop at some yard sales. Once we pull up to someone else's junk, something inside her clicks. She "get's it." She has always been a big bargain hunter. What better place to hunt for bargains than at a yard sale? Jenna makes it part of their routine to look through the paper each week to see where the best yard sales might be.

Some days, Granny has trouble comprehending what we are doing, rummaging around in a stranger's carport. On those days, Jenna just does a little sight-seeing with her and makes a stop at Sonic. But we realize that Granny is still having some sort of adventure.

I have been asked into several nursing homes to paint with the residents and was impressed with one home in particular in Lafayette. Our friend Kelsey is in charge of activities there. She has shown me amazing pictures of the trips they have taken their elders on. Most of the residents need daily meds, oxygen, and full-time care, but this home feels that adventure is so important to the residents' health that they take them anyway. They have taken them to theme parks, to shows, to zoos—anywhere and everywhere.

Now, do I think that is best for them? No. In an ideal situation, the residents' families would be taking them on their family outings, and they would be making those memories with them. But when the situation becomes less than ideal—and we all know life has a way of messing with our plans—then a place like this *is* the next best thing. It was so nice to know that a "home" like this exists. The staff at this facility knew what I know— that adventure makes life worth living. Why allow AD to change that?

9. Picture Perfect

A picture is worth a thousand words. It also brings back a thousand memories. One of the tricks I learned to do with Granny is really more of a mental stimulant, but I list these here because we did a whole category of things that involved pictures and media.

As you can tell, I do not advocate sitting in a chair all day, simply existing. Why not make the most of that time? Let's be honest; when we hear the dreaded diagnosis of Alzheimer's disease, one of our biggest fears is that our loved ones will reach a point of not knowing us. If they live with the disease long enough, then that time will come. I have had to face the fact that there may come a time when I walk in the door, and Granny and Papa have no idea who I am. That time has not come for us yet, and I am doing everything in my power to stave it off completely. I am doing that, one four-by-six photo at a time.

I purchased several cheap photo albums from the store, a batch of blank address labels, and a good Sharpie permanent marker. I took recent photos of everyone who is significant in Granny's life. On the left side of the album, I placed a picture of people around the time that Granny remembers who they are. For most people, it is a photo from five or six years ago. Then I placed current pictures of the people on the right side of the album. Jenna and I wrote everyone's names on labels with a Sharpie and then placed the labels on the plastic covering over the photos. We go through these books with Granny every day and review each family member's name.

I have a theory—maybe it's a reverse theory. There is an old saying: "Out of sight; out of mind." So I got to thinking … what about "in sight; in mind"? Why wouldn't that work?

Important note: Don't waste your time using an ink pen. I will discuss permanent markers in depth later on, but I have made a discovery about markers. (This is strictly a Lorrie McDonald discovery. I hope to someday have official research done on it, but for now, I just know that it works!) For whatever reason, if I leave Granny a note written with an ink pen, she can read it a hundred times, but it will not register with her. However, if I write the same note—written exactly the same way, on exactly the same sized paper—but written with a Sharpie or other marker, it seems to register with her. I don't know why. It must have something to do with the left side/right side brain issue, but it is worth sharing this information with you. (Just because I don't completely understand how electricity works doesn't mean I will sit around in the dark because I can't explain it!)

Marilyn helped me with the albums, and we use them with Granny every day. One has just family in it, starting with my stepson, the oldest grandchild, and descending down to the youngest, the most recent great-grandchild. I also try to keep a recent picture of Granny with that person, just to remind her that she really does know that person. Oddly enough, she has the hardest time remembering Mike. He is her third grandchild. When she starts naming all them for me in a family picture that we have from Cory and Megan's wedding, she can name everybody except Mike. She always calls him John (his brother). Strangely enough, Mike was always Granny's fishing buddy when he was younger. He is away at college, so I encourage him to visit Granny and Papa every time he comes home for a day or two. We can laugh or cry about AD, so being the warped family that we are, we just make fun of him and call him the "other John."

Some days, Granny names everybody in the photos; some days, it's hit or miss, but we still do it—every day. Routine. Routine. Routine.

Another way we use pictures to help Granny's recall is by playing old home movies for her. I often use some movies that I shot, but I really like to use the ones that she took herself with her video camera. She will watch one of her Christmas plays from twenty years ago and recall every child's name in it. It truly is amazing.

Break out the home movies and stimulate your loved one's mind; enjoy taking a walk down memory lane. Don't hesitate to have other family members bring some of their home movies also—anything that will help your patient recall important people and places in his or her life.

Another method I use to identify people in pictures, involves the family photos sitting around her house and hanging on her walls. I suggest taking index cards and with your trusty Sharpie, right the names of all the people in the pictures on the cards. Tape those to the pictures. This way, day in and day out, your patient will have a reminder of who these "strangers" are. We know where AD eventually leads, but I have seen that with a little ingenuity, we can slow down the journey on that path quite a bit. No one completely understands how the brain can be fully engaged one minute and completely rewired the next, but that doesn't mean we can't "cheat" it at every opportunity.

Skype is amazing! If you are unaware, Skype is a software program that allows you to have video chats via your computer. You can use it stay in touch with people across the country, but you also can use it for those AWOL family members who can't seem to find time to stop by very often. Don't be worried if your patient doesn't feel quite comfortable using Skype at first. Talk to an old family friend or a great-grandchild across town, just get them connected. If you don't have Skype ability but have an iPhone, you can use a similar program called FaceTime. Other brands of cell phones have similar programs; I am just not familiar with the names of those. Modern technology can be a wonderful tool to help you stay in touch with loved ones.

Another great use of your phone is to call family members, and then put them on the phone with your patient. There have been numerous times when Granny and I have been riding down the road, and I just can't cope with her asking me the same thing over and over any longer. I take out my cell phone, hit the preprogrammed number for Aunt Mildred (or another of Granny's sisters), and hand the phone to Granny, saying, "It's Aunt Mildred. Ask her how she's been." I sometimes put the phone on speaker phone before I hand it to her. This way, I know what's being asked on the other end and can offer suggestions for answers and ways to keep the conversation flowing.

She is probably going to say something crazy. She may ask something embarrassing. But it will give her brain a much-needed workout. They say talk's cheap, but a phone conversation with a grandson off at college can be priceless—even when Granny hands me the phone, I hit "end" and ask, "So how was Mike?"—and she responds, "Who is Mike?"

Trust me … you did the right thing by making the effort to make the call, whether you realize it or they ever remember it. You did.

10. Dignity

I feel very passionate about the topic of dignity. Just because the person you are helping may not know what's going on around him, *you* certainly do. *Never* use this illness as a way to degrade another human being. As I have so often mentioned, with this disease you sometimes can cry or laugh, but that laugh should *not* be one of degradation.

One night we all went out to eat at a little mom-and pop diner. As everyone walked to the table, Papa was in front of me. We had been sitting in the waiting area for several minutes, and he apparently had loosened his pants. Unfortunately, he was not wearing a belt. As he was shuffling to the table in front of me, his pants just slipped down to his ankles. There was a mass "oh-h-h" from the crowd, and he and I both quickly jerked them back up, and he secured the button.

He turned to me in utter shock and said, "I can't believe that just happened!"

I assured him that no one saw him and that I was standing so close behind him that those who might have seen it didn't really see it. I assured him that no one even noticed.

I mention this incident not to humiliate Papa but to show that you need to be prepared for situations that will be awkward to you, the patient, and possibly a restaurant full of people. Everyone in that restaurant had enough class to pretend they didn't see it, and I, fortunately, had enough sense to pretend it didn't happen. Be prepared. Guard your loved one's dignity. Someday, *you* may be caught with your pants around your ankles.

I have already mentioned Granny and the Depends. I had to insist she wear them not just out of convenience for Jenna and me but for safety. I was very careful in choosing my wording about her wearing a "diaper." There was absolutely no reason to rant and rave or talk down to her. Just imagine if your child came into your room tonight and insisted that you start wearing adult diapers. You would swear up and down you did not need them. An AD patient may think he or she is about the age you are now. Be gentle; be sneaky; tell them Aunt Mary wears them. Just don't be degrading.

Don't allow others to take away your patient's dignity. Be especially careful around children of all ages. Teenagers can be extremely cruel (the world does revolve around them, doesn't it?). Get control over how your children address the patient from the start. Remember that in fewer years than we may care to admit, our time will come. The majority of the population will wear diapers and drool on themselves eventually, if they live long enough. Your children will look back and remember how *you* handled this situation. Give them a noble example. Otherwise, you may just find yourself the butt of a joke or two.

I admit that this next subject grates on my nerves about as much as anything people do to AD patients. *Do not discuss the patient in front of the patient, as if the patient doesn't know you are speaking about him!*

If you have company or you run into someone while you are out and about with the patient and that person asks about the patient, be kind enough to address the patient. For example:

A well-meaning neighbor might ask, "So how is Mrs. Lois doing?"

I turn to Granny and say, "Granny, Mr. Smith wants to know how you are doing? I think you are doing great! What do you think?"

Of course, you can have a short conversation without involving the patient, but don't assume that just because she doesn't recognize this person or won't remember this conversation in five minutes that you shouldn't show enough respect to engage her in the dialogue.

The doctor's office is another place where it can be extremely touchy to maintain the patient's dignity. I learned some easy tactical moves and handle doctor visits in one of three ways:

1. I type a list of things that the doctor needs to know before we get to the doctor's office and then hand it to the nurse, who puts the list front and center in Granny's chart. This way, Dr. Lim has a chance to see the things that really concerned me without having to go into a deep discussion in front of Granny—I know that she will deny having any of the problems I bring up anyway. This way, he can ask her about certain symptoms and then offer a suggestion to me in case they "should" occur.
2. If it's something I need to verbally tell the doctor, I listen for him to be outside the door, and then I tell Granny I'm going to check on what's taking the doctor so long. Then I leave the room and try to quickly tell him before he walks in the room. Again, it just takes a few extra minutes of my life to ensure a little more dignity in hers.
3. Sometimes I call ahead and speak to the nurse and have her make a note in the file. The head nurse often knows Granny as well as the doctor and can give valuable advice without having to talk about Granny in front of her, as if she is a toddler just learning the English language.

I have had to correct several family members who were ignorant of the situation. One of them once said that it didn't matter what we said in front of Granny because she wasn't going to remember it anyway. I didn't handle that very well. As a caregiver, you too will become protective of your patient—and rightfully so.

Be aware of taking another person's word over your AD patient's word. I will never forget Granny telling me that Aunt Ruth and Uncle Gary had brought her lunch one day. When I asked Cordell about it, he said he didn't know what she was talking about. He hadn't seen Ruth at all that day. "Granny must be making that up."

That weekend, as we were having Sunday lunch at the Hotel Restaurant in town, Aunt Ruth and Uncle Gary popped in. Just as I was about to ask them about it, Aunt Ruth hugged Granny and asked her if she had enjoyed her lunch the other day. Granny was clearly confused and didn't remember what she was talking about. "Lunch? When did you bring me lunch?" she asked, trying to recall.

"Tuesday. Gary and I were in a terrible hurry. We popped in and just had time for a quick hello. We yelled out to Cordell, who was out back, feeding the horses, but I don't know if he heard us," explained Aunt Ruth.

Papa clearly had not heard them. Chalk one up for Granny.

Situations like this actually happened a lot. Granny and even Papa would tell us things in front of all the family members, and someone would pipe up and dispute whether or not that was true or a figment of their imaginations. More often than not, there was truth to what they were telling us, even if some of the details were sketchy. When your patient sees or hears you doubting what she is telling you, it brings on more doubt to her already cloudy thinking. Show a little class and assume that he or she is telling you the truth. You can sort out the details of the truth later, without bringing undue confusion to the patient.

You will offend some family members when you make them walk out of the room to have certain conversations, but they are not your number-one concern. Your patient deserves the dignity of being spoken to, not spoken about.

Rain, sleet, or snow may not stop the mail from getting through, but scam artists will bring the mail delivery to a screeching halt. Marilyn began to notice that Granny was writing checks for all kinds of gizmos and gadgets—multiple times. She said she thought she needed to keep an eye on Granny and Papa's checking accounts, and I agreed wholeheartedly. She put all their bills on automatic draft, and then she would check their incoming mail each week. Sometimes as a person gets older, he or she can't look at a piece of mail and realize that it is not a legitimate bill. That is what scam artist are *banking* on. Literally.

Recently, someone we know bought five different extended warranties on her vehicle. From five different companies. Each one sent her what looked like a real letter from a real company. She even got a phone call, saying that she wouldn't be allowed to legally drive her car since the warranty had expired. It had not. They lied. She was eighty-three years old and very trusting. So she paid them. All of them. It was a mess, until her son got involved and started keeping a closer watch on her banking. Just stay aware.

You may need to forward their mail to your home to protect them from some of the cleverest scams out there. This does *not* take away their independence. Quite the opposite. You are enabling them to stay at home—safer and longer.

This same son came to visit his mother from a different state and realized that she was giving out personal bank information over the phone. The scam artist this time was from Jamaica. He would leave sob stories on her answering machine, and she is such a trusting soul that she offered to send him several hundred dollars. Thankfully, her sister-in-law caught her just before she mailed it out. Instead of taking out her home phone, her son forwarded her number to his cell phone. She has a cell phone, and anyone who really needs to talk to her has that number. This way, if she needs to use her home phone, she still can, but the Jamaican scam artist can't tell her any more sob stories. Mr. Scam was quite resilient. He called her for over six weeks on the forwarded line. Finally, her son had her home phone number changed and unlisted. This was just another way to aid in keeping her at home as long as possible. Genius!

It all boils down to working at keeping AD patients' dignity, while protecting them at the same time.

11. Helpful Hints for the Help

* Make cheat sheets.

I bought a pack of card stock and a Sharpie, and I make "cheat sheets" for Granny. I fold the paper in half so it will stand up, and then I write her a note. Such as:

> Today is Wednesday.
> Lorrie will be here
> at 6:30 for church.

I write the notes about anything she needs to remember for longer than a fleeting moment. Here is a current one:

> Do not unwrap the presents under the tree!
> Lorrie knows where the list is
> that tells you what is in them.
> *Do not unwrap the presents under the tree!*

This little jewel came about when I came in one night to find Granny surrounded by dozens of half-opened Christmas gifts.

"*Granny!* What on earth have you done? Why did you unwrap all those gifts? Oh, my goodness!"

She huffed and said, "I couldn't remember what I had bought, so I unwrapped them to see."

In the calmest voice I could muster, I said, "Granny! You can't do that! Do you have any idea how long it's going to take to wrap all those again? Don't unwrap them anymore, okay? I have the list of what's in each one. It's back in the bedroom."

"Humph. I bought 'em. I can unwrap them if I want to!" she growled.

I was too tired to have this fight. I put the gifts back under the tree—half opened, ragged edges pulled back—and came to an executive decision that re-wrapping the gifts would be a good job for Granny and Jenna tomorrow.

I put her to bed, and as I was leaving, I glanced under the tree and chuckled out loud. "Hm-m-m. No wonder the song says, 'He's making a list and checking it twice.' From the looks of this mess, ol' Santy Claus has a memory problem too!"

—⟨ℴℴ⟩—

A Sharpie will do wonders. If you are going to be in the laundry room, write a quick note:

> I'm in the laundry room. Be right back out.

We write Granny little notes all the time. We have taught her to glance at the table in front of her and read her note. It works more than half the time. And with AD, those are good odds. It is well worth your effort to try it.

Write in large, bold letters (use a wide-tip Sharpie).

Use print, not cursive.

Make the note short and to the point.

Make a note when you are going to go somewhere in the car.

> We are going to the doctor.
> Dr. Lim. He is your neurologist.
> We will go eat afterwards.

Lay it right in her lap when she sits in the car, or if she tends to fidget, tape it to the dash of your car, right in front of her. Instead of losing your cool and snapping at her that you have already told her a dozen times where you are going, just point to the note. Have her read it out loud to you.

Another great use of the cheat sheets is to forewarn visitors of things to avoid discussing. You tape this information to the door. For example:

> Lois is having a particularly hard day.
> We would love for you to come in and visit, though.
> Please *do not* bring up the church picnic.
> It seems to cause her to get extremely confused.

Most people will completely understand, and it will help you maintain the patient's dignity by not talking about her in front of her, as though she is not there.

I came upon the idea of using a Sharpie quite by accident. I was in a hurry one day and scribbled Granny a note and placed in on the table in front of her. To be perfectly honest, when she continued to ask me the same question repeatedly after I made the note, I grabbed a marker and wrote out the answer in huge black letters out of frustration.

Voila! One of the most valuable tricks we have used had been born.

After that, the conversation went much like this:

"Whose birthday party are we going to? Oh, wait, here's a note right here. It says, 'Going to Marilyn's house tonight at 6 for Jay's birthday party. You have a card with money in it already.' Okay, Lucy! If you say so!"

She had another note that said exactly the same thing, but it was written in ink and in smaller lettering. She had ignored it all forty-seven times she had asked me where we were going and whose birthday it was. Both notes written on the same sized paper and both were directly in front of her.

Just like that, the *size of the letters and the thick black lines* clicked somewhere in her brain. I would love to know the neurological reason behind this. It must have something to do with a lobe here and a neuron there, but at that moment, all I cared about was that it worked!

* *Use a journal.*

Even if you are the only caregiver, write down a synopsis of what went on during the day. Take it to all your patient's doctor appointments. Make a note if it was a good day or if it was a particularly bad day. Did she have hallucinations? What was the weather like? Did he eat something different? Did she have company? Who stopped by? How did he react to that?

Particularly if you have multiple caregivers, write it down. Write down anything that will make the transition from day care to night care easier. Jenna always tells me if they do anything out of the norm today. Then, for mental stimulation, I ask Granny about it. Even if she cannot recall doing it, it stimulates her brain to think about it.

You will be surprised at how excited you become when you ask your loved one if he had company that day, and then he remembers who it was! It's like being able to give the Alzheimer's monster a black eye!

The journals have become somewhat of a photo album for us. I keep them out of Granny's and Papa's sight, but sometimes, Jenna and I will review them. We can see when we were on one of those downhill slides, and on some of our darkest days, we have been able to have a good laugh or two, recalling some of Granny's antics.

You will be glad you took the extra few minutes each day to record your patient's progress or, in the sad case of AD, perhaps his or her decline. Either way, the information gathered in your journals will be very beneficial for your whole family. I use these as valuable notes for Dr. Lim as well. You can get a quick snapshot of your patient's current mental status by simply scanning over a few short notes on the pages of these journals.

—⁂—

* *Make signs that that tell your patient the day of the week.*

Today is Monday

I have one in front of Granny's chair and one at the eating table. We use three dry-erase boards daily also. I used permanent marker to write the part of the sign that stays the same each day and a dry-erase marker to change the information from day to day.

Today is: Thursday
The date is: June 12, 2008
We are going fishing today!
Put on the clothes that are laying by the sink.

These signs come in very handy for the "changing of the guard" also. Jenna and I leave notes on them to each other. One quick tip: do *not* leave the marker or the eraser out where the patient can find them. Put them in a drawer or cup—out of sight, out of mind. *Trust* me!

Even a well-meaning AD caregiver gets to the point in the day when she just wants to scream! That's okay. Go outside, breathe deeply, and then outwit this monster.

When your patient is in the "broken record" stage and is stuck on one question *all day long*, do yourself a favor and write the answer down on a card-stock sign or a dry-erase board, and then hand it to her or put it within her sight. Simply smile and point to it as many times as need be.

These simple signs will save your voice and your sanity. Plus, we have found that Granny actually has taught herself to look on the table to see if there is something there she needs to remember and, of course, ask Jenna and me about.

———∽∽∽———

* Record conversations with the doctor.

When I first started caring for Granny, there was no such thing as a smartphone. So I carried my little video camera to the office visits. When Dr. Terry would tell Granny she had to stand up straight and walk, she never believed me when I later reminded her. So I just shot a video of him telling her exactly what we were telling her, and I would show it to her when she balked.

I would tell her she had to stand up and quit leaning over so far, and she would spout out, "Who says I have to do that?"

I could pull out the video and show her that she was in the doctor's office, nodding her head to what Dr. Terry told her to do. She could hear and see Dr. Terry explaining all this to her.

I outsmarted her!

Now, with smartphones, you have it made. Take a video of the doctor telling the patient whatever your patient's Achilles' heel happens to be. With us, it has always been, "Granny stand up straight!"

———∽∽∽———

* Limit the choices!

I cannot over emphasize this one point enough. This is one of the most humane things you can do for your patient. You are *not* taking away his or her independence. You are removing a horrible trigger for disaster.

Again, this wonderful tip happened out of frustration. Somewhere in the patient's AD mind, certain questions send him or her into a tailspin. Have you ever had a computer you were trying to get to run an application? It just sits there with that horrid little arrow spinning around and around in circles? Or that silly little hourglass telling you just wait … I'm thinking … I'm thinking …

I have a feeling that is what happens when an AD patient is forced to make the simplest of decisions. We had a houseful of people, and someone asked Granny what she wanted for supper. She turned what should have been a simple, quick answer into a near nervous breakdown episode. I was trying not to be the bossy, take-charge person I am often accused of being, so I just sat there and watched for nearly fifteen minutes while Granny tried to sort out the question.

"Do you want a salad? Or would you rather have soup? I see you have leftovers in here. Would you rather I just fix you a plate?" the person asked.

Granny had *that* look on her face. I know it all too well. Deer in the headlights. Broken record. Meltdown coming. "Do I want *what*?" she asked.

"Do you want a salad? Soup? Or leftovers?" the family member asked.

"What do you mean, do I want a salad, or soup, or what did you say? What was the other thing you mentioned? I don't understand what you are saying." She was more and more confused by the minute.

This went on until—clearly flustered at the three ring circus I had just witnessed—I got up, made Granny a quick salad, heated a bowl of soup, and put them both in front of her. "Here, Granny. Here's your supper," I said.

"Oh, thank you, honey. What are you going to eat? I think someone said there's salad, soup, or leftovers in the fridge. Help yourself!" she replied as she tasted her food.

See? She just had to be jolted out of the broken-record mode. I begin to notice that anytime she was given a choice—what to eat, what to wear, where to go—it just made her confusion worse.

So I started limiting the choices. Oh, I can hear the scoffers now. "But you are taking away her autonomy. You are taking away her independence." No, I am shielding her mind from going into craziness over peanut butter and jelly or pimento cheese.

People who have not worked with AD patients will be happy to tell you how you should treat elderly people. Well, unfortunately, that rule book gets thrown out the window when the Alzheimer's monster gets involved. Those people mean well, I'm sure, but they should trust people who are actually dealing with these patients on a day-to-day basis.

I have seen Granny sit on the side of her bed in total confusion because she had one white sock in one hand and pantyhose in the other. There were just too many options for her brain to sort through. I have also walked in that same room, gathered up the plethora of garments, handed her one complete outfit, and said, "Here. Put this on." And I have watched as the cloud of confusion rolled back, and then she proceeded to switch gears into auto-drive. She began getting dressed and asked me how I was doing.

There are several things for which I have stopped giving her a choice. As rude as it may seem, I simply give her the item she needs, and we move on. This may seem overbearing *if* you have not worked with AD patients, but if you *have* worked with them, this will click and make all the sense in the world.

I now tell her, "Granny, go to the bathroom and get ready for the day."
I now lay out the clothes she will be wearing that day.
I now tell her to take her medicine.
I now tell her to come to the table for breakfast.
I now tell her to do her exercises.

I now get the mail every day and only give her what will *not* cause confusion.

I remind myself and Jenna and all those who help me with Granny that we are not taking away her freedom. We are taking away her fright. If your patient says, "I think I want green beans for lunch." Then by all means, don't interfere! But when he reaches the stage when a simple question (such as, "Would you rather have green beans or broccoli?") becomes confusing, then it's time to simplify—for your patient's sake, never just for your convenience.

I am reminded of this verse: *"Verily, verily, I say unto thee, When thou wast young, thou girdedst thyself, and walkedst whither thou wouldest: but when thou shalt be old, thou shalt stretch forth thy hands, and another shall gird thee, and carry thee whither thou wouldest not." (John 21:18)*

As long as you understand that you can help your patient by taking away his or her confusion, then you are making a wise decision. Never undermine his or her independence just for the sake of your preferences.

———≈≈≈———

* *Make every day a special occasion.*

Learn to use this horrible disease for your good. One day, in the middle of September, Jenna called me, laughing. "Mrs. Lorrie, you are not going to believe what Granny's just done."

"Oh, no. What now?" I was almost scared to ask.

"I was cleaning up all the cards off the table in the living room. You know, the ones she got last month for her birthday?" There was more laughing.

"And?" I said. It's always been hard for Jenna to get through a funny story.

"Well, I laid them down on the kitchen table where Granny was sitting and went to change out the laundry. When I came back, Granny was reading them and was beaming from ear to ear! She told me, 'Just look at all the cards I got in the mail today!'" More laughter.

"She doesn't remember getting them before?" I wondered out loud.

"No, ma'am. Not at all. And the funny thing is, she has made the exact comments about each one that she did the day she got them the first time."

So now we take cards out from time to time and hand them to her. We even try to give her note cards to fill out to send to family and friends. Sometimes this is just too taxing on her, and we just have her sign her name. But either way, it's always pleasant to get a card in the mail. Even for the fifth, sixth, or seventh time.

I recently saw a greeting card that made me laugh and think of Granny. The outside showed two middle-aged women, and the caption read, "We will be good friends until we are old and senile!" The inside of the card read, "Then we'll be *new* friends!"

When you find something that makes your patient happy, use it *every day.* You have to remember, it is new to her. But if it brings her joy, then it will be joyful tomorrow, and the next day, and—oh, look, something new and wonderful. Use the disease to your advantage to help the patient.

—◦/◦/◦—

* Become a medicine man.

I leave Granny's medicines on the table. Of course, I have filled up her seven-day pillbox each week for years. In the beginning, I would just leave her medicine bottles on the table, but I would fill up her and Papa's weekly boxes and leave them sitting out. That seemed easy enough.

But nothing stays simple for long when dealing with AD. At first, Granny could remember to take Monday's pills on Monday, Tuesday's on Tuesday, and so forth. Until she no longer remembered the day of the week. Was today Thursday? Was it Sunday? Let's say it was Monday. She took her Monday meds just like she was supposed to. But then, while Jenna was making lunch, she turned around to see that Granny had Tuesday's day opened and had just swallowed tomorrow's medicine too.

After the initial, "No! Granny! What are you doing?" was out of the way, she realized that Granny had no idea what she was doing—the very definition of AD.

So … what's a girl to do? I went to Walmart and bought twenty-eight cute little containers. I got out my handy-dandy Sharpie and went to work. Seven containers were for Granny's a.m. medicine, and seven were for Granny's p.m. medicine. Although Papa is still cognitive enough to know which day's meds to take, Granny sits at the same table with Papa's medicine. So there have been days when she took her meds and then, knowing it was Wednesday and seeing a pillbox with medicine in Wednesday, she took *his* too.

If you're wondering why I didn't just hide the medicine boxes, we tried that. And we found out that Granny rummaged through her cabinets, found both hers and his, opened every compartment, and poured out *all* the medicine into one very colorful pile. So my cute containers just made more sense. (Tupperware makes adorable little boxes that are great for this, but I just bought the cheap ones from Walmart, and they served the same purpose. Get as creative as you wish.)

On the top of each one I wrote either "Granny" or "Papa," along with the day of the week and time of day to take the meds. For example, "Granny, Monday, Morning," or "Papa, Tuesday, Night." I fill these each week and hide the rest of their medicine in the top of the kitchen cabinet. Jenna gets out *only that day's* medicine and puts it with their breakfast and supper plates. She oversees that the correct pills go down the correct throats, and then she hides the containers. Nothing sits out on the counter.

I was lying in bed one night when I had the most terrifying thought. This was in the beginning stages, when Granny was only mildly forgetful. It dawned on me that sometimes Granny would take an Ambien to help her sleep if she absolutely thought it was necessary. I got to thinking that she might take one, forget that she'd taken it, and take another. And another. She might take half a dozen or more before they took effect and knock her out like Rip Van Winkle.

I took all medicine that potentially could be life-threatening out of the house. I keep them in the glove box of my car. That way, if Granny acted like she might have trouble going to sleep, I could get her one, but the pills weren't left where she could accidentally take too many. You don't have to take them out of the house, but you do need to be clever where you hide them. Perhaps a lockbox hidden away in a guest bedroom closet would work for you. Just be sure that all the caregivers have a key and know the location.

Another word on medicine: Just because the patient has been taking a certain medicine for as long as you can remember doesn't mean he or she actually needs it. Check with the doctor on a regular basis and question the validity of the medicines the patient is taking. Every medicine has a side effect, so the fewer medicines taken, the fewer chances of adverse side effects. Just be sure to work with the doctor's on this. If the medicine is needed, so be it. But you can talk with the physician to be sure that the patient is not continuing a medicine that is no longer relative.

---

* Once a man twice a child.

The longer I work with the elderly, the more I realize that old adage is completely true. One of the other "jobs" I have always had is working with children. I have taught the two- and three-year-olds at church for about twenty years. Before that, I worked as a daycare teacher of young children. My degree in early childhood education and psychology has come in handy when working with Granny!

The longer I work with Granny and Papa, the more I put that early childhood training into practice. I do it in a nondegrading fashion, but it helps tremendously to think about their care in the terms of childcare. The same tips apply to both ends of life's spectrum.

Here are a few examples:

1.   When your patient is cranky, it is usually because something is bothering her, and she doesn't know how to tell you what it is. Treat her just as you would an infant—figuratively, of course. Go through your mental list of what might be bothering her—hungry, wet, tired, over stimulated? You get the picture.

2.   Patients need snacks and treats. Time and time again, when Granny or Papa is in a foul mood, I suggest we get a snack. I cut up some apples and spread peanut butter on them. I give them a yogurt with some berries. Sometimes I even tell them we are going to run to Sonic for some ice cream. Who can be grumpy when eating ice cream?

3.   Fresh air does a body good, whether that body is a fussy eighteen-month-old or a fussy eighty-one-year-old. Get him or her to go outside and get some fresh air and new scenery. *Do not* just turn on the television (for either age) and say, "Watch this." Get your patient outside in the fresh air.

4.   Never underestimate the power of a nap. I am amazed at moms who don't make their children take a nap. They are doing *them* and *themselves* a huge injustice. I have heard mommas ask their five-year-olds if they "want to take a nap." They might as well ask them if they would like some Brussels sprouts while they are at it. Let me help you with that, Momma. No. They do not want to take a nap. No. They are not tired. The problem with that thinking is that they may not be tired at one thirty when you ask them, but at six thirty, when Daddy gets home from a long, hard day at work, they will turn into a sleep-deprived monster. Don't do that to Daddy, your kiddo, or you.

The answer? You tell them, "Okay, it's one thirty. It's time to lie down and take a nap." No ifs, ands, or buts. The rule at our house was that the kids had to lie there with their eyes shut for thirty minutes. Then, if they still weren't asleep, they could get up. Guess what? Ninety-nine percent of the time, after lying still for thirty minutes in a quiet, darkened room, they'd conk out, usually for an hour to two hours. Obviously, somebody's body needed some rest.

The same goes for Granny. Every afternoon, after Jenna has Granny clean up the lunch dishes, they head to the potty, and then Granny lies down for thirty minutes to "rest her back." Granny is adamant that she never takes a nap during the daytime. I don't know why that is such a big deal to her, but it is. It was a source of great contention at first—until we outsmarted the AD. Since she complains about her back hurting all day, which I'm sure it does, then we say we are doing "back exercises" when she lies down. Why? Because Dr. Terry and Dr. Lim told her (at my suggestion) to lie down every afternoon for thirty minutes to "rest her back."

It is amazing how a woman who adamantly denies ever taking a nap during the day has to be awakened around two thirty every day to get up and do our afternoon routine. And what happens on afternoons when she lies there, all big-eyed, and doesn't fall asleep? She typically ends up hurting worse, whining more, and basically needing a time-out. So it's just better for all involved to make it a part of the daily routine. Our days are filled with activity. Although we do not advocate lying in bed all day, we do highly recommend a time of relaxation and renewal—for your four-year-old and your seventy-four-year-old.

5. While on vacation one year, I potty-trained my great-nephew, Jordan. He lives with his dad and his grandparents. It had been over twenty years since Marilyn had potty-trained anyone, so I offered to help. I told Jordan that during the week of our vacation, I was going to teach him to use the potty like a big boy, and we would buy him a big prize when he stayed dry all day. That suited Dad, Grandma, and Pa just fine.

What is my amazing "potty-training a two-year-old" trick? It works 100 percent of the time! Ready? I *don't* train two-year-olds to go potty. I train a twenty-something-year-old mommy and daddy to take the two-year-old to the potty.

That's it. Problem completely solved. See, the two-year-old has been wetting at random and walking around in it until some tall person thinks, *Hmmm, I need to see if he's wet.* So the two-year-old is never going to know when he is supposed to tell you that he has to go. That's why children first learn to tell adults that they *went!*

The real trick is that I set my watch to beep every hour on the hour, and I got Jordan and told him it was time to go "pee-pee." At first, we stood there, and he looked at me like I was clueless. Then, as he was standing there, I slowly poured a glass of warm water over his "pee-pee-er" and watched as the magic began. I did this the first six times or so. Sometimes he went to the bathroom, sometimes not. But I was training the adults in his life that every hour on the hour, take him to the potty. *Do not ask him if he needs to go. The answer will always be no!*

Top: Granny with baby Jordan
Bottom: Jordan (completely potty-trained)
has turned into quite a fishermen, just like his great-Granny!

Just as I didn't want Jordan walking around in a diaper all day, I don't like Granny to do that either. We may get there someday, but that day is not today. Just as I put Jordan in a diaper when he lay down for a nap or went to bed, I put one on Granny when she goes to bed at night. Otherwise, we do the same routine with her that I did with Jordan. Every hour, Jenna will lead her to the bathroom. Just like with Jordan, Granny always tells us she doesn't need to go. Just like with Jordan, once we get her in there, she almost always does go. Even on trips when she doesn't actually use the bathroom, we have still accomplished a goal by not allowing her to sit for too long at a time.

When we head to Nashville, which is almost an hour away, or if we are going to be somewhere and I'm not sure we will be near a convenient bathroom, then I do just what I did when my children were small. I try to get her to wear a Pull-Up, just in case, and I always carry and extra pair of undies with us.

Speaking of peeing, let's address bedwetting. (Are you beginning to see how as you get older, you truly do revert to your childhood? That's not always a bad thing, especially when you have a team of caregivers who are on your side and have no desire to humiliate you for what just comes naturally.)

As I have already explained, Pull-Ups (or Depends—whatever brand name you use) work great—but let it be the patient's idea, or at least trick the patient into believing it is his or her idea. Another thing to remember (as with small children) is to limit the amount of liquids the patient has right before bed. It took trial and error on our part to realize this was part of the problem. The first few weeks of bedwetting were a nightmare. Granny was getting up sometimes two or three times a night and changing her sheets. The first thing I did was buy a mattress pad. Then we tried the potty chair next to her bed. This worked for a short time, but as with all body processes, patients with AD go through stages, and you have to come up with your Plan B.

I realized that Granny was always thirsty for water when it got time to put her into bed. There were nights when I would watch her drink two full glasses of water out of the bathroom faucet and then lie down to go to sleep. No wonder the falls were gushing!

I did two things. First, I took the glass out of the bathroom. Again, I was using AD to my advantage. Once the glass wasn't sitting there, she looked for it only a couple of times. After that, she just cupped her hand and got a few swigs but not a full liter anymore.

The second thing I did was increase her water intake during the day. I realized one of the reasons she was so thirsty at night was because she just wasn't getting hydrated enough during the day.

Jenna and I made a conscious effort to give her a full glass of water with each meal, and then we made sure she drank it, especially early in the morning. Another reason we upped her water intake during the day was because older people tend to not drink enough water. Without sufficient hydration, the body becomes dehydrated. One of the signs of dehydration is mental confusion. Your patient's memory may improve just by increasing the amount of water he or she takes in each day. So we made sure Granny was taking a full glass of water with medicines and with meals.

This seemed to help with her asking for water right before bed. Then, just like I used to do with my kiddos when they were younger, I explained to her that she could only have a few sips before bedtime because we didn't want her wetting the bed.

"Humph! Wet the bed? Why, I have *never* wet the bed in my life!" This was her response every time. (Of course you haven't. Silly me!)

6.   When you think of how to deal with AD patients, you really do need to recall how you dealt with small children. Learn to do this without being degrading. The elderly love to put puzzles together, color, and paint, and you will be surprised by how much they like to be read to at bedtime. They like to feel independent, just like toddlers. "I can do this by myself!" So, you should allow them to keep their independence for as long as possible and just assist.

Just as parents of small children learn to "help" without children realizing they are being assisted, you can do the same thing with your patient. And never underestimate the benefits of praising them for their accomplishments. Every kid needs an attaboy and a pat on the back every now and then. Even weary caregivers.

12. There's a Vitamin for That

Not long after David and I got married, his right knee began to bother him, to the point that he felt it was time to get a knee replacement. He was only in his mid-thirties, and I was very leery of him whacking off body parts. I took him to see a reflexologist named Howard Daily.

A reflexologist is someone who presses on the pressure points on the bottoms of your feet and can usually diagnose what is ailing you by the little crystals that form at your nerve endings. I have found that people who have seen a reflexologist are firm believers, and those who have not are firm skeptics. I had been and was amazed at how accurate his findings were.

I told David that for his birthday, I was taking him to see Howard. He was very skeptical, but I've grown use to that. Howard began mashing on David's feet and told him he sure must have a sweet tooth. (He had already eaten four pieces of birthday cake that morning.) Then, as Howard pressed on the bottom of David's left foot, he told David that his knees were in great shape. At that statement, David turned and looked at me with an "I told you this guy is a quack!" look. About that time, Howard mashed on the bottom of David's right foot, and David's hind end came up off the recliner where he'd been lying. He screamed, "*What* was that?"

"Well," said Howard, "I stand corrected. Your left knee is just fine, but your right knee is shot! But I can fix that if you let me."

And with that, my hubby became a believer in reflexology.

Howard put him on glucosamine/chondroitin. When David went to see Dr. Terry, our orthopedic surgeon friend, he told Dr. Terry what he was trying. Dr. Terry laughed and told him, "You can try that if you want to, but there's no proof that all those herbs and vitamins work."

But David began to faithfully take glucosamine/chondroitin and drink black cherry juice, and within just a few weeks, he was feeling better. Soon, he actually was able to run again. No surgery needed.

Ten years later, when David went back in for a different ailment, Dr. Terry said, "Have you ever tried glucosamine/chondroitin for your arthritis? It's been proven in the last few years to really help."

"Uh, yeah, Doc. I've been on it ten years now! I'm the one who told *you* about it."

One of the great things of the great things Dr. Lim told me was that as long as I was not giving Granny anything harmful, he thought supplements would be a good addition to her medical treatment. So it began. I took Granny to see Howard, and he gave me several things to help her. First, he started her on glucosamine/chondroitin for her joint aches and pains. We give her two tablespoons of black cherry juice every morning in a little juice glass and fill the rest with water. She takes fish oil. We also give her two or three different herbs that are strictly for memory. The following herbs have been known to help with dementia: ginkgo biloba, omega-3 fatty acids, Huperzine A, vitamin E, magnesium, and ginseng.

It was during this time that I realized that most elderly people are low in calcium and vitamin D. So I give her those supplements, along with a dose of sunshine every day. Again, I cannot stress too strongly how important it is to get your patient outside every day for fresh air.

Some of Granny's medicine makes her drowsy. Jenna fixes her a strong cup of coffee every morning to prevent drowsiness. Because my Sundays are usually very time-sensitive, I keep small bottles of Coke in the fridge, hidden from Papa, who would drink them nonstop. I grab one and Granny's cup of medicine and give her that on the way to church. Anything to help save a little time.

Aricept works for Granny, but many of the other medicines we have tried do not. I have found that adding natural supplements have helped tremendously. I suggest you do an Internet search for "herbs and nutrition that help memory functions." We live in an amazing world, and new things are being discovered every day. Always discuss any supplements with your patient's neurologist. I am very fortunate that Dr. Lim was on our side when trying to fight this disease.

I suggest adding supplements slowly; to make sure that your patient doesn't have a reaction to something. If you give her more than one new item, you will have difficulty telling which one is causing the problem.

13. Cracker Barrel

As you know by now, you need to know your patient. Knowing what he or she likes and dislikes will be invaluable as you come up with your game plan. Knowing that Granny loves to shop makes it easy to choose where we are going to lunch. Although there is an O'Charley's right next door to her doctor's office, I know where she wants to eat most of the time—Cracker Barrel.

How can you go wrong with a place that serves home-cooked meals, just the way Granny used to make them, *and* shopping, all under the same roof? Genius! I cannot tell you the number of hours that we have spent shopping at a Cracker Barrel. (Plus, they put up a Christmas tree on July 5, it seems. Okay, it may be early September, but they are the first business we patronize that has Christmas out so early. I know that irritates some people, but not me.)

I am dealing with a woman who has AD. Some days, I have to *work* to bring her joy. If it is an impossible day, I know where to head—to Cracker Barrel, where I turn her loose. She is a like a kid in a candy store. Granny loves fried chicken livers, fried okra, and fried apples. But she insists on serving me salads with extra celery—go figure. She also loves shopping, and she loves Christmas, so going to Cracker Barrel is a no-brainer for us.

When we go there in winter, I always ask to sit at a table in front of their roaring fire. So far, we have never been seated anywhere else. The staff is always amazing, and for that brief time, Granny is content. To see the smile on her face as she buys a basket full of ornaments is worth a lot—worth more than whatever our bill for the day may be. It is priceless.

14. The Power of Suggestion

Have you ever felt just fine until someone looks at you and asks, "Are you feeling okay? You look a little sick." Then, amazingly, you notice that scratchy feeling in the back of your throat. And wait—is that a chill you feel? You had hardly noticed it until now, but your head feels a little warm. Maybe you should go lie down.

The same thing can happen in reverse. If I am around someone who says something like, "Wow! You look great! Have you lost weight? Are you working out? Man, you look good today." even though I previously may have felt "blah," I perk up and feel better—better than I have felt in ages.

I saved this topic for the end of this chapter because I want it to *stick in your mind*! Let this be the secret weapon of all caregivers everywhere. Here is the reason you bought this book:

"A word fitly spoken is like apples of gold in pictures of silver." (Proverbs 25:11)

What does that mean?

Basically, it means the words that are chosen carefully can bring about great pleasure or a sense of pleasantness. Your words are powerful. All too often, we simply don't stop to think before we speak.

We live in a hurried world. People are too self-absorbed to give much thought to bringing simple pleasures into other people's lives. Once I became aware of the effect that words—mine and other people's—have on Granny's physical outlook, I became quite the "Word Police."

Let me demonstrate:

I walked into the living room, and Granny was sitting in her chair, staring out the window with a gloomy look on her face.

"Granny, you okay?" I asked. "You look like something's wrong. You feeling okay? Is your back bothering you?" I had asked before I realized it.

"Oh, my aching back," she complained. "Honey, I just can't go with you today. I feel bad. I don't know what's wrong with ol' Granny today. I just don't feel quite right."

Then I had an epiphany.

The great thing about Granny and Papa's house is that it is built with open rooms—you can walk from the back of the house to the den without going through the living room, where Granny sits. So I experienced what I believe was divine intervention. I thought, *What if I had worded that differently? I'm the huge advocate of making this stupid disease work in my favor... Let's just see if what I've believed all this time really* does work.

And with that, I very quietly walked through Papa's bedroom and circled back out to the den. I waited about ten minutes and then came back into the living room.

"Hey, Granny!" I said, all chipper. "Don't you look spry this morning! You look like you slept great and are raring to go. We'll just hop to it and get you dressed so we can get outside and enjoy this glorious day!"

"When did you get here? I thought you had already come by this morning," she said, a little confused.

"Oh, I had. Anyway, you must have slept great. You look wonderful. Your hair is as wild as a betsy-bug, but we can fix that up in no time." I just fluttered around, smiling from ear to ear at her. And what do you know? Her whole demeanor began to change! She got up from the chair by herself, without complaining. Hallelujah! She headed back to the bathroom, and we were dressed and out the door. Talk about a breakthrough moment!

In the game of golf, it's called a mulligan, a "do-over". If you hit a sorry shot off the first tee, then you get to take another ball and call out "mulligan," and you get to start again, just as if that sorry ball never happened. So that morning, my mulligan changed my whole game plan.

I went from a certain "bogie" (a terrible golf shot) to a "birdie" (a great golf shot)—just with one simple adjustment.

I told Jenna about it at the "changing of the guard" the next day, and she said that she had begun doing exactly the same thing. She had completely stopped asking Granny *if* she felt good in the mornings and simply told her she felt good. (Eliminate the option of feeling bad, and your patient just might believe she doesn't!)

"Heaviness in the heart of man maketh it stoop: but a good word maketh it glad. (Proverbs 12:25)

You may think that is the stupidest thing you have ever heard of—that you could change the way a person physically feels with a few rosy words and smiles. But I am sharing with you the things that I learned the hard way. After that day, I did real-life experimentation. I know my friends and family thought I had suddenly started taking a mood-altering drug because everywhere I went; I interrupted people when they addressed Granny. I would rephrase questions as soon as I realized they were opening a can of worms. I ran "emotional interference" for Granny.

"Mrs. McDonald, how you feeling today, honey? Is your old back still giving you fits?" some sweet, well-meaning friend would ask us while we were out and about. I would quickly turn to Granny and before she had time to fully process the question, I would reword it.

"Granny, he said you're looking good! He wants to know if we're having a good day. We *are*, aren't we? We're having a *wonderful* day!" I would say to her, beaming.

Granny would automatically smile and say, "Hi there. I'm doing okay for an old woman, I guess. How are you?"

Looking back over the last couple of years, I noticed that instead of it being "out of sight, out of mind," it was more "out of mind, out of mind." In other words, when Granny wasn't thinking about her back hurting, her back didn't hurt. But as soon as someone brought it up … oh, boy, here we go. Jenna realized the same thing. When she worded her questions and comments to Granny in nothing but a positive outlook, then Granny almost always responded in a much better frame of mind than when we brought up one of her aches and pains. I figured if Alzheimer's could steal her memory of what day it was and who some of her grandchildren are and some of her joys, then we could use it to our advantage and let it steal away the memory of the bad.

I went on a public campaign to let people who visited often know that they should never ask Granny about aches and pains; they should encourage her. All that is well and works great—except for that one dear family member who drinks sour lemons for breakfast … Papa.

Papa is a different story. Since he is fighting his own demons, I never can get him to fully understand the method to our madness. He often pops his head into the living room and says things such as, "Lois. It's raining today. You ain't got any business going anywhere today. It's just going to make your back hurt that much worse." And then he turns and heads back to his grumpy-bear den. (Well, thank you, little ray of sunshine.)

Fortunately, Granny long ago learned that Papa is that little rain cloud on her sunny day. And she has learned to ignore him—most of the time. We *love* Papa. He is a total sweetheart. I like to think of him as a cute, cuddly porcupine. He's precious until he throws his quills up, and we just have to learn when to walk a wide berth around him. (Feeding him a chocolate milkshake every now and again doesn't hurt, either.)

Let me stress to you to begin practicing your new, sunny power-of-suggestion therapy. I also stress that you to try it on your spouse and your other family members. We all tend to be too hasty in our words.

"Seest thou a man that is hasty in his words? there is more hope of a fool than of him" (Proverbs 29:20).

One of the most profound statements I have learned is found in Proverbs. *"For as he thinketh in his heart so is he" (Proverbs 23:7).*

I practiced this verse a bazillion times with my children. You should always be your children's number-one encourager. That does not mean that you don't have to discipline them at times, but if you constantly remind your child how smart, how kind, and how compassionate they are, then that becomes ingrained in who they are.

I probably come across as very rude at times by cutting into someone's conversation with Granny. My apologies to them, then and now. But after they spoke to Granny, they would go on their merry way, leaving me to deal with the fallout. I would rather—as politely as I can muster—interrupt and "reword" their comments and leave them a little confused than have the next twelve hours ruined because they were unaware of the damage their genuine concern was going to cause.

This not only applies to AD patients but to all people with whom we come in contact. I spend a lot of time with Granny's sister Aunt Mary. I have noticed that when people—people who love her dearly, mind you—walk into the room and say, "Mary Nell, I'm concerned about you. You don't look well to me," I want to blow a gasket. (And I'm sure I sometimes do!) I always lean in and pat her hand and say, "Actually, she's doing great, aren't you, Aunt Mary?"

When I do this, I get looks from family members who think I am trying to "cover up for Mary Nell," or they think I am some "positive-thinking lunatic." Either way, I just know the power of suggestion! *I have witnessed the effects thousands of times!* Begin making this one simple change in your caregiving methods today, and you, too, will see that a spoonful of honey makes the medicine go down.

"Death and life are in the power of the tongue: and they that love it shall eat the fruit thereof." (Proverbs 18:21)

Why not use your tongue to bring about a better life for your patient?

Here are a few other verses that God used to confirm this solution to me:

"And the Lord answered the angel that talked with me with good words and comfortable words" (Zechariah 1:13).

"So shall my word be that goeth forth out of my mouth: it shall not return unto me void, but it shall accomplish that which I please, and it shall prosper in the thing whereto I sent it" (Isaiah 55:11).

I realize this is the Lord speaking about His words going forth, but if we are His, and He lives in us, then I think it safe to say this verse would apply to the words we allow Him to speak through us as well. Words are powerful.

Chapter 9

If They See Monkeys, I See Monkeys

Recently, after a particularly hard morning dealing with Granny, I was at the dentist office, talking with my daughter-in-law, Megan. We had what I call "a teachable moment." When my kids are trying to understand something, I try to give them a real-life scenario that lets them put themselves in the other person's shoes.

I was explaining to Megan how confused Granny had been about something, and Megan couldn't understand why Granny just couldn't "get it," even after I explained that the mind just loses track of time. Granny had thought her mom and dad were still living and was very adamant that I needed to take her to check on them. Meg just couldn't believe Granny couldn't understand they had been dead for nearly thirty years. That's when my "teachable moment" occurred.

My granddaughter, Ellie Beth, had been sitting at the kitchen table in the break room with us, coloring. I noticed that at some point in the conversation, she had gathered up her crayons and coloring book and had gone to explore the prize box Pops keeps for young patients. Meg had been so engrossed in our conversation that she had not noticed that Ellie Beth had left the room.

Suddenly, Meg glanced around and said, "Where's Ellie? Where did Ellie Beth go?"

For whatever reason, I took this opportunity to give Meg a glimpse into what an AD patient lives through.

"Ellie Beth? What do you mean, where is Ellie Beth?" I sweetly and confusingly (on purpose) looked at Meg, took her hand, and patted it.

"Ellie Beth! She was just sitting here with us, coloring, and now she's gone! When did she get down? Where did she go?" asked a genuinely concerned Meg. She was afraid Ellie would go somewhere she didn't need to be.

I continued to hold onto Meg's hand and told her in a very convincing way, "Sweetie, Ellie Beth's not been here. Ellie's thirty years old and has children of her own. She's not a little girl anymore. You were just *imagining* that she was here."

Meg's eyes got wide as saucers as she looked at me, thinking her dear mother-in-law had lost her mind.

Then I changed my voice and said in my normal tone, "She hopped down to go get into the prize box. But now do you see how panicked Granny and Papa feel when we tell them that something they *know* just happened is not real?"

"Wow!" said Meg. "I get it. To Granny, her mom and dad are still alive and living up the hill, even though they've been gone for years. How sad."

"Yes. Very."

—◦◦◦—

Without a doubt, the number-one thing family and caregivers of Alzheimer's patients ask about is lying.

In the beginning, it starts out with dealing with the patient's so-called lying. I call it "so-called," because as I have dealt with this subject over the last several years, I have come to a truth about this lying. Is it really a lie if it is true to them?

Stop and think on that for a moment. It took me months of dealing with Granny and Papa for me to come to this understanding, so it may take you a few minutes to comprehend that statement.

When I first started spending hours on end caring for them, I noticed that they would fib. Well, actually maybe we should call it a half truth? Let's just call it what is was—a lie! A bald-faced lie.

I can remember standing right beside Granny while she was talking on the phone with Aunt Mildred, and all of a sudden, she said, "Hang on, Mildred. I didn't hear you. I dropped the phone. Now, what did you say?"

I couldn't believe my ears! She had most certainly not dropped the phone. She just couldn't hear her or understand her.

Soon, I would come in, and she would tell me something, and then David would come in, and she would tell him something completely different. In the beginning, I really fussed at her for this.

"Why, Granny! You were a Sunday school teacher! I can't believe you would lie!"

She looked at me as if I had just slapped her. "Lie? Well, I most certainly did not lie. What in this world would you think I lied for?" she demanded.

Then I explained it. She denied it. (Another lie.) And soon our whole evening was blown up over something she couldn't even remember saying.

As time has progressed, so have the lies. Whether or not we can justify the dropped phone incident is not up to me to decide. But as time has gone on, one thing is for sure: things happen in her mind every day that are just as real to her as you reading this book. They really happened to her!

I began to get pulled into these lies, and at first, it tore me to pieces. One morning, on the way to the doctor's office, Granny started fretting.

"I forgot to turn off the iron! We've got to go back. Cordell's not there, and I've left the iron on. We've got to turn around and go back," she insisted.

"Granny, you didn't leave the iron on. I laid out your clothes last night. The iron and the ironing board are both in the hall closet. They aren't even out. It's okay," I assured her.

"What do you mean, they aren't out? They most certainly are! I would know. I'm the one who ironed these clothes this morning! I'm not crazy! It is on!" She was clearly upset now.

This went on for fifteen or twenty minutes, until she actually started crying. I tried everything in my power to convince her that she had not even gotten her clothes out, that I had done that for her last night. Of course, she could not remember my being there last night. Then it dawned on me.

I knew the iron was not on. But she really believed that it was. So what I needed to do was to turn the iron off in her mind.

"Granny, you know what? I turned the iron off. Yes, ma'am. That iron is off. I turned that iron off, sure as the world. Wow. Am I glad I remembered that! That iron is turned off." I blurted out of nowhere.

She started slowly getting a grip and said between sobs, "Are you certain you turned it off?"

"Granny, that iron is turned off. I am positive." Finally, I had her calmed down.

Everything I told her was the truth. I *did* turn the iron off—in her mind it was on, and now it was off. The iron actually was off, so when I kept reminding her of that, all of it was true.

I lay awake a long time that night, thinking about that. You may not see what the big fuss was about. You may think, *Tell her what she needs to hear, lie or no lie, and go on.* Well, I am a born-again Christian. Lying is number nine on the top-ten list of our faith (the Ten Commandments). It goes against everything my faith and my conscience tell me are true and honest. I hate liars. So does God. He really hates it.

"These six things doth the Lord hate: yea, seven are an abomination unto him: A proud look, a lying tongue, and hands that shed innocent blood" (Proverbs 6:16–17).

So for me—and for millions dealing with AD patients—this is a moral issue.

Thankfully, after much serious prayer about it, God took me to several places in my Bible that gave me the peace I needed to do the job He had called me to do.

First and foremost is the story of the Hebrew midwives. In the book of Exodus, Moses tells the story of how the king wanted to rid the land of all the Hebrew babies. He ordered the midwives to kill all the baby boys. *"But the midwives feared God, and did not as the king of Egypt commanded them, but saved the men children alive." (Exodus 1:17)*

It goes on to tell that when the pharaoh called them in for questioning they told him, *"for they are lively, and are delivered ere the midwives come in unto them" (Exodus 1:19).* You know, they lied. How did God handle their deception?

"Therefore God dealt well with the midwives: and the people multiplied, and waxed very mighty. And it came to pass, because the midwives feared God, that he made them houses" (Exodus 1:20-21).

I would never try to justify lying for any reason, but I read more into this than lying. God blessed these women for doing what He had called them to do in the way He gave them orders to do it. I know it messes with a lot of people's doctrine, mine included. I just know that God tells us that His ways are higher than our ways.

But these were not the only passages that showed me how to handle incidents when they arose. I will explain this in depth because I know people just like me truly struggle with this. Time and time again, when I discuss this with people and offer them counsel on this topic, this seems to help them come to grips with this aspect of the caregiver. I truly hope it helps you too.

"The wicked is snared by the transgression of his lips: but the just shall come out of trouble" (Proverbs 12:13).

The Bible tells us that God looks on the heart. I got peace that the Lord will judge what was wicked and deceitful and done with a wicked heart and what was just, like those Hebrew midwives.

One of the things I realized, after much prayer over this subject, was that ***it is not a lie to them. In their minds, this is really happening***.

I have coined a term: ***the truth of their mind***.

I believe with all my heart that God showed me that as a caregiver, I need to be aware that I sometimes cannot see what is right in front of *Granny's* eyes. It is real to *her*. I may be sitting in 2014, while she is very much living in 1974.

Fortunately for me, when I came to grips with this and it made sense to me, caring for Granny and Papa became much easier for them and for me. It did not cause me to tell big whoppers to everybody else in my life, but as you will see in the stories to follow, at some point, as a caregiver, you need to realize that if *they* see monkeys, then *you* see monkeys!

One afternoon after work, Melanie stopped in to check on her daddy, Uncle Bob. As she walked in the door, she noticed he was putting on his work boots. When she asked him where he was headed, he told her it was time to go feed the cows.

Really? The cows? thought Mel. *How many years has it been since they sold off all his cattle?* "Well, I don't know if that's such a good idea. Where's Barbara?" she asked. Barbara was Uncle Bob's other caregiver.

About that time, Barbara showed up in the doorway. "Uncle Bob, you about set to go feed those cows?" she asked cheerfully.

Now Mel was beginning to question her own sanity—and Barbara's.

"Barb," she whispered, "what cows is he going to feed, pray tell?"

"Ah, the same ones we feed every day about this time." She winked. "Mel, it's like this. Every day for more than sixty years, Uncle Bob fed the cows. It's just wired in him. So instead of upsetting him like I used to do and explain over and over and over to him that he doesn't own cattle anymore, I simply caved in one day and told him, 'Alrighty then, let's feed those cows!' And we've been doing the same routine since. Bob gets excited, puts on his boots, and we head out the door, but by the time we get out in the yard a little ways ... well, he's worn slap-dab out! He tells me he doesn't think he feels up to it today, and then I tell him not to fret over it, that Stanley [Mel's brother] will take care of it. Or I tell him I'll take care of it. We meander around the yard a little while and then we head back in. Uncle Bob's content, and I'm pleased as punch that we have not gotten our feathers ruffled over something that is very real to him." Barbara explained this in a matter-of-fact tone.

"Barb, you're a genius!" exclaimed Melanie.

"Mel, it's like this." Barbara leaned in to explain to Mel. "If *he* sees monkeys, then *I* see monkeys. It's just as simple as that!"

Uncle Bob, "checking" on the cows

It's funny; I didn't hear this story until after several years of seeing monkeys myself. God's funny that way. I would have had peace over dealing with Granny and Papa so much faster if I had heard this. After all, it makes all the sense in the world. But I think God wanted me to work that out with Him. I had to come to grips with my convictions. Ironically, I had been seeing monkeys for years and putting out all kinds of fires without knowing that anyone else had come up with their own methods, much like mine, of being in the truth of their patients' minds. Once you get a handle on this, you will be amazed at the truth behind this verse:

"Heaviness in the heart of man maketh it stoop: but a good word maketh it glad" (Proverb 12:25),

———◈◈◈———

Not all caregivers come to grips with this. Melanie had hired one lady who refused to "partake" in lying to Uncle Bob. She finally had to quit because Uncle Bob became so quarrelsome. Well, I reckon so! How was he supposed to feel, knowing he had all those heads of cattle out there, just starving to death?

Some of my helpers have a hard time with my methods of "seeing monkeys." One afternoon, I walked into the den, and Papa was nervous as a cat. He was pacing back and forth and sitting down on the edge of his chair and wringing his hands. Then he got up and went to the door but never completely went out, and then he started the whole cycle over again.

I was in a huge hurry that night. David and I had somewhere we had to be, so I was going to pop in, give Granny her shot, check on everybody and then be out the door.

After I walked through the den, I asked Marilyn, who was in the kitchen, cutting up apples, what was wrong with Papa. As I got the Forteo shot out of the refrigerator to give to Granny, Papa was in the den, mumbling something about the golf carts.

Marilyn, who had been there at least an hour and had heard enough to be irritated (which happens to all of us on a daily basis), turned and told him (probably for the umpteenth time), "Daddy! There are *no* golf carts to be put up! You sold the golf course ten years ago. Quit getting yourself all worked up. For heaven sake! You're making yourself and everyone else crazy!"

What happened next happened so quickly—I just reacted—probably because I was in such a hurry, and I knew that we were leaving Carthage and headed to Nashville. I wasn't going to be able to put out a fire here tonight.

I flew into the den and looked Papa square in the eyes. "I put them up," I said.

"What?" he asked, calming down slightly but with a confused look on his face.

"Yeah, when I pulled up, there were golf carts everywhere, and I just thought I'd help you out, and I parked them all." Where in this world was this coming from?

"Under the shed? Did you park them under the shed?" he asked, beginning to completely relax.

"Yes, sir."

"What did you do with all the keys?" he asked quickly. (Not putting the keys in order under the counter was one of Papa's huge pet peeves when we did own the golf course.)

233

"I put them all under the counter. In order. It's all okay. You just sit down and watch golf. It's all taken care of."

And with that, he took off his blue windbreaker and reached for his tobacco. "You know, I kinda thought you might put them up when I saw you walk through the door." And with that, his monkey was back in its cage.

Until—and be prepared; there is almost always an until—I walked back in the kitchen. Marilyn was so mad at me that she could have cut me with that knife she was using to slice apples.

"*Why* did you lie to him? That's not going to help him! That's only going to make him crazier!" My sister-in-law rarely gets angry, but this was a doozy.

Unfortunately, I was in too big of a hurry to worry about anything else, other than getting Papa calmed down and giving Granny her shot. "I did what needed to be done to calm him down at the moment. To him, Marilyn, those golf carts are very real! *In his mind*, we are at the golf course. I didn't lie to him. I told him what he needed to know in his mind, to be able to settle down. And, by the way, he's not crazy!"

And with that, she threw the knife in the sink and left, mad and crying, and I stormed off into the living room to give Granny her shot.

Remember, everyone who is involved in your "circus," for the lack of a better word, will not agree with your seeing monkeys. You will have enough to deal with that you will have to let everyone else work out their own understanding of this disease in their own way and time. But don't let that stop you from doing what needs to be done for your patient. Hopefully, others will get a better understanding of the game plan and join in, but if not, you have a circus to run.

—⟨૦/૦⟩—

Jenna and I have had hours of discussions on this subject of *the truth of their mind*. She had come to terms with handling it the best way she knew how when she was staying with Mrs. Beatrice.

One evening, Mrs. Beatrice got into a terrible shape, worrying about when her husband would be in. He had "gone out fishing," and she was concerned that he was not back yet. Jenna tried over and over to console her, saying that he'd be home any minute and that she should not fret over it. Then Jenna would try to get her busy thinking about something else.

The problem was he had been dead for many years. But not to Mrs. Beatrice. She could vividly tell you what he had on that afternoon when he went out the door. She could still smell his skin as he brushed her check with a good-bye kiss. Yes, for all practical purposes, in Mrs. Beatrice's mind, he was terribly late, and she had cause for alarm.

After hours of this—and it only escalated by the minute—Jenna took matters into her own hands. Literally. Jenna reached into her pocket, pulled out her cell phone, and secretly dialed Mrs. Beatrice's house phone. When it rang, Jenna jumped up to answer it. Mrs. Beatrice said, "I bet that's him right now."

Sure enough! Who would have thought it? Jenna picked up the house phone as she hid her cell phone out of sight.

"Hello? Yes, sir, we were just wondering what had happened to you. Yes, sir, I'll tell her. Okay, then. Well, you just take your time, and we'll see you when you get here." And then she hung up the phone.

"Was that him?" asked a sweet, caring Mrs. Beatrice.

"Yes, ma'am. And he said he wanted you to go ahead and eat your supper without him. He's having a big time where he is. Let's just go ahead and have our supper, and he'll be in directly."

And with that, Mrs. Beatrice's heart could quit racing in panic and fear. Her sweet husband was just out fishing and having a good time and would be in directly. She would be seeing him before she knew it.

What happened, though, when he didn't show up "directly"? The mind is the most complex part of the body. Once that dilemma was resolved, Mrs. Beatrice's mind felt at peace and could return to the here and now. Or at least to a whole new delusion.

I've seen it happen hundreds of times. I cannot explain, but again, I refuse to sit in a dark room because I can't fully explain electricity. I just know that this trick works, and therefore, I highly recommend you start seeing some monkeys yourself.

———◈◈◈———

Let me take a moment to completely contradict myself.

When Granny starts in, "What day is it? Where are we going today?"

I do not answer her the first time she asks. I don't ignore the question; I simply give her brain time to fire up the ol' furnace and figure it out herself. Otherwise, I would literally spend all day answering the same questions, over and over and over.

"Granny, look at your board. What day is it?" I'll prompt her. "Look at what clothes you are putting on. Where do we go when we get dressed up like that?" I'll ask.

"Well, I don't know. Sunday? Church, I guess."

I nod my head and smile.

"Well, let me ask you this: what day is it? And where exactly is it that we are going?" she asks anew.

Smile, point, and nod. There is no sense in answering the same three questions asked repeatedly. I just get her to look at those signs and notes.

I also do not just jump on the "monkey wagon" every time we are involved in a little delusion. I always start off by trying to bring her back to reality. I give her mind a gentle nudge to see if she can adapt. Sometimes I can correct her and help her realize when and where we are. Other times, because AD tends to wreak havoc on emotions, I just save her a lot of unnecessary sadness, and I speak *the truth of her mind.*

The other night, I was giving Granny her supper when all of a sudden she looked up at me and said in a panicked tone, "I've got to go check on Mother and Daddy! I told them I would bring them supper, and I've completely forgotten."

"Granny," I said, reaching for her sweet shriveled-up hand, "Granny Amy and Pa have been dead for nearly thirty years. David and the kids and I are living in their old home place while we build our new one. It's okay. They're in heaven. You don't have to worry about them anymore. I promise."

"*Dead?* Are you sure?"

"Yes, ma'am," I said, just waiting to see where this road was going to lead. Jenna and I noticed that more and more, Granny had been talking about needing to go take care of her momma and daddy. It happened at least two or three times a week now.

"You know ... I think ... somehow ... I've missed some family member's funerals. You know ... I think I remember someone telling me

236

that Frank died, and Ray, and if I'm not mistaken, I think I heard something about Dave Manning dying. Surely I've not missed all those funerals." She was staring somewhere out into time and space, trying to bring all these thoughts back to make sense.

"Granny, I want you to listen, okay? Really listen, deep down inside the crevices of your heart and not just your mind. You planned the most beautiful funerals that have ever been for your mom and your dad. You did an unbelievable job helping to orchestrate all of that. You also were right there at Frank's, Ray's, and Dave's. I know because I took you. You can quit worrying about everybody. You have spent your whole life taking care of everybody else, and now it's your turn to be repaid for all that. That's why I'm here, Lucy! You're stuck with me, taking care of you now."

"If you say so, Lucy. But there's one thing I want you to take me to do tonight, okay?" she said, clearly lucid and back to the present.

"Sure, Lucy! You just name it," I said, relieved to have her back. "What do you need me to do?"

"Take me up to Momma and Daddy's. I've got to take them something for supper."

So much for the present.

"Granny, how about I just drop them off something on my way out. I'm going to be going right by there." Monkeys.

"Are you sure? I hate to be a bother," she said, perking up—but dare I guess what year she'd come back to?

"No bother. Be glad to. I was already heading that way," I tell her as I got up to head out the door. "After all, I *do* live in *their* house now," I mumbled to no one but me and the monkeys.

Sometimes, your patient not only has you seeing monkeys, but you end up with a whole three-ring circus, and everyone gets to join in the fun. I have mentioned that our family has been involved heavily with a nursing home ministry for years. The kids go on the fourth Saturday of every month, just like clockwork. One particular Saturday was December 25. That Christmas morning, after the gifts had been opened and the house brought back to some order, Collin looked at the calendar.

"Oh, no! It's nursing home day. What should we do?" he asked, more to himself than to anyone else.

"What a great opportunity! We'll all go!" exclaimed a very excited David McDonald. He loves Christmas as much as his momma. "What better way to celebrate our Savior's birth than to minister to those who are truly in need of some love and attention today."

So, at two thirty, our family showed up in the dining room of the Smith County nursing home. (Much to the surprise of the nurses and staff, I might add. They marveled that we would take our family time to come minister. What better way to celebrate Christ's birth?) We stayed an extra long time that day. We all sang Christmas carols, and all kinds of residents were in attendance. Two very special people in the crowd that day were Aunt Mary and Uncle Tommy. This was just a few short weeks before he went home to celebrate the Savior in person.

As we sang, Uncle Tommy, who had been a preacher all of his life, began to conduct the "church service" … from his hospital bed. It was great! He leaned up in his pajamas and told the "congregation" that he had heard this wonderful group sing, and he had invited them especially for the "service" today. He continued to conduct the service from his bed, and we all joined right in with him. He explained to the "congregation" that they must trust Jesus Christ as their own personal Lord and Savior. He even asked if there was anyone who would like to come forward and give their heart to Jesus. He quoted John 3:16, Galatians 2:21, Ephesians 2:5, Titus 3:7—all from the trusty old King James Version from which he had been preaching for more decades than I had been alive. Funny how AD couldn't take out the Scriptures that he had hidden in his heart.

"Thy word have I hid in mine heart, that I might not sin against thee."
(Psalms 119:11)

No one there shushed him. No one tried to make him be quiet. We all joined him in his delusion. It was great that day that my kids and my husband learned a wonderful trick of the trade: "If they see monkeys, I see monkeys." And to be honest, I think Jesus was quite proud to be a part of our circus that day.

Christmas Day 2010
Our family and Uncle Tommy, conducting service from his bed

Someone once said, "Memory is the power to gather roses in the winter." It has an amazing ability to smell certain odors, and we are transformed to a beach we visited years ago. Or smells take us to a Christmas spent at our grandmother's home as a child. The memory actually transports us physically to another time and place.

I have thought about something funny that happened years earlier and actually laughed out loud over it. Was it actually happening right now? Of course not. But the mind plays tricks on our emotions. That's the reason Hollywood can make billions making movies.

We get so enthralled with a love story that we will cry our eyes out, but when we come out of a movie with wet cheeks, no one threatens to put us on antidepressants and lock us away. Why not? Were we really on that mountainside with those soldiers who lost their lives? Were we really in the hospital room beside that loved one's bed as he drew his last breath? Of course not. But our brains didn't know that. They transformed us onto that movie screen with the actors. When it is a well-made movie, we become part of the emotions that take place on the screen. Whether that movie is set fifty years in the future or a hundred years in our past, we were there! It becomes real to us.

Then why is it hard to accept that your patient is crying over a lost parent from forty years ago, or that he is commanding a platoon from sixty years ago? William Shakespeare said, "Life is a stage, and we are all the actors." You would never walk up to a total stranger as you left a movie theater and tell her, "Stop that crying! That wasn't real! That happened over forty years ago! What's wrong with you?" Yet when a lone, fragile woman looks out the window for her husband who has been fishing all day, we are ready to put her in a padded room. You might try joining her and have her tell you all about it. It may be that this current generation is losing out on a grand opportunity to learn a little more about the past. We call these walks down memory lane delusions and medicate the people who are reliving them in order to stop them.

I read a wonderful book called *Healing of Memories* by David Seamands. In this book he delves into the ministry of allowing God to heal harmful memories of our past by revisiting those events and experiencing them anew. But this time, he suggests going back in your mind and dealing with the person who hurt you the way you would have liked to have done but didn't get a chance to. He speaks of allowing an omnipresent Holy Spirit to let you relive the moment by intervening and allowing you to experience some closure on what harmed you the most.

It was a very insightful book. With all that I have learned about AD by trial and error and then reading Seamands' book, a lot of things I saw Granny and Papa experience daily made sense. The mind can transform you to the point of giving you chills when sitting out in the sun but thinking of a snow-covered mountain that you once skied on. It heats you up when you daydream about the beach. Why wouldn't it upset Uncle Bob to think his cows needed to be fed and when a strange woman in his house was telling him that he didn't have any cattle?

When you learn to be in the *truth of their minds* and gently lead them back to the here and now, you are not making them think they are crazy;

you are acknowledging that what they are seeing is very real *to them*. Lead them gently back to the room they are in and the place they are now. Pray for God to lead you in this, and you will be amazed at how much better your patients will get.

As you can see, you will have to be like a parent with a new baby. Just as the mother or father has to learn the baby's cries well enough to know when the baby is hungry, wet, or tired, you will have to know what sets off your patient and how to defuse that situation. I suggest always starting by trying to remind him of where he really is in the present moment. But there will be times when you need to throw caution to the wind and simply see the monkeys.

This won't make you crazy; it will make you an incredible caregiver!

"To the weak became I as weak, that I might gain the weak: I am made all things to all men, that I might by all means save some." (I Corinthians 9:22)

Chapter 10

Gone Fishin'

It was a sad day. I had known it would come, but I just wasn't ready for it. We all knew it was coming. It happens to everyone. Eventually. There was no reason to mourn. It could not have been avoided. I just wish I hadn't been the only one so sad over it! It was like adding insult to injury, the way all my friends and family actually rejoiced over it. The very nerve of some people. No class. That's what's wrong with today's society.

The date? August 1, 2009. The event? My fortieth birthday. Yes, it was a sad day indeed. Or should I say it *would* have been, if not for my precious, thoughtful thirteen-year-old son, Connor. See, Connor took it upon himself to orchestrate a surprise fortieth birthday party for me. He had done this *all by himself.* Well, mostly.

He had gone to his daddy and told him of his master plan. He thought since I had thrown his daddy surprise fortieth and fiftieth birthday parties that he would jump at the chance to return the gesture. Connor was so excited! It was not going to be a big event like I had pulled off for his dad, just two hundred or so of our closest friends and family. David, being the David McDonald we all know and love, handed Connor a credit card and said, "Here. Call Mrs. Gina and Mrs. Lucinda. They'll know what to do." And with that, he got out of feeling guilty for not planning it himself.

Looking back, I'm kinda glad that David didn't get more involved. It is one of the sweetest memories I have. To find out all the time and energy my baby boy put into this event was very heartwarming, to say the least. Don't get me wrong; Cory, Meg, Collin and Delanie helped Connor, with the execution of the party, but the planning and scheming were all his. That made the event incredibly memorable.

So memorable, in fact, that two weeks later, while I was driving down the road, thinking about how wonderful it had made me feel to be shown that kind of love, an idea came to me. Granny would be turning eighty-two years old on August 25. That still small voice said if anyone deserved to have some love and affection showered upon her, it was Granny. I called my sister-in-law and told her of my idea, and she was all for it.

I printed out invitations and had them in the mail the next day. We were less than two weeks away from the party, and we got busy planning. Granny was incredibly excited when we would remind her about it. Of course, by this time, the AD was so bad that each day, the party planning gave Jenna and me something "new" to talk to her about. We'd tell her, and she'd say, "Oh, honey, don't go making a big fuss over me." Then she'd ask who I thought would come. She'd smile like a Texas debutante, waiting for her big debut. Granny *always* loved a party, even when she couldn't remember why we were having a party.

The morning of her party was a beautiful August day. Her birthday fell on a Tuesday that year, so we had the party on the Sunday after. We figured we'd have a better turnout if we made it convenient for people. After all, most of them were already "gussied up" from church anyway.

As most of our Sundays went, it was quite an event to get her dressed and out the door.

"What day is it? Where are we going? Why am I getting so dressed up? Is it Sunday? Are we going to church? Is today the party? What party? What day is it?"

Her broken record was so bad that morning that Papa went ballistic more than once. He stomped into the living room where I was curling her hair and yelled at her. "Lois! Why do you keep asking all these questions?" Papa shouted at her, not waiting for an answer. "Tell me why in the world you just keep asking over and over and over, 'What day is it? Where are we going?' on and on and on! You know good and well what day it is. You're driving us crazy!" He stomped out to his chair.

What I wanted to say was, "Papa, can you say 'Alzhemier's'? Remember that little disease we are battling here?" But even I knew not to mess with him that day. He was in a foul mood. They were both dealing with a change in schedule the way they typically did.

Papa was a grumpy Gus because he hated being made to clean up and go somewhere, and David had made him bathe yesterday and was coming to get him right after church. Granny always went into "broken record" mode when some part of her brain knew something was different about today's schedule. She couldn't put her finger on it, but she knew just enough to know she didn't know what was going on.

It was an eventful morning! I dressed her and herded her out the door (think herding turtles), having to pass by Billy Goat Gruff's chair to get to the door.

"Granny, stand up," I reminded her.

"I can't. My back hurts!" she whined.

"Stand up, Lois! Your back hurts because you're slumped over like a center on a football team!" Papa "gently encouraged."

With that, Granny stood up stick straight, turned around, and glared at him. "Cordell McDonald! You just mind your own business! I know when my back's hurting! You just shut up!" And then she turned back to me, slumped over—she did look like a football center—and mumbled and grumbled all the way to the door.

Well, that went as scheduled.

—◦◦◦—

Once we were in the car and headed to church, I did what I do every Sunday morning. I took twenty or thirty deep breaths and reminded myself why I even bothered. I thanked God there was no bloodshed and then handed Granny the eight-ounce Coke that I gave her Sunday morning.

"Here Granny. Drink this on the way to church, please."

"Church? Is today Sunday?" That would be the seventy-fifth time she'd asked that.

"Yes, ma'am! And the day of your party. Drink this so you won't be so sluggish." Drats! Did I *really* just mention the party? Oh, no! Not smart. Not today. And then the floodgate opened.

"Party? What party? Did I hear something about a party? We're headed to church right? Is there a party at church today? Seems like someone said there was a party." As she was reciting her dissertation, she wasn't really paying attention to opening the Coke. That's when it happened.

As she unscrewed the top, she held onto to the top but completely let go of the Coke It poured into her lap. Of all the mornings! I jerked the car over, ran to the passenger side and practically yanked her out of the car, with her squealing about her back the whole time. Too late! She was soaked. I grabbed what napkins I could find and wiped her and wiped the seat and the floorboard and the door and the glove box. This was going to need a beach towel, not a fast-food napkin. We had no choice. We had to go home and change. And with that, I made a U-turn and headed back to the battlefield. That's when an idea hit me.

"Granny, don't worry about it. I'm going to take you back and get you a change of clothes. But with the kind of mood Papa is in, I'm not taking you to your house. We'll go up the hill to my house, and I'll find you something to wear," I said with stern determination to get through this day.

"What do you mean, 'the kind of mood Cordell is in'?" she questioned. "Why, as far as I know, Cordell was in a great mood this morning. Did he say something to you that I don't know about?" She was clearly confused.

"To me? Granny, he yelled and screamed at you all morning! How can you not remember that?" I asked.

"Cordell? Screamed? At me? Why, Cordell has never raised his voice at me a day in his life!" She was clearly delirious at this point. What else could explain her not being able to recall the shooting match that had happened less than fifteen minutes ago?

"Okay. Whatever. It doesn't matter. We're going to my house so you can change your skirt," I stated as I sped past her house.

"Where are we going? You just passed my house. Is church over? Did we go to church this morning? Honey, you passed my house. Cordell's going to be worried if I don't come straight home from church. Aren't we going to church today? By the way, I think I must have peed on myself, my whole skirt is soaked! Well, I've never! What in the world?"

The questions went on nonstop the whole time I was getting her out of the car and herding her into our new house, which completely confused her. She couldn't figure out whose home we were just waltzing into. I ran to my closet and found a skirt that had elastic in the waist so it would fit her. She was wearing a bright fuchsia blazer with a white blouse. So I grabbed a long navy skirt with bright fuchsia flowers on it. She thought it was a little bright, but I didn't give her a choice. I washed her off the best I could, threw a slip on her and her new wardrobe, and out the door we went.

We were back on the road and approaching the spot of the Coke incident when the questions started up, right where she had left off when we were there the first time.

"Where are we going? Is today Sunday? Are we headed to church? Did I hear someone say there was a party after church?"

"*Yes*, Granny." I was too exhausted to think anymore. "Yes, it *is* Sunday, we *are* headed to church, and the party is for *you*. We are having an eighty-second birthday party for you down at Marilyn and Steve's right after church. It's going to be wonderful!"

"For me? You have got to be kidding me!" She clearly was pleased. "A party for me! Wow! I wish someone had told me! Because I sure would have worn something nicer. I sure wouldn't have worn this wild thing! I don't even remember buying something this wild! Oh, well, too late now."

And with that, she kept flipping up my skirt, completely out of sorts with my fashion sense. Happy birthday, Granny!

—⁓⁓—

The party was a huge success, wardrobe malfunction and all. Eighty-two people showed up. I thought that was the coolest thing ever that eighty-two people had shown up for her eighty-second birthday celebration. Every single one of them knelt down next to Granny, who we planted in a big comfy chair. They each took time to wish her well. They told her happy birthday, and all of them showered her with hugs and love. It was a beautiful day, outside and in. The sun was shining, and it was not too hot. I really couldn't have planned a more perfect day.

She asked more than one person, "Whose party is this? Whose house is this? Isn't this a nice turn-out? Do you know whose party this is? Were we supposed to bring gifts? Whose house is this? Why in this world am I wearing this wild skirt? I *must* have gotten it on clearance!"

I took her home and let her rest before we headed back to church that night. It had been a great day, and as I tucked her into bed that night, we discussed all the people who had shown up and wished her a happy birthday. I thought, *I am so glad I listened to God's leading and had this party for her now, instead of waiting until next year.* I couldn't get over the urgency I felt that we should do it this year. He probably knows that as bad as her memory is getting, she might not recognize any of those people at this time next year. Yes, I am glad we went to all this trouble.

As I wearily drove up the hill toward home, I made up my mind. I would have another party next year for her eighty-third birthday party. We would have it at my new house then. We had only been in the house for a few weeks and still weren't completely unpacked. But next year ... yes, next year we would definitely do this again. And that was the last thought I had as I got out of my car and headed inside, right after I grabbed an item from the passenger seat—one very wild skirt.

Granny at her last birthday party ... in her very wild skirt
Left to right: Aunt Mildred, Aunt Mary Nell,
Granny, and Aunt Ruth Jean

———

Two weeks later, on another glorious Sunday night, I pulled into Granny's driveway and got her out of the car. It had been a long day, and David and Delanie decided to say their good nights from the car. They each told her that they loved her and that they would see her tomorrow. The boys jumped out and stuck their heads in the back door to say hello to Papa and to check on the scores of the Sunday night football. I led Granny to the bathroom and started getting her out of church clothes and into her gown. I went to my chair and wrote in the journal all that had happened that day so Jenna would know what to expect tomorrow. I had spoken with Jenna earlier that day, and she had mentioned that the weather was going to be beautiful tomorrow and what did I think about her taking Granny fishing. "That's a great idea, Lucy! She'll love it!"

So I wrote on Granny's dry-erase board:

Today is: Monday
Date: September 14, 2009
Wear old clothes.
Jenna's taking you *fishing*!

As Granny climbed into bed, I told her all about going fishing tomorrow. She was so excited. She loved to fish. Loved it. Her memory was getting so much worse so much more quickly lately. We had hit a downward slide, and I was ready for it to stop and for us to get back to some level ground.

She had started wanting to check on her mother and father several times a week now, and she could not name all seven of the grandchildren's names from memory any longer. She had prayed so many times that God would not allow the disease to get so bad that she couldn't remember her family. It was so hard to see us heading in that direction. But fishing? That she remembered! So with a quick hug and kiss, I headed out the door. I hollered over my shoulder, "Get a good night's sleep, Lucy. You've got a big day ahead of you tomorrow!"

"Thanks, Lucy! You're the greatest! I don't know what ol' Granny would do without you," she called after me.

"The feeling's mutual," I said, but by that time, Granny was already falling asleep, no doubt dreaming about catching "the big one."

———

The next morning broke with all the promise of being a perfect day to go fishing. The phone rang, and I noticed the caller ID read "McDonald, Cordell." It was just a little after 7:00 a.m. "I'll call him back in a minute," I said. Granny was probably already up, getting ready to go fishing, wondering where Jenna was and wanting her to hurry up. Papa was probably tired of hearing her questions already. I was in a hurry to get David's clothes ironed and get him out the door to the dentist office. I let it ring. *I'll call him back.*

Twenty minutes passed.

Phone rang. This time the caller ID read "Sloan, Dennis."

Hmmm ... that's odd. The Sloans are Granny and Papa's next-door neighbors.

"Hello?" I answered.

"Lorrie, this is Gladys. Cordell is here and says Lois has fallen, and he can't get her up. He's standing right here. I'll let you talk to him."

"Lorrie?" It was Papa, but he sounded horrible.

"Papa? What's wrong?" I asked cheerfully.

"It's Granny. She must have fallen getting back into bed. I can't get her to get up. I can't get her to do anything."

"Papa, it's okay. I'm on my way. Just go tell her to sit in the floor. I'll get her up. I'll be right there. It's okay, Papa. She'll be okay."

"Lorrie ..."

"Yes, Papa?"

"There's blood ..."

"It's okay, Papa. She probably cut herself when she fell. I'll be right there."

There have been about a half a dozen times or so in my life when that still small voice has spoken so loudly and clearly that I *knew* better than to disobey. This was one of those moments. As I pushed "End Call," I was going to jump on the Gator (our all-purpose farm utility vehicle) and go check on Granny. I was still in my pajamas.

That still small voice said, "Get dressed. Take your Tahoe."

Oh, Papa sounds desperate; I'll just go like this, I thought.

"Get dressed! Take your Tahoe!"

"Okay! Dressed. Tahoe. Got it," I actually said out loud to no one I could visibly see.

As I pulled into the driveway, Papa was standing under the carport with his cordless phone still in his hand. "I tried to call you. It looks bad. I don't know what else to do." He was clearly shaken.

Guilt rushed over me. "I'm sorry, Papa. I should have answered the phone. I was trying to get David off to work. It's going to be okay." I patted him on the shoulder and started into the house. "Lucy! What have you done now? Are you being stubborn to Papa and won't let him help you get up? Granny? Where are you? Granny?" As I called out to her to let her know the cavalry was there, I kept peeking around doors. First into the living room, where her chair is. No Granny there. Next to the left, into the bathroom. No Granny there.

"Lucy … where in the world are—" I stopped cold when I glanced to the right to her bedroom floor. There lay Granny. There was a pillow on the floor right above her ankles. Oh, dear God! *Help!*

I grabbed the phone from Papa, who actually leaned over on me, almost collapsing.

"I can't get her up," was all he could mumble.

"It's going to be okay," I said, knowing neither of us believed it but both needed to hear me say it.

"9-1-1, what is your emergency?"

"This is Lorrie McDonald. I am at Cordell McDonald's home. 107 McCall Street. I have an eighty-two-year-old white female who has fallen and is unresponsive. Hurry!"

"Ma'am, I will need to ask you some questions and keep you on the line."

"Tell Ricky Slack to *get here now*!" And with that, I slammed down the phone and ran to Granny. Ricky was the chief of paramedics, and he and I use to coach soccer together. It was a small town, so I could have said, "This is Lorrie McDonald. I'm at Granny's house. Send help!" And they would have known where I was and who I was talking about. This was *not* a time to play by some phone operator's manual, written in some big city somewhere. I was not staying on the line. I was throwing myself down on the floor next to Granny to see if I could get her to respond.

"Granny, it's me, Lucy. What have you done?"

Nothing.

"Granny, can you hear me?"

Nothing.

"Oh, dear God in heaven. Lord, send *help*, now!"

Sirens were in the driveway. I hugged Papa. "Go tell Ricky to come back here, Papa. And Papa … this was *not* your fault. It's going to be okay."

Nothing.

I knelt beside her. Her eyes were open but staring out into a space somewhere I couldn't see. Her breathing was slow and gurgling. Not good. I was certified to teach CPR when I was the head lifeguard at the golf course. It all came rushing back. Lots of information. Information I would never need, right? Gurgling was bad—that much I remembered.

"Lord, help."

Ricky and several others were behind me with a stretcher. "Hey, Lorrie, what happened?" Ricky asked as he and another paramedic squatted down and checked Granny's vital signs.

"I'm not sure. But from the looks of it, she must have gotten up to go to the bathroom. There is a wet Pull-Up on the floor by the toilet. She must have knocked her pillow off on the floor when she got up and tripped over it when she came back to bed. Ricky, look—both of her arms are down by her side."

"That means she fell so quickly, she never had time to try to brace herself," Ricky said. "And Lorrie"—he paused to make sure what he was telling me was sinking in—"since both her arms are down by her sides, that means the blow knocked her unconscious immediately, and she never tried to struggle to get up. I just thought that might help you and Doc if you knew that."

"But she's not unconscious. She's blinking. Her eyes are open. She's not … Ricky … she's not … I can see her breathing …" I practically begged him to tell me she was going to be okay.

"You better call Doc and tell him to meet us up at Riverview. And Lorrie … tell him to hurry." And with that, he was out the door, sirens blaring.

I told Papa that he could ride with me. As I stuck the key in the ignition, I said a quick thank-you prayer to the Holy Spirit for telling me to get dressed and bring the Tahoe. He knew what lay in store for me when I walked through Granny's door. He also knew what lay ahead at the ER. And at this precise moment, all He brought to mind was a familiar passage:

"Yea, though I walk through the valley of the shadow of death, I will fear no evil: for thou art with me." (Psalm 23:4)

———✂∾∿∾✂———

I don't remember the exact order of phone calls I made on that short drive from Granny's house to Riverview Regional Hospital, but I called my mom, Nana, to go to my house and get my three kids and get them to the ER as quickly as possible. I called Cory, Granny's oldest grandchild, at Rite-Aid, where he was the pharmacist.

"What do you mean, you don't know if she's going to make it?" Cory asked. "How bad of a fall could it have been? Lorrie, Granny's the toughest person I know. Tell her I'm on my way!"

Unfortunately, Mike, and Jay were both an hour's drive away at college. John and his wife lived just a couple of roads over from the hospital, but he didn't pick up his phone. I left a voicemail. It all runs together now. I got in touch with Marilyn and Steve, and soon we were all standing around Granny's bed in the emergency room.

Tina Tyree, a good friend of ours from church, was on duty that bright, beautiful fall morning. She's a good nurse. She stood there and cried right along with the family. That made her a great nurse. She told me that Granny was still breathing on her own, and she could probably hear us. We each took our turns leaning down to tell her that we loved her and good-bye. Collin, Connor, and Delanie were very brave for being only fifteen, thirteen, and eleven. Steve loved his mother-in-law and held Marilyn as they both told her good-bye. I thought David would melt into a puddle onto the floor; he was crying so hard. Then Cory got there.

Cory had told the techs at the pharmacy he had to leave. It was an emergency. I don't think he had any idea just how serious it was until he walked through those sliding ER doors. He looked at the faces of those he loved most and flew to Granny's side. He looked up at me with a pleading face, but all I could do was tell him, "She can still hear you. You need to tell her good-bye right now. While she still can."

"*What?* Lorrie! This can't be happening!"

"Cory, I'll explain later! Tell her whatever you want to tell her—now!"

Cory wailed uncontrollably and told her she was the best grandmother in the world. Which was true. He told her that he loved her with all his heart. Which was true. He told her life would never be the same without her here. Which was true. Then he told her that he wouldn't tell her good-bye, because someday he would see her again. Which was true!

After everyone had a chance to kiss Granny's cheek, I noticed she still seemed to be lingering. Almost waiting. Then, knowing her like I do, I knew what it was.

I brushed that beautiful gray hair away from her ear and leaned down and whispered to her, "Granny, the other boys are away at school. We can't get in touch with them. Granny, they know how much you love them. You don't have to wait for them. They can't get here it time. It's okay. You can go home now. We all love you more than you'll ever know. And Lucy, you're the greatest."

And with that she took one last deep breath and crossed over Jordan. God was faithful. She didn't have to go home alone. She was surrounded by family and a room full of love. Suddenly, it dawned on me—Alzheimer's had lost! She never got to the point of not knowing all of us. God had been faithful even in answering that prayer. It didn't seem like an answer to our prayers at the time. But looking back, he took her quickly, just as *she* had asked Him to do. God is always faithful.

—◦◦◦—

One of the most important pieces of information I can give you is this: have your patient fill out a living will. You need to have it as soon as possible, especially if he or she is already in the beginning to middle stages of AD. Granny and Papa both had been thoughtful enough to fill one out years before. Neither one of them wanted to be hooked up to a machine and kept alive when it was obvious to the doctors that they were beyond coming back to us. Boy, were we thankful we knew her wishes that morning.

When the paramedics took her into the emergency room, it was obvious that there was very little brain activity. One of the first questions we were asked was if she had a living will. She did. She absolutely did not want to be kept alive by some machine. All of us knew her wishes, but if we had not had that legally binding document on file at the hospital, then if just one person had fought us, we would have had to watch as she lay there and suffered for who knows how long. It was a blessing to know that we were doing exactly what she wanted.

Take the time to find out if your patient has a power of attorney in place and a living will. There is no time to waste. Your patient will need to be coherent enough to be deemed legally able to make these decisions. Thankfully, Granny had always been thinking of all of us. She had never wanted to be a bother. Bless her heart … she never was!

—◦◦◦—

We all stood outside the ER, sobbing and consoling one another, when my cell phone rang. Oh, no. How could I have forgotten?

"Hey, Mrs. Lorrie. I'm running a little late. I stopped and got us some worms. Granny and I are going fishing today!" Jenna chatted up a storm, so excited about the great weather and fun day she had in store for Granny that day.

Oh, how I dreaded telling her this.

"Jenna, do you have your key?" I asked.

"Yes, ma'am. Why?"

"Well, Jenna, there's been an accident. Granny fell early this morning, and she's … Jenna … Granny's gone. She passed away just a few minutes ago. Can you go on into the house and go to her room and tidy up for me before we get there? She had the accident in there. I am so sorry to ask you to do this. But I don't want David and Marilyn to see it."

"What? But Mrs. Lorrie …" Jenna was stammering.

"Yes, Jenna?"

"Mrs. Lorrie, Granny *can't* be gone. We were goin' fishin'."

Granny's fishing chair, sitting empty

———=<><><>=———

We spent the rest of the day at Granny and Papa's house, going through photographs and getting all the arrangements in order. We laughed, we cried, we sat silently. But most of all, we stared at one another in disbelief. How could she be gone? She was goin' fishin'!

David stayed with Papa until he knew he needed to go home. Papa swore he was fine. He was not. We offered to bring him home with us, but he thought he needed to be there. The next morning, we found him asleep on the couch, still in his clothes from the day before. He told us he could have sworn he heard Lois call for him.

He never slept in his bedroom again. When I finally realized what was going on—he was troubled by being back there in that part of the house—I took action. I brought his bed out in the den, right next to his ugly green chair. Everyone warned me that he would fuss at me. He thanked me. I understood. I really did. I begged him to come live with us just up the hill. He said he'd think about it.

———=<><><>=———

The night after Granny died, we had been at the funeral home almost all day for visitation. She was so loved. Hundreds of people came by that day, and hundreds more would come the next. We were absolutely exhausted. Emotionally and physically. As I was getting ready for bed, I noticed the clock. I hopped up and looked at David and said, "Oh, no! In all the commotion, I forgot to stop by and get Granny ready for bed!" He turned his head sideways and then, with the saddest smile I've ever seen, reached out his arms for me. Then it hit me. She's gone. She's really gone.

As a caregiver, I didn't see Granny two or three times a week. I saw her two or three times a day. She was my buddy. She was my sidekick. She was my partner in crime. And now, she was gone.

Chapter 11

Lucy, You're the Greatest!

Sorrow is better than laughter:
for by the sadness of the countenance the heart
is made better.—Ecclesiastes 7:3

The summer and fall of 2009 was the year of a terrible drought. We had not had rain in months. Granny talked about how dry it looked every time we got in the car to drive anywhere. Jenna said it was the same thing every morning on the front porch.

"Would you just look at how dry that pasture is. *Why*, I don't believe I ever remember it being this dry. We need some rain," she would always say. Same way. Each time. Same emphasis on the word "why," each and every time. That's a sure sign of AD. Over and over and over. The patients gets in that broken-record mode and experiences the same emotions over and over.

That's exactly how I felt in the days that followed Granny's death. I was in such a fog. Dozens of times, I would think about having to get to the church or get to the funeral home and automatically, I'd reach for my cell phone to call Granny to tell her to be ready to go when I got there. Too late; she was already there. I was dumbfounded.

Everybody in the family took it hard. All of us loved dear, sweet Granny. I knew David and Marilyn were hurting because they had lost their momma. Cordell was hurting because he had lost his wife of sixty-two years. All the grandkids were devastated. None of us could believe how empty our lives would feel now that she wasn't sitting in her chair in the living room any longer. But there were two people that I knew were going to experience an ache that no one else would understand.

257

Those two people were Jenna and me. We had lost our "baby." We took care of her. Jenna during the day. Me at night. We had been doing it for so long that we both sat and looked at each other, simply bewildered.

"Now what am I supposed to do every day?" Jenna asked me on the morning of the funeral. I knew this question had absolutely nothing to do with her job security or her livelihood. Nothing at all. I knew *exactly* what she meant.

David had told Jenna immediately that we wanted her to stay on and help us take care of Papa. We gave her a month's severance pay and suggested she take at least a couple of weeks off to mourn. This was the hardest part of being a caregiver. This was where the caregiver's job ultimately ends. Then, she moves onto her next patient. Jenna confided in me that she didn't know if she was going to take on another caregiving position. It was too hard to deal with it when she got this emotionally attached.

Jenna had always cleaned houses on the side, and she knew that she would have more work than she could do. She would work for us, and we would go from there. But Jenna still felt lost.

Every waking minute of Jenna's life had involved Granny up until now. At night, she would plan what she would wear the next day, depending on what activity or adventure she had planned for Granny. If they would be running errands, then Jenna would dress up. If they would be riding around on the farm or fishing, she knew she would plan on wearing old clothes. All of Jenna's meals were planned, cooked, and eaten at Granny's kitchen table. It had been forever since she had actually eaten supper by herself in her own kitchen.

Jenna and I spent many hours following Granny's death basically counseling each other. No one else understood. We didn't expect them to. A family member overheard someone tell Jenna and me that they realized *we* were taking it harder than anyone else, and I could tell that did not sit well. That was okay. She was a big *part* of their lives, but she *was*, in a way, *our lives*. Every part of our day-to-day living involved giving thought to how it would affect Granny and her upkeep. I really didn't expect them to understand. They hadn't understood while she was alive; why would they "get it" now?

Granny got her wish, and on the day of her funeral, the drought stopped. It rained like I have never seen it rain before. It poured down all day and all night without stopping. When I spoke at her funeral, I jokingly said that Granny had probably gone fishing first thing on the banks of the Jordan River and had gotten her hook stuck in the bottom and had sprung a leak in heaven! That was probably where all this rain was coming from. Everyone got a kick out of that. As a matter of fact, her funeral proved to be one of the most joyous occasions I can remember in a long time.

We decided to hold her ceremony at our church, Cornerstone Baptist Church. We knew that is where Granny wanted it, and we also knew that there would be such a large attendance that the funeral home wouldn't be able to seat them all. We were right.

None of us had to wonder how Granny wanted her service conducted. In true Granny style, she was not about to be a bother to us, even after she was dead and gone. Several years earlier, Granny had taken matters into her own hands. She decided to plan her funeral for us.

One day not long after Dr. Lim had diagnosed her with Alzheimer's, we were driving back from his office. She was only at the beginning stages and knew enough to know that things were going to start getting bad.

"Lucy, I want you to do me a favor when we get home," she said after thinking for a long time.

"Sure, Lucy! What's that?" I asked, thinking this was going to involve a fishing pole.

"I want you to sit down with me, and I want to tell you what I want you to say at my funeral." There. She had said it.

"Granny! What in this world would make you say a thing like that?" I said, clearly shocked.

"That doctor said I've got Alzheimer's, right?"

"Yes. But there's medicine ..."

"I'm going to get bad, aren't I?"

This was way too serious of a moment for me to play it off.

"Yes, ma'am. You are," I answered in a hushed tone.

"Okay, then. I want to tell you what I want each of my grandchildren to know that I *remember* about them. Who knows? I may not be able to remember anything someday. I don't want them to ever forget that ol'

Granny loves each and every one of them dearly, and I couldn't have asked for better grand young'uns. Why, I have loved every minute of it!"

"Granny! You're still going to get to enjoy doing things with them!"

It was no use. She knew what she wanted to do, and I was honored that she asked me to be the one to share it. Besides, I knew that by the time we pulled up on McCall Street, she wouldn't remember this conversation anyway.

——◦◦◦——

But she *did* remember. As soon as I took her in the house, she walked straight to the dining room table and grabbed a notebook and an ink pen.

"Here. Sit down. I'm going to tell you my favorite memory of each of my grandchildren." And she did. Granny style. We laughed until we cried.

She also told me which dress she wanted to be buried in and which songs she wanted the kids to play. She *loved* to hear Collin, Connor, and Delanie play the piano and their other instruments. She told me to have the four older boys read passages of Scripture and her obituary. She knew exactly what she wanted and how she wanted it done.

And with that, I took the notebook and hugged her good-bye. I kissed her on the cheek and told her I'd put it in safekeeping, but that we weren't going to need it for a long, long time!

She kissed me and hugged me tightly and told me what she always had: "Thank you, Lucy. You're the greatest!"

No, Granny, *you* are.

——◦◦◦——

One of the best things you can do for your patient, your family, and your sanity is to sit down with your patient and preferably one other family member and have your loved one tell you *exactly* how she wants her funeral to go. It may be an awkward conversation, but there was such a peace of mind, knowing we had held the exact service Granny wanted.

Another thing that would be of more benefit than you can imagine is if your patient can tell you, in front of at least one witness, to whom he or she wants to leave his or her personal belongings. This will keep peace when people's emotions are already running high anyway. Write it down, have him or her sign it, have your witness sign it, and then tuck it away. Even though Granny and Papa had a basic will it would have been nice to know to which grandchild they wanted to leave each personal item. In the long run, you'll be glad.

———◦◦◦———

When we went back to Granny's house on the day we left the ER, everyone set about gathering pictures and mementos to sit around at the funeral home. Marilyn told me she was going to take Granny's jewelry box with her to her house for safekeeping. That was fine with me. I told Marilyn, there were only two things I really wanted; to me they were worth far more than any silver or gold.

I went into Granny's room and took the old quilt off her bed and just buried my face in it and cried. I stayed back there so long that David finally came in to check on me. He wrapped his arms around me when he saw *what* it was that was so important to me.

Granny, under her quilt, and Delanie, on Granny's last Christmas night

Ellie Beth on *the* quilt with her great-Granny!

"I pulled this up under her chin *every* night for the last four years. I want this quilt," I said in between sobs.

"Granny wouldn't want anyone else to have it," he said.

The other thing I wanted was in the kitchen: her recipe box and the church cookbook that she used all the time. They were full of her handwritten notes. They were priceless to me.

I don't know whatever became of all of Granny's silver serving pieces. I'm sure we will all split them up among us eventually. And Granny had more horse tack than jewelry. I'm sure there will come a time when we will all sit down and go through what she did have. But there is hardly a day that goes by that I don't sit under that quilt and read my Bible in the mornings or pull out Granny's copy of the "yellow cookbook" and read her hen-scratch. Those are far more valuable to me. Priceless, actually.

Those cookbooks and that quilt even had special meaning to Jenna. She met her Prince Charming shortly after Granny's death. Jenna asked me to do her engagement and wedding photography and I gladly accepted. She knew she wanted to have a part of Granny with her as Jenna started this new life. Jenna and Jimmy moved to Alaska, but they have a beautiful reminder hanging on their wall that part of Jenna's heart will always be back in Tennessee.

For Jenna's engagement pictures, there was one very special
item she wanted in her picture … Granny's quilt.

—⟨ϙ/ϙ/ϙ⟩—

You can never tell how a tragedy will affect someone. Some people
become quiet and reserved. Some people become introverted and lock
themselves away from public eyes. Some people become angry and bitter.
But what Papa did shocked all of us.

Granny's funeral was held on Wednesday afternoon at our church.
When we walked into the sanctuary that rainy day, I looked over to where
we always sat and saw Granny's green Community Bank fleece blanket.
She was cold-natured. Our pastor, Brother Ron Ralph, loved Granny just
as much as the rest of us loved her. Although he liked everything done
decently and in order, he allowed one item to remain in the sanctuary week
after week, without sending it to Lost and Found. That was Granny's green
blanket.

I spied it and just smiled. My first thought was, *Oh, good, Granny's
going to need that.* Then it dawned on me: Granny wouldn't be sitting
there today. She would be, quite literally, front and center. Then I had a
little touch of Granny's mischievous side. Why wouldn't Granny need
her blanket? After all, she was in the church. She always was freezing at
church. She always put it over her lap. So …

I marched over, grabbed it, and headed up front to the casket.

Our precious youth pastor, Brother Jim Britton, was turning on lights and checking things out in the sanctuary when he saw where I was headed. He stopped and grinned and nodded his head in complete agreement. "I am *so* glad you are doing that! When I first came in here this morning, that is the first thing that caught my eye. And then the thought crossed my mind, *You need to pick that up to make the church look nice for the funeral.* Then the next thought was, No, *Mrs. Lois always gets cold. I'll just leave it there for her.* Then it dawned on me what I was thinking. I couldn't move it. I just couldn't. I'm so glad you're doing that." He smiled again.

And with that, I sashayed up to the casket and laid it, rolled up, beside her. Now she wouldn't get cold! I guess as her caregiver, it was just in me to see to her right up to the last minute.

The family all sat together. Of course, Jenna sat right there with the other grandkids. She had become one of us, just as she had become an honorary member of the Kemp family when Mrs. Beatrice died. You can never underestimate the love of a good caregiver.

Collin and Connor went to the baby grand piano and played the most beautiful duets: "Amazing Grace" and "It Is Well with My Soul." That's what Granny wanted. Check that off her list she'd given me.

John and Jay each read a passage of Scripture. Check.

Michael read her obituary. Check.

Then I got up and read off all the wonderful memories she wanted me to share. She had something delightful to say about each one of her grandkids. Check.

The last words I said were directly to her. I shared all that she cherished about her family, and then I closed it by telling everyone there that I never left her side without her hugging me and saying, "Lucy, you're the greatest!" So I closed it by telling her that I had forever been changed by being her daughter-in-law, and I truly meant it when I looked down at her, lying so peacefully asleep and told her, "Lucy, *you* are the greatest!"

Then Cory, her oldest grandchild, stood up and told the couple hundred people there why his Granny was the greatest woman he knew. He said that in the Bible, we are taught to be Christ-like and that Christ was the greatest servant of all times. Jesus showed us how to love by loving others. Then he told us that Granny, Icie Lois McCall McDonald, was the greatest example of a servant he had ever known.

Granny didn't ask me to put that on her list of things to do at her service, because deep down, I think she thought that as tender-hearted as Cory was, there would be no way he could make it through it without crying. Which he didn't. He cried. We cried. Granny looked down on us and smiled. I'm not just saying this because he's my stepson, but it was one of the most touching things I have ever heard said at anyone's funeral. Period.

Delanie played her violin, graveside, and played the sweetest rendition of "Sweet Hour of Prayer" that I've ever heard. Granny loved to hear her play it. Check.

All in all, I had never felt so satisfied about carrying out someone's wishes in all my life. I know that Granny nudged all those family members who had gone on before her and said, "I wish you would look at the fuss they have made over me. Well, I've never! I hate to have been such a bother! But aren't my grandkids so talented? Each and every one!"

"Wherefore seeing we also are compassed about with so great a cloud of witnesses, let us lay aside every weight, and the sin which doth so easily beset us, and let us run with patience the race that is set before us, Looking unto Jesus the author and finisher of our faith; who for the joy that was set before him endured the cross, despising the shame, and is set down at the right hand of the throne of God" (Hebrews 12:1-2).

When we left the graveside, we all went back to Granny and Papa's house for a while, and then, one by one, we all went home. I promised Papa we would be back to check on him later.

That night about six o'clock, we heard stirring upstairs. David and I had been sitting on the loveseat together, just talking and resting, for most of that afternoon.

"What are y'all doing up there?" he called up the stairway.

"Getting ready for church," yelled down one of the kids.

David looked at me and said, "Are we going to go to church tonight?"

"Why wouldn't we? Granny would have a fit if we used her funeral as an excuse," I deducted.

About that time, our phone rang. It was Cory, asking us how we were doing. When David told him that we were getting ready to head back to church, he said that was sort of what he had figured. He, Meg, and Ellie Beth would see us there.

As we headed down the hill, David said he wanted to pop in and check on his daddy. I told him to ask him to come with us.

"Ha. You better come in if you want him to even consider it. He hasn't been to a church service in thirty years. But if you want to ask him, come on in. Who knows? They say miracles still happen." He chuckled as he headed into the carport.

"Hey, Daddy. How you doing?" David asked once inside.

"Just sittin' here, son. Just thinking about Momma," Papa said, sitting up on the edge of his ugly green chair.

"Hey, Papa, why don't you come to church with us tonight? You're still dressed nice, and everybody there was so nice to you today. It would be good for you to get out of the house for a while," I said hopefully.

David gave me his "I told you not to expect too much" look. And then the miracle we had been talking about happened right in front of our eyes.

"You sure I'm dressed all right?" asked Papa, standing up and buttoning his pants button. "Might as well …"

"Absolutely!" I almost shouted.

David almost staggered backwards, he looked so shocked. "Well, let's go then."

And we were out the door.

———⟊ᴓᴓ⟊———

Granny, waterskiing

Different people grieve in different ways. Lots of times, it completely alters their personality. That is an understatement when it came to the transformation that took place in Papa after Granny's death.

David stopped by every day at lunch and picked him up. He brought him up to the house, where we all had lunch together. David would take Papa back home and then stop back by after work and fetch him again. He'd come back up to the house, and we'd have supper.

The first week of this, we all sat just dumbfounded when he started telling us what an amazing woman Lois was. We sat there and just ate as he told us about the first time he took her waterskiing. He told us,

"Lois was amazing. Why, there wasn't anything she was afraid to tackle. Did I ever tell you what a great water-skier she was? She really was something!"

I sat there thinking, *You've got that right! After all, she married you!*

My father-in-law could be a sweetheart, but the older he got, the more stubborn and set in his ways he became. Granny never minded. She loved him in spite of himself.

He always had a great sense of humor. One day I when I was pregnant with Delanie, I was walking onto the carport as he was walking out with his keys in his hand. He stopped for just a moment and gave me that mischievous chuckle of his.

"I'm headed over in town to get my truck tag changed ... *again.* I'm planning on applying for 'PAPA7' this time. But you could save me a lot of trouble if you could just go ahead and let me know should I apply for PAPA8 or PAPA10? Just wondering." He chuckled to himself. He was referring to the fact that David and I had given them three new grandkids, one every two years or so. He was the grandpa to seven, thus the vanity tag.

"I think PAPA7 will be just fine," I replied. "Smarty pants."

Since he was often reserved, when he did say something comical, we all found it *way* funnier than it would have been had someone else said it.

I remember one time when the whole family was down at their house having one of our many family suppers. David was showing off some new dress pants I had bought him for work. He was thrilled with them and had never seen any quite like them.

"Look, Steve, these are the neatest pants Lorrie found me. They are a size 36, but they have these hidden elastic straps on the side that give me an extra two inches!"

"What are those called?" asked my brother-in-law, Steve.

"Thirty-eights," came the quick reply from the ugly green chair.

Delanie, Papa, and his ugly green chair

—⟨ᴑᴑ⟩—

After that first amazing Wednesday night, Papa never missed a church service again. Each time we got ready to go, we would ask him if he wanted to come. He would say, "Might as well." On Wednesday night after David would bring him up to the house for supper, he would just hang out with us until time for church. On our way home from church, we'd let him off at his house.

One particularly hectic Wednesday night, I was still running around in sweat pants and a grungy T-shirt at about six thirty. Papa was sitting up on the edge of the love seat, wringing his hands. I could tell he was confused about something.

"Papa, is something wrong?" I asked as I was putting stuff back in the refrigerator.

"Well, I kinda had it in my mind's eye that tonight was prayer meetin'" at church," he said.

"It is," I answered, still not sure why that had him confused.

He straightened up and inquired, "Well, you ain't going lookin' like *that*, are you?"

And with that admonition, I headed into my bedroom to change into something more suitable. Might as well!

——⟲⟳——

The whole family was flabbergasted at the "new Papa." He was the biggest chatterbox in the world after Granny's death. David theorized that since Granny had been the life of the party, maybe Papa never felt like he needed to say anything before. Well, he was certainly making up for lost time.

He was constantly going places with us and seemed to want to be a part of everything going on. It didn't matter where I was headed. He'd grab the remote control and turn off the Golf Channel, and he was out the door. It was as if when Granny reached heaven, she broke into the "happy dust" and sprinkled it on him during his sleep!

We were excited about spending *many years* with this new and improved version of Papa.

He began referring to his house as his "room down yonder." I don't think he ever thought of it as home after Granny passed away there. He didn't have any reason to go back into the back of the house anymore. Except when David made him take a bath, but that was only once a week or so. Even then, David stayed there with him until he was able to get back to the den.

Papa began sticking around my house after David went back to work after lunch and staying until bedtime. David finally talked to him and reasoned with him that it only made sense for him to let us set up an apartment for him, downstairs at our house. I clinched the deal when I grinned at him and told him he could even bring his ugly green chair. He decided that sounded like a deal.

We had already set up the house for that purpose when we built the new house. Of course at the time, we always thought we would have to move

Granny in there eventually. It was always Granny that everyone assumed was going to need around-the-clock supervision someday. When we built our house, we did so with her in mind and made a handicapped living quarters downstairs. Of course, we were just as happy to think that Papa was going to get to live with us. But that wasn't God's plan.

—ꙮ—

Top: Papa and Granny when they were first married in 1947
Bottom: Papa and Granny at their fiftieth wedding celebration in 1997

Apparently, it wasn't in His plan for Papa to move in with us either. Just six short months after we lost Granny, I got a call from Papa's doctor. I had taken him in for his yearly checkup and got a call one

morning that said his blood work showed that he was in renal failure and would need to go into a hospital in Nashville overnight to have some dialysis done.

We stayed by Papa's side while he battled a horrible cough and began having his kidneys flushed out. I went down every morning and stayed with him until 6:00 p.m., when David could get there from work. He would stay until 8:00 or 9:00 p.m. and then head the hour drive home.

After Papa had been in the hospital for a few days, they began to "medicate" him for delusions. I noticed his delusions were getting worse and worse. So again, we made a decision. I talked to David on Wednesday night after Papa had been in the hospital several days. I told David I wanted to transfer Papa back home to Smith County from Nashville. I just felt like he would be more comfortable back home, and the staff at our hometown hospital knew him and would treat him with more respect.

The next night when David arrived at the hospital, Papa's mental state was almost scary, he was so confused. David let him know we would be moving him back home tomorrow. I was going to arrange for his transfer the next day. Unfortunately, during the night he got worse.

They ended up putting him on life support and giving him a week of induced coma. He went in on a Monday, and ten days later, David had to adhere to Papa's living will and make the heart-wrenching decision to pull him off life support. At the end of the week, just like that, Papa was back with Granny. We lost him six months after losing her.

In August 2007, Gina Dillon and I flew to Detroit, Michigan, for her cousin's wedding. It was an incredibly swanky event and one of the most fun weekends I have ever had. On the flight up there, she asked me what I would be called when Cory and Megan started having children. I told her I wasn't sure. I was only thirty-eight years old, so I was a little young to be a "Granny Mac." My mom is Nana, and Granny, of course, was Granny. So I figured I would know when I heard it.

I didn't give that any more thought until we arrived in Detroit. Her cousins picked us up from the airport, and off we went, excited about the

weekend's activities. As we were driving along, Gail's fifteen-year-old son kept referring to her sister, his aunt, as "Cha Cha."

"Hey, Cha Cha, where are we going to eat lunch? Hey, Cha Cha, what time is the dress rehearsal?" Cha Cha this. Cha Cha that.

"Okay," I announced, "if I am going to be with you guys all weekend I need to know why Jessie keeps calling Roxanne, 'Cha Cha.'"

"Gladly!" answered Roxanne, aka Cha Cha. "When Jessie was born, his mom and I were standing outside the nursery window, looking in. Two ladies were arguing just a few feet away from us about some random baby behind that glass. They each kept declaring that they were going to be the baby's 'Cha Cha.' So just like you, we asked what in the world a 'Cha Cha' was. One of them twirled around and exclaimed, 'A Cha Cha is the *only* person who loves you as much as your momma loves you. Every family has *one*, and I am this baby's Cha Cha!' And with that, she turned her attention back to the other family member, who was just as adamant that she deserved the sacred moniker. So Gail and I decided that I would be Jessie's Cha Cha!" she explained, pleased as punch.

"That's it!" Gina declared, looking at me. "*You* can be a Cha Cha!"

So that's what I have been ever since Ellie Beth McDonald came into this world. And just like Granny, I am Cha Cha to *everybody*. I have the license plate to prove it. All my Sunday school kids call me Cha Cha, and so do all my kid's friends. It is my own personal ode to Granny. Everybody in town referred to her as Granny. I feel very honored to be known as everybody's Cha Cha.

Everything I learned about being a good grandmother, I learned from Granny, Mammie, and of course, my mother, Nana. They are completely selfless and make coming to their house the most fun ever. I hope that from all the time that I spent caring for Granny, I learned from her how to be a servant. She truly was the picture of putting others first. Mammie taught me how to be tough and keep on keeping on. Nana has always been available, day or night, when I needed her. I feel blessed to have had these three incredible women in my life. I will have done well if I turn out to be half the grandmother these ladies have been.

—◦◦◦—

I don't regret a moment I spent caring for my in-laws. They both deserved to be honored, and I am glad I was able to help give them a life worth living. David and I were able, along with a lot of support from a lot of people, to keep them at home and see that they didn't just "exist"; they "lived"!

We were able to keep them involved with their family, right up to the end. That's all they ever hoped for. That's what I hope for. I hope that my children and my grandchildren will someday remember all that I did for Granny and Papa and will put forth a little effort to keep me home too. I also hope that when I get to be Granny's age, I can look back and remember how stubborn she could be at times, and perhaps I will make things easier on them. But I'm not making any promises!

Not too long ago, when it was just getting warm outside, we had turned on the heater for our swimming pool. Our oldest granddaughter Ellie Beth has gills! She loves to swim, and we are excited to teach her younger sister to swim this summer too. Her sister, by the way, was born three years after Granny passed away. Her name? Annsley *Lois* McDonald.

When Cory called home to tell us they were having another girl and what her name was going to be, David and I cried. Granny was the greatest person Cory has ever known. There will always be a part of her with him.

Then David and I looked at each other and died laughing.

"Oh, no!" said David. "Do you think since they are naming her after Granny, she will grow up to be a ringed-tail tooter like her?"

"Probably! I hope so! We all need a little dose of Granny inside us. Every family needs someone who is sweet to the core and dripping with mischievousness. I certainly hope so."

We have not been disappointed. Annsley Lois McDonald has turned into the biggest joy we could have ever imagined. She dances to her own beat. She, too, has been given her own moniker: Lulu. It seems only fitting that someone named after Lois, who called everyone Lucy, would end up with the nickname Lulu! I think Granny looks down from heaven with a smile on her face at the little angel her namesake is becoming.

Annsley Lois "Lulu" McDonald

⸺◈⸺

So earlier this year when we turned on the heater to the pool, I couldn't wait to tell Ellie Beth. By the way, we call Ellie "Moochie." (Nicknames are just what we do in our family.) As soon as she ran into the house, I squatted down in front of her and looked her square in the eyes.

"Moochie, what is your most favoritest, most wonderfulest thing in the whole wide world?" I knew she was going to scream, "*Swimming*!"

Then she wrapped her arms around me and looked straight into my soul and said, "You is Cha Cha!"

Moochie and Lulu

I realized right then and there that I *am* going to be okay someday. Someday, when I'm old and senile, somebody will go to bat for me. Because those are the seeds I have planted, and God's Word is true. You do indeed reap what you sow. My children watched Granny be a caregiver and then they watched me be a caregiver to her. That's part of who *they* are now. It's what they know to do. So all those days and nights when Granny made me want to pull my hair out … well, they were all worth it. Every last exhausting one of them.

I will spend my short time I have left here on earth practicing what Granny preached with her life, being a servant. Or a caregiver. Or just the best mom and Cha Cha I can be.

There's one other thing I will practice, too. Because someday, when I'm sitting in Dr. Lim's office, I want to be able to fool them all into thinking I'm just as sane as they are. So I think I'll start memorizing it now …

Blue, baseball, Virginia.

Blue, baseball, Virginia.

Blue, baseball, Virginia!

"And there are also many other things which Jesus did, the which, if they should be written every one, I suppose that even the world itself could not contain the books that should be written. Amen" (John 21:25).